THE RED FLAG RIOTS

Raymond Evans is a senior lecturer in History at the University of Queensland. He specialises in social history, race relations and conflict studies, and is particularly interested in the treatment of non-Anglo Europeans during and after World War I. Dr Evans has published widely in this area and is the author of *Loyalty and Disloyalty: Social Conflict on the Queensland Homefront 1914-18* (1987), and a co-author of *Race Relations in Colonial Queensland: A History of Exclusion, Exploitation and Extermination* (new edition, UQP 1988).

What next? (*Worker*, 7 November 1918)

THE
RED FLAG RIOTS

A STUDY OF INTOLERANCE

Raymond Evans

University of Queensland Press
ST LUCIA • LONDON • NEW YORK

First published 1988 by University of Queensland Press
Box 42, St Lucia, Queensland, Australia

© Raymond Evans 1988

Typeset by University of Queensland Press
Printed in Australia by The Book Printer, Melbourne

Distributed in the UK and Europe by University of Queensland Press
Dunhams Lane, Letchworth, Herts. SG6 1LF England

Distributed in the USA and Canada by University of Queensland Press
250 Commercial Street, Manchester, NH 03101 USA

Cataloguing in Publication Data

National Library of Australia

Evans, Raymond.
  The red flag riots.

  Bibliography.
  Includes index.
  1. Race discrimination – Queensland – Brisbane.
  2. Brisbane (Qld.) – History – 1918-1922.
  3. Brisbane (Qld.) – Race relations. 4. Russians
  – Queensland – Brisbane – Social conditions.
  I. Title.
994.3'1041

British Library (data available)

Library of Congress

Evans, Raymond.
  The red flag riots / Raymond Evans.
    p.   cm.
  Bibliography: p.
  Includes Index.
  1. Riots – Australia – Brisbane (Qld.) 2. Brisbane (Qld.) –
  History. 3. Russians – Australia – Brisbane (Qld.) – Politics
  and government. 4. Anti-communist movements – Australia –
  Brisbane (Qld.) I. Title.
DU278. E93 1988
994.3'1 dc19   87 30189

ISBN 0 7022 2073 6

*For my parents
David Leslie and Maisie Evans
who were both born
in these troubled
times*

Contents

Illustrations

following page 120

The Women's Peace Army calendar for 1917
Jennie Scott Griffiths, radical journalist
Queensland's Police Commissioner, F.C. Urquhart
A much younger looking Urquhart drilling Native Police
    troopers in North-Western Queensland
Jeremiah Joseph Stable was Chief Queensland Military Censor
    from January 1917 to May 1919
A rare cartoon displaying the obsessive concern for secrecy,
    suppression and surveillance
Herbert Brookes campaigned forcefully for the suppression of
    all republican and revolutionary influences in Australia
    towards the end of World War I
Dr Ernest Sandford Jackson, organiser of the United Loyalist
    Executive and the King and Empire Alliance
Dr Jackson's dramatically opulent home, *Glenolive*
Herbert Ebenezer Sizer, returned soldier, politician and
    loyalist polemicist in the back seat of his Rolls Royce
Two candid photographs of crowds drawn to the Brisbane
    Domain
Acting-Premier Theodore struggles vainly to welcome home
    Victoria Cross holders
Herman Bykov (alias Resanoff) arrived in Australia as a
    fireman
An artist's impression of eleven of the fifteen Queensland
    Red Flag prisoners
A passport photograph of Alexander Michael Zuzenko
Zuzenko with a cane-cutting gang in North Queensland
A much altered Zuzenko on the bridge of a Russian vessel

Maps

Acknowledgments

My late, great aunt, May Collins — although she never knew it — had a lot to do with my becoming an historian, and writing the kind of history I do. At times, when I was young, she used to talk of those wild Queensland mining frontiers of Mount Mulligan and Collinsville in the twenties and thirties: of the initial, petty torments visited upon the "pommie" migrant — for she was Welsh — and about the later solidarity struggles of the miners, of whom my great-uncle Dave, proudly Communist, was one. I never met the man, for he had died, "dusted" in the lungs, in the 1940s; but my Auntie May would bring him alive again for my cousin and me in her stories of those rough, deprived and bawdy days.

It was she, therefore, who whetted my appetite for a past which was never really appeased by the Australian history I learned in school or at university. Gradually I came to see that there was another kind of history, of which her recollections formed a legitimate part — an untidy, sprawling history of unknown workers and their uneven struggles; of "ordinary" (though, often, extraordinary) men and women, white and black, migrant and native-born. What beckoned therefore was, for want of a better term, a people's history, even though most of those very same people had been encouraged, generation by generation, to cast it aside as "over and done with" and of little intrinsic account, in any case. That past does not perish so easily, however, as I hope this book will help attest. Yet we still know so very little about it. If only we could revive it as effortlessly and as vividly as my great-aunt's fond memories of her late husband, Dave.

Kay Saunders first suggested the feasibility of this study to Craig Munro of the University of Queensland Press, so it is to them both I must offer my thanks initially that it has now become a book. Two colleagues, Tom Poole and Eric Fried, those perennial Russia-watchers, offered me sterling support, including bringing many new archival sources to my notice. My fellow founding-members of the Koala Club — a loose alliance of radically-inclined Queensland social historians, who are far from being grey and full of sleep — have all offered encouragement in their various ways: Bill Thorpe, Lyndall Ryan, Denis Cryle, Helen Taylor, Kay Saunders, Tom Cochrane and Jan Walker. The comradeship born of our initial meetings and the informal links we have since maintained by letter and personal contact have much to do with conveying a sense of purpose about this history-that-matters, with getting it researched and written. Bill, Helen and Kay have read sections of the manuscript — Bill actually, read it all — and offered numerous constructive suggestions, as did Judith McKay of the Architecture Department at the University of Queensland. Kathryn Cronin and Joseph Ury deserve special thanks for putting me up — and putting up with me — in London during 1984, when some of the research was undertaken.

Closer to home, my parents — to whom this book is dedicated — have always given me every encouragement by believing in the worth of what I am writing. My father even reads it. My daughter, Erin, also takes the greatest interest in my academic pursuits — a preoccupation most uncommon in a seventeen year old. Sandie Evans (who is happy to be recorded here as my wife) has been my close companion throughout the writing of this book. We face life together, arm in arm. Anthony and Shane, my stepsons, also contributed, however unwittingly, towards the production of this volume. For it was their (often loud) teenage traumas which frequently kept me closeted in my study, my mind resolutely tuned to 1919.

The staff of the following institutions made the task of research easier, indeed sometimes pleasurable: Queensland State Archives, Fryer Memorial Library, Oxley Library, Australian Archives (Brisbane, Canberra and Brighton), Mitchell Library (Sydney) and the Public Records Office (London). The manuscript was expertly and painstakingly typed by Robyn

Eastgate, and a fine editing job done by Diane Penney. Bernadette Brunott did the excellent cartography. The History Department, University of Queensland, where I have worked for twenty years, was generous in providing funding for the illustrations and maps.

Introduction

> . . . strange things occur in Brisbane, now and then.
>
> W.A. Watt (1919)

Episodes of riot, disturbance and protest abound at times of heightened conflict in Australia's past — as the enterprising scriptwriter of the television mini-series has been quick to discover. Yet the raw intensity of such episodes seems to have largely escaped the attention of professional historians. With rare exceptions, the dynamics of the religious-sectarian clash, the race or xenophobic riot, the class disturbance, the election sortie, the frontier dispersal or the jingo outburst are left obscured in the dust of their own disorder. Academic avoidance seems most pronounced where vigilante activism — that form of "establishment violence" which flaunts the rules ostensibly to defend them — is concerned. Australia's past, this historical silence implies, has been relatively untroubled by such lawlessness.[1]

Overall, it is as if the cautious academic peers down upon each crisis from a peaceful study; then, with notes unruffled, quietly closes the window against all the noise. Perhaps it is a profound commitment to rationality in this eminently rational discipline which keeps passions muted and the historiography of this continent mainly a quiet one. Speaking generally for all Australians, the historian George Arnold Wood concluded earlier this century, 'Nothing can be so completely without importance to us as the study of what is both bad and past'. Perhaps, too, an ignorance of street conflict is, in many cases, a reflection of more privileged class backgrounds and an avoidance of political activism in these historians' own contemplative lives. Few in-

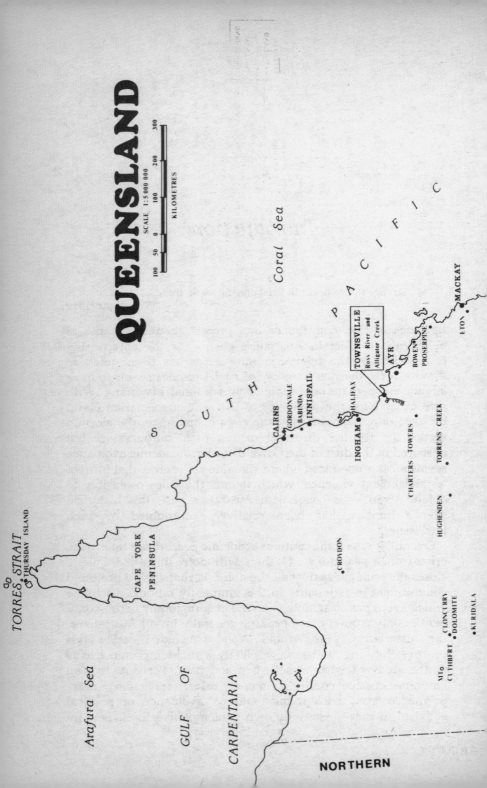

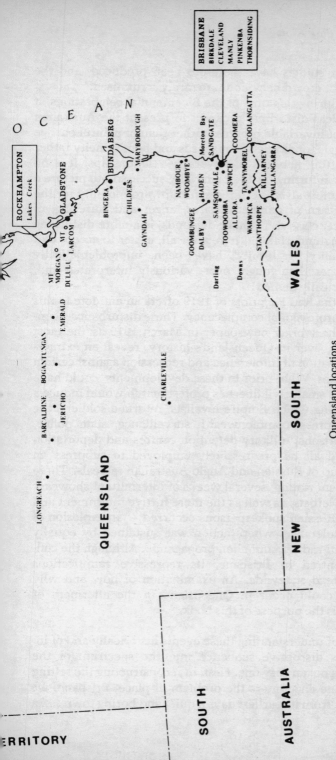

Queensland locations

depth conflict studies have therefore been produced, and the past vagaries of crowd behaviour are rarely scrutinised.[2]

Especially during this time of the Bicentennial celebrations, it may seem a less disturbing prospect to present the Australian story as one of invariable progress rather than of painful change through struggle; or as one of consensus and homogeneity rather than of a shifting network of adversary relationships. It is no doubt more comforting for the materially successful to picture a past which almost always offered swift upward mobility for the worthy. To learn of damned desires, anger and suffering, of frustrated race, class and gender demands, is a more disturbing and perplexing undertaking. It is, after all, easier to accept that 'liberty, equality, fraternity' have been unproblematically achieved, rather than fought over, variously interpreted and, often, emphatically denied.

A study of the Red Flag riots of 1919 offers an antidote to this popular and professional complacency. These disturbances, condemned by the *Worker* newspaper in March 1919 as 'the most serious rioting' ever in Queensland's history, reveal an extraordinary mobilisation of intolerance and repression against certain targetted groups. Who, prior to these developments, could have credited that a small civil liberties protest march would induce a backlash, during which Empire loyalists, returned soldiers, the conservative press, commonwealth surveillance, state police, law courts, prisons, military detention centres and deportation vessels would all be progressively employed to suppress an ebullient group of Russian and Anglo-Australian radicals? Three nights of violent rioting, several weeks of intermittent showcase trials of local leftists, as well as the more furtive internment and expulsion of Russian spokespersons occurred — an explosion of organised intolerance, where action was sustained by equally aggressive anti-radical, anti-alien propaganda. Although the conflict was centred in Brisbane, its repressive ramifications gradually spread statewide. An examination of how and why such events could occur in Queensland in the aftermath of World War I is the purpose of this book.

Yet the task of understanding these events historically and of integrating this disruptive sequence into the spectrum of the known past is not an easy one. First, in reconstructing the setting of conflict, one encounters the problem of place: Brisbane, we are told, was 'from its earliest days a quiet and boring town . . . a very law-abiding community'. This observation is invariably capped with a nod towards Ronald Lawson's *Brisbane in the 1890s*, which unfolds a gently graded social order, where dullness was the price paid for tranquillity in this drowsy, over-grown village. That popular image is challenged, however, by a newer historiographical strand, which emphasises that the Queensland capital ‘– much like any major urban centre – possessed its seamier side, its wilder side, its more passionate, articulate side: that, from its convict roots to its present-day con-servation, land rights, civil liberties and trade union struggles, it grew in conflict and travail as well as in its dusty, suburban sprawl. How this allegedly 'classless' town of the nineties played host, in 1912, to Australia's first general strike, is a question which historian Glen Lewis has pertinently asked. And, I would add, how did this purportedly law abiding, 'homogeneous' com-munity produce the savagely xenophobic and loyalist rioting of 1919, much as it had the worst anti-Chinese violence on the eastern seaboard in 1888? Do we truly stand upon a tranquil ur-ban plain to witness the sudden tumult of 1919? Is the tumult, perhaps, a mirage; or is the plain really a shaky historical paradigm which the evidence of tumult interrogates and, ultimately, disowns?[3]

A second problem requiring some attention is the time se-quence within which this post-war rioting occurs. In 1973, A.G.L. Shaw claimed that:

> in the 20th century violent agitation and protest have been less fre-quently resorted to than in the 19th, and until the recent Vietnam moratoria and anti-conscription campaigns, were almost confined to some of the activities of the IWW, the conduct of some enthusiasts on both sides during the World War I conscription campaigns, and the plans of the New Guard and the All for Australia League during the Depression.

The social dislocation which followed immediately upon the Great War is here nowhere in sight. Yet, in opposition to this sweeping conclusion, Michael McKernan asserts: 'The im-mediate post-war years gave no indication that Australian socie-ty would revert to *its pre-war innocence and placidity* . . . The ex-perience of war blew all that away. The people were forced to confront division and class antagonism.' McKernan's conclusion, therefore, sets Shaw's upon its head. Further confirmation of the era's conflictive nature is provided in the works of both Malcolm Waters and Richard Morris who find it to be more seriously disruptive, industrially, than the 1890s. Overall, Gavin Souter detects a 'new strain' of social ferocity after the war, making 1919 'the strangest, most violent year the Commonwealth had ever known'. Dwelling less upon the terrible novelty of this period than upon its social and temporal repercussions, Humphrey McQueen then reminds us that, via a revamped 'combination of violence and ideas . . . modern Australia was spawned in 1919'. And, if the evidence of civil disorder, Australia-wide, is intimately addressed, blood in the streets was clearly a feature of those birth pangs.[4]

As this work is intent upon showing, therefore, the Red Flag riots were not simply an isolated moment of sub-tropical madness. The disturbance forms part of a pattern of antipodean and global conflict, linked to the interplay of revolution and counter-revolution in this turbulent age. It also merges into a continuum of local conflict which – sometimes muted and sometimes strident – highlights those major, interactive themes of race and class relations in Australian society.

A third difficulty arises in encountering a mainstream historiography which infers, by omission, that non Anglo-Celtic ethnicity is not a significant issue in Australia until problems of refugee migration, assimilation and multiculturalism are negotiated after the *following* world war. If such a perspective remains unchallenged, then the ethnic background of some major players in this earlier drama is far too brusquely obscured. Russians in Queensland, politically engrossed, socially visible and highly vocal, were largely a legacy of Czarist persecution after the failed 1905 uprising in their homeland. Locally, these Russian émigrés heightened revolutionary consciousness among a minority, while providing the occasion for the manipulation by loyalist organizers of anti-Muscovite distaste among the general populace. That other small thorn in capitalism's side, the Brisbane Industrial Workers of the World (IWW), smiled incredulously in mid-1915 when, as 'hardworking British subjects', they were warned by police 'not to let those Nihilists from barbarous Russia lead the IWW astray, for those fellows are only here for murderous purposes'. Yet it would be a combination of such mounting xenophobia and well-honed anti-revolutionary ardour which, during 1918–19, targetted both of these groups for the major thrusts of loyalist reprisal.[5]

The problems of dealing with these preconceptions of place,

time and personnel, however, are merely fractions of that larger difficulty posed by the generally 'harmonious' approach to our history. Overall, those Australian histories which keep both revolutionaries and ruling class personnel in the shadows; which exalt the fighting Anzac but ignore the problems of the broken war veteran; and which segregate politics and society into artificially distinct research categories would each, in differing ways, find the events unfolded here both mystifying and disquietening. Several works, written by Souter and McQueen, Denis Murphy, Joe Harris and Ross Fitzgerald, have dealt fleetingly – and sometimes peremptorily – with these disturbances. Additionally, one necessarily limited, though insightful history honours thesis by Trevor Botham was completed in 1975, but never published. My own *Loyalty and Disloyalty* attempts to give some temporal and social context to the conflict, but this amazing series of events deserves a much closer examination than the span of that study allows.[6]

Because of an accident of timing, the tumult of March 1919 was never debated in any parliament, as both commonwealth and Queensland state legislatures were in extended recess at the time. After several weeks of press sensation, the matter faded in the public memory, as did the fate of its victims. Following an official query from London in May 1920, the Governor-General, Roland Munro-Ferguson informed the Secretary of State for the Colonies that he knew nothing whatever 'of the alleged persecution of Russians in Australia'.

By mid-1920, such amnesia was no doubt convenient. With the most volatile period of social disorder now safely behind him, it was possible for the 'Imperial pro-consul' to exhibit such dismissive absent-mindedness. Three years earlier, however, distracted by the intensity of homefront conflict, the Governor-General's reports had struck a distinctly different keynote. Writing 'Home' in late October 1917, on the brink of the second conscription campaign, Munro-Ferguson had warned how 'the complete separation between classes' in Australia was even more apparent that the social 'gulf' existing in Great Britain. Consequently, he declared, "bitterness grows, and 'war to the knife' is the sole expedient either side believes in".[7]

As this study reveals, that homefront 'war', of which Sir Roland wrote, was no mere phantom of conservative disquiet. Between the years 1917 and 1920, the knives of conflict were out in Queensland, and seldom, if ever, sheathed.

Chapter 1

This Damn Slaughter

A stands for Armaments, the Capitalists' pride,
B stands for Bolshie, the thorn in their side . . . [1]

The Red Alphabet

With the sharpened perception of hindsight, we know today that the year 1918 marked the dying days of the Great War, that the vast juggernaut of extermination was at last grinding to a halt. Yet, to contemporaries, their imminent deliverance was hardly as apparent. Indeed, by Christmas 1917, an end to the daily warfront horrors did not appear so clearly ordained as it had seemed before Christmas 1914. Australian soldiers wrote sardonically of the war continuing until 1939 and of the lost legions hearing W.M. Hughes's 10,378th 'Win the War' speech as they carved out permanent residences amidst the debris of twenty-five years' carnage. By the early months of 1918, the Allies hardly seemed to have a military success to their credit. Italy was reeling and Bolshevik Russia and Roumania had withdrawn from the struggle. Then, in mid-March, the tense stalemate of attritional trench warfare was ended, not by a victorious Allied advance, but by a powerful German offensive which was not halted until July, nor finally turned until August and September.[2]

Upon the Australian homefront, more and more non-combatants had grown exhausted, anticipating a promised victory which never seemed to eventuate. The columns of dead, wounded and missing no longer seemed to balance against the paper triumphs concocted by military censorship and political propaganda. A Queensland returned soldier, en route through Brisbane to his small farm at Woombye after being gassed at Messines, told commonwealth policeman Constable Hubert

Foote in early 1918 that, although his moral convictions were liable 'to get him six months', "If any man asks me if he should enlist after what I have seen at the front, I should say *No* . . . I voted 'No' at the referendum and I would not vote another man to go through the same as I have".[3]

The second conscription referendum of December 1917 had miscarried more conclusively than in late 1916, and the propaganda barrage of both campaigns had accomplished little more than underscoring the ominous realities of technological slaughter. 'Yes' and 'No' proponents had both paid obeisance to such grim facts — the former to plead the desperate need for conscripts and the latter, more successfully, to warn against national suicide in the muddied slaughterhouse of Europe. 'They're beginning here to ask, what are we fighting for?' wrote a Dutch resident of rural Queensland on Christmas Day, 1917:

> The Australian born say, "what good is all that to us? Have we got to give up our men etc. for these selfish plans of European nations?" . . . Methinks Australia's fed up and will have nothing more to do with this war. The upper class papers (who make pots of money out of the war) believe in everybody fighting. Those who won't are curs, unpatriotic rebels, I.W.W., Sinn Feiners etc. [But] it's the capitalist class who's forced the workmen to act . . . This war, replacing class war has made things worse. Everywhere . . . the desire for the end of the war increases . . . I should not wonder to hear about more revolutions breaking out.

War-weariness, then, seems to have burst through the dykes of official control by early 1918 — a fact that the capitalist press itself could no longer avoid facing. The *Brisbane Courier*, for instance, in its New Year's address, castigated this 'ugly decline in popular morale'. Why had the blood of the Australian 'race', it raged, become so 'weak and watery' and its patriotic spirit so anaemic? The danger was not so much that the war would be lost 'in the field', but that the complementary 'strength to endure at home' should now fail.[4]

An obscure Dutch rural worker and the influential *Brisbane Courier* thus diagnosed similar homefront symptoms in the aftermath of the second referendum, although these seemed as much a sign of hope to one as an index of 'selfishness and insensibility' to the other. Disillusionment had certainly not baulked at class boundaries; yet the centres of loyalty were by now more clearly located among the ranks of the rich and powerful than within the hearts of the wage-labouring masses. Large numbers of war-committed workers no doubt still existed, but the stereotype of

The fortunes of War (*Worker*, 6 November 1919)

'loyalism' had increasingly assumed the form of that ogre of plutocracy, "Mr Fat", in the cartoons and diatribes of the workers' press. The profile of the committed loyalist, the man or woman who helped organize recruiting drives, patriotic fundraising and war loans, was more exactly that of the Anglophile, Protestant, ruling and propertied classes by 1918 than a typification of the national mood which had so vociferously entered the war in 1914. 'Loyalty' and 'disloyalty', indeed, had gradually assumed their own rough social dimensions, the former emanating from the upper social orders and the latter from society's lower echelons — particularly from its radical, its Catholic and its non-British minorities. If conscription clearly had divided the nation, so too, increasingly, had a pro- and anti-war stance. And, with each embittering defeat of conscription, such fundamental postures had become more firmly locked in open combat, even as war's ordeals swelled the 'disloyalist' ranks.

Just as leftwing voices typified loyalists as a 'capitalist class urging the people to war frenzy from upholstered couches', so too did conservatives via press, pulpit and political outlets, spread images of disloyalty which became more forbidding and detailed as the war dragged on. Commencing at the founts of radical and pacifist war opposition, the stereotype was extended to include all who avoided enlistment; all who struck work at such a time of national emergency; and all who resisted a 'necessary' onset of military compulsion. To these variegated ranks, virtually all non-British sectors had eventually been added; and, despite their war record, almost all the Catholic Irish, depicted now as openly or covertly in league with the Sinn Fein. This coterie of dissidents was known by many names — 'shirker', 'saboteur', 'wobbly', 'Hun' and more recently 'Bolshevik' — but behind the invective, the loyalist analysis of their presence was always the same: revolutionaries working cheek-by-jowl with enemy nationals 'within our gates' had played upon the sentiments of the weak and cowardly, the self-interested, the uncommitted and un-British, effectively seducing them into un-cooperative and seditious poses.[5]

Here was an analysis which seemed at once glibly circular and self-fulfilling. The blame for all war malaise now could be directly sheeted home to those 'low and filthy' beings, those 'garrulous, blatant, ill-balanced demagogues' who openly advocated either warfare's end or even some fundamental political and industrial reconstruction of Australian society. Why else had Queensland's

The joy riders (*Worker*, 17 August 1918)

enlistments plummeted from a peak of 3,886 in January 1916 to only 283, exactly two years later? Why else were workers shunning war loan appeals in such numbers that federal authorities were contemplating a 'resort . . . to compulsion' to require 'all persons to subscribe . . . in proportion to their means'? Why too, did loyalists, by 1918, detect increasing 'public diffidence in volunteering financial assistance' to the glut of patriotic funds? Many organizations were suspending activities, meatworkers were receiving Red Cross collectors 'with obvious disapproval', and copper miners, who once gave 'most handsomely', were offering 'today not a penny'. And why else had industrial disputation in Queensland leapt from seventeen strikes involving 2,000 workers in 1915 to eighty-four in 1918, involving almost 11,000, if not for 'the IWW germ infecting the veins of the industrial body'?[6]

Working class analysts, however, could suggest very different causes for the discontent. Despite the 'terribly critical stage' the war had reached, the formerly unquestionable 'righteousness' of the Allied cause no longer seemed so credible. The struggle, instead, was depicted as a sordid 'trade war', in which workers, after providing much of 'the blood and treasure . . . always lose', no matter which side won. Because of militarism's demands and the revived clamour for conscription, it was vigorously argued, 'all our civil rights are jeopardised'. Australia had entered the war, trade unionists somewhat fancifully suggested, 'because she loved Civil Liberty and loathed Military Tyranny'. Yet the gradual impositions of the *War Precautions Act* and its extensive panoply of regulations, military censorship, espionage and internment procedures, the *Unlawful Associations Acts* and the *Alien Restriction Orders* had all contributed to a repressive situation, whereby: "[Australia] has no longer free speech; she has no longer a free press. Public meetings, even private homes have been invaded by the police . . . [and] it is proposed to complete this work by conscription."[7]

Even conscription's second rebuff, confided the Governor-General, Sir Roland Munro-Ferguson, to the Colonial Office, was not regarded by Prime Minister Hughes as being 'final'. Instead, 'he . . . considers it releases him from all pledges and clears the deck for further action'. 'His autocratic ways excite alarm', Munro-Ferguson candidly observed, for, unlike governments 'in other British communities', the Hughes regime seemed to operate as 'a secret, or open autocracy', wherein 'Ministerial

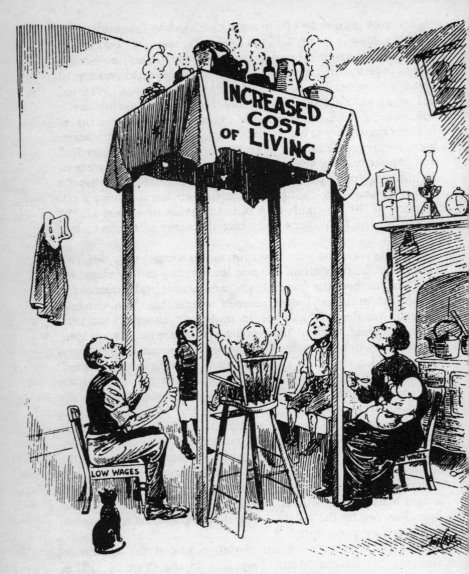

The table has got to come down, or else the chairs must go up.

The alternatives (*Worker*, 2 May 1918)

and Parliamentary responsibility is evaded, the Executive Council becomes an instrument of registering the will of the Prime Minister, or even civil servants; while, in moments of crisis, responsibility is apt to be constantly shifted to the Governor-General'. Although not as privy to such intimate political machinations as the nominal Head of State, workers were nonetheless sensitive to the increasing coercion, as it invaded and restricted their daily lives.[8]

Yet, for many, the impact of civil regimentation was by no means as acute as the socio-economic hardship which wartime conditions had imposed. In the commonwealth, the cost of living had climbed by 222 units between 1914 and 1918, whilst wage rates lagged far behind. In Queensland, both right and leftwing sources adduced that there the increases had been greatest — the former blaming them upon ministrations of the Ryan Labor Government. Overall, Queensland's retail prices rose 60 per cent, compared with a 47 per cent commonwealth average. Complaints against exorbitant rents, high grocery prices and undue 'profiteering' were constant. A Sandgate worker, whose family was £40 in debt to several business establishments, wrote to Premier Ryan in early 1918, 'We want to live, but very often have no beef or butter — dripping has to do us. War times are bad . . . believe me.' Additionally, high unemployment had remained a constant scourge since the war began, when it had soared to almost 18 per cent. In 1917, it equalled the commonwealth figure of 7.1 per cent and was again rising. During 1918, it reached 9.2 per cent and continued to grow. For the truly destitute, meanwhile, charity was in scarce supply because of the war effort. Contributions to patriotic funds had meant a serious 'shrinkage of revenue' to local charitable organisations. The Society for the Prevention of Cruelty reported in 1918 that there were few welfare bodies 'who are not experiencing a curtailment of their accustomed support'.[9]

Such privations cast a shadow across all loyalist appeals for equality of sacrifice, self-denial and thrift. For a statistical analysis of real wealth had undermined any claims about social equity among the Australian population, in terms of either earnings or material assets. As the 1915 War Census of 'The Private Wealth of Australia' had discovered, substantially similar levels of gross inequality existed in all the states. In Queensland, only 0.5 per cent of the adult population enjoyed incomes exceeding £1000 per annum, whilst 90.5 per cent of all wage and salary earners received less than £200 per annum. An elite of 8.5 per cent held more than 70 per cent of all material assets, whilst a full 73 per cent had to share just 8.5 per cent of the "wealth" amongst themselves. Trade union leaders were not slow to display their anger at these findings. As a Queensland labour pamphlet asserted at the war's end:

> The great bulk of the wealth . . . is owned by a ridiculously small minority of people . . . how glaring is the disproportion between the incomes . . . of the workers, from whose ranks the majority of our soldiers come, and the minority who form the so-called "upper" and well-to-do classes . . . the great majority are working . . . for just a bare living and nothing more . . . There is something radically wrong somewhere.[10]

To this injury of substantial inequality, the insult was added of excessive war-induced profits being pocketed by the 'rich money bugs'. War was simply the capitalists' 'weapon', it was argued, wielded to enrich them as it bludgeoned the workers. In the manufacturing industries, the Governor-General calculated in 1918, the average value of output per employee had risen by 75 per cent in six years, while shipping profits had multiplied more than twelve-fold between 1913 and 1916. Additionally, in assessing warfare's margin of gain bestowed upon Australian business, banking, wheat and wool sales in January 1918, Munro-Ferguson myopically deduced, 'the only conclusion . . . is that Australia has not suffered – *except in loss of some of her best blood* – in any material sense, but rather has been benefited'. To this litany of "successes", a *Brisbane Courier* columnist added in September, 'Queensland has actually done a larger trade and realized higher profits than usual from this war'. Its population should therefore be gratified, this writer reasoned; and he demanded, without any apparent sense of the moral discrepancies involved: 'Does Queensland think that she is to receive only and not to give? . . . The war will not wait. The best are being killed and maimed daily . . . there should be no complaint of want of reinforcements to the firing line.'[11]

Perhaps more than anything else, it was this coldly calculated war ledger, balancing capitalist profit against human loss, which the working class had come to loathe. "One of the most awful aspects in connection with this war is the ghoulish process by which 'mouth patriots' are making enormous profits out of the holocaust", wrote a correspondent to the Brisbane *Worker* in August 1918. They seemed to find satisfaction only in 'dividends

The pig that stayed at home (*Worker*, 1 November 1917)

— fat unspeakable dividends'. Thus, in answer to the continual 'Win-the-war-by-jaw' appeals for conscription, trade unionists responded: "If these people are in earnest, they would say, 'we can't give our lives, but take our property, our gold, our sheep, our bullocks.' Instead of doing this, they make reckless charges against the eligible, and call those who disagree with them disloyalists, slackers and shirkers . . . " Yet, were not the "real shirkers", these writers contended, "the Beef Brigand, the Banking Bandit and the Commercial Cormorant [?] . . . MAKE THEM PAY UP!"[12]

By 1918, therefore, the lines of social and ideological disagreement were no longer simply margins of debate in an unequal society, but angry barricades of entrenched opposition. In a metaphorical sense, it almost seemed as though the trench warfare of the Western Front had shifted to the homefront, with a lonely 'No Man's Land' of incomprehension stretching between increasingly implacable foes. At times, however, hopeful couriers still crossed these lines, offering negotiations or some message of reconciliation.

Such an attempt occurred on 9 January 1918, when Captain R.H. Cottam, Secretary of the Queensland War Savings Committee, approached trade union delegates to arrange a discussion upon workers' contributions — and was sent sharply packing. George Gavin, Secretary of the Brisbane Industrial Council (BIC), replied, 'In view of all that has happened locally in connection with war matters during recent months, and the attitude towards the workers adopted always by most of those whose names we note upon your official letter paper, we are somewhat surprised that you should approach us at all.' These representatives came exclusively from commercial and banking concerns — men who had increasingly displayed bitter opposition to 'every move made by our class to better our material conditions', Gavin noted. 'It is therefore surely the refinement of cruelty', he continued acidly:

> [as] many of them today are responsible for the soaring prices of many of the workers' necessaries of life, that this appeal . . . should come from such persons and at such a time. With the cost of living out of all proportion to our earnings, it seems a studied insult to our intelligence . . . to talk of workers' "savings". It is quite evident that whatever little your committee may know of war . . . it knows less of the working class fight with low wages and evil economic conditions . . . had we, as workers any savings to invest, we could and ought to

AN EXCURSION TO EUROPE!

The Famous A.I.F. Personally Conducted Tours Round the World.

JOIN a PARTY NOW, and Take a Trip to the Land of the HOHENZOLLERNS!

Do you enjoy country life? Germany is the ideal holiday resort!

Magnificent views! Bracing air! Thrilling experiences! Glorious appetite.

Climate cooler than Kosciusko! Better than the Blue Mountains or the Barron Falls!

Visit the famous (and infamous) Rhineland!

Through service at frequent intervals by perfectly appointed steamers from Australia to Somewhere-in-France.

Refreshing sea trip, with interesting shore visits.

Be in time for the opening of the Potsdam Exhibition.

Magnificent Display of Fireworks by Pyrotechnists of the Allies.

A Ten-thousand-Mile Tour, and not a dull moment!

Exceptionally liberal rates and special privileges.

A visit to historic Berlin will completely cure that great Australian Tired Feeling.

Don't you want to witness the triumphal procession along Unter-der-Linden?

OUTDOOR SPORTS.

Tenting, Target-shooting, Tramping, Bombing, Motoring, Aeroplaning, Riding, Mountain-climbing, Swimming.

A unique opportunity for hunting and shooting in the most primitive part of Europe. Hunting begins the day you arrive. Ammunition and rifles provided free of charge. More wild beasts and savages than Darkest Africa ever knew!

Everything conducive to a lively and exciting time!

Enjoy life in the open under skies of Prussian blue!

The A.I.F. management furnish complete camp outfit gratis.

A progressive holiday from camp to camp is just the thing for a man who wants to get away from the humdrum, workaday grind, and escape from the conventions and artificialities of modern business and social life.

Good fellowship and not style is aimed at.

Al fresco meals by the chefs of the A.I.F.

Don't you want to see the Kaiser's wonderland?

Periscopes provided free!

The staff of the A.I.F. will arrange everything for you! Terms on application.

For detailed information apply to the

State Recruiting Committee, Preston House, Brisbane,

OR TO ANY RECRUITING OFFICE.

An excursion to Europe! (*Worker*, 2 August 1917)

use it in a much more desirable and Christian way than that which you propose.

This stinging rebuff had undoubtedly been salted by observations made during a walk around the inner-city streets. For everywhere, upon prominently displayed hoardings, the posters of the War Savings Committee had imprudently informed potential investors of what their contributions might purchase: '17/6 will buy 140 cartridges or four hand bombs . . . 47/6 will buy two shells for big guns . . . £8/15/- will keep one soldier in the field for 16 days'. The BIC members were singularly unimpressed by these grisly bargains. 'When the workers of Queensland have money to invest', they ventured, 'it would be wiser for them . . . to spend it, not on bullets and shells to maim the bodies and blow out the brains of other workers . . . — equally as guiltless of provoking this war as they — but to perfect the bodies and develop the brains, not only of themselves, but of the children for whom they are directly responsible.' The pressing necessity was now peace, the BIC concluded, 'and in the securing of it lies all our interests. Hoping, we have made our position clear to you . . . '[13]

As if to underscore that commitment, the Brisbane Labor-in-Politics Convention began on 28 January 1918 with an address focussing upon the 'danger of miltarism' and the spread of war-weariness. Delivered by Labor moderate, William Demaine, MLC, the President of the Queensland Central Executive (QCE), it vividly exemplified how the call for peace was now re-echoing throughout labour's ranks. 'I attribute the big majority against conscription to this growing desire for peace', Demaine stated:

> We are told that the majority of Australians do not realize what war means, but I deny this . . . there is hardly a home that has not suffered bereavement, had its sons returned maimed or that does not suffer the anxiety that attends having . . . a relative at the front. Our streets filled with an ever-increasing number of maimed, halt and blind, or otherwise afflicted returned soldiers give striking evidence of how much the war affects Australia . . . The horrors of it shriek to high Heaven and the peoples of the world are sickening of them all, and in this sickening lies the hope of peace.

The so-called 'righteous' war had been caused by 'Imperialism . . . the arch-enemy of Democracy', he argued, and, in this regard, the Russian Revolution represented 'the most hopeful sign of the times' for peace by negotiation and a world-wide 'democratic' solution to social injustices. In Queensland, however, he was quick to add, socialism should come about, not by force, but under the evolutionary auspices of Labor in power, increasing 'class consciousness' educatively among workers and eventually putting the Tory 'boodle jingoes' to rout.[14]

Among pacifists to the left of labour's mainstream, concerted calls for 'immediate peace' had been publicly made as early as August 1917. During the second referendum campaign, leading 'peace cranks' had combined with socialists and syndicalists of the IWW upon the Anti-Conscription Coordinating Committee (ACCC) in the surge towards a 'No' victory. Out of the anti-conscription movement, as William Demaine recognised, a revitalised 'Stop-the-War' crusade had emerged as, with renewed vigour, the local anti-war movement led by the Australian Peace Alliance (APA) and the Women's Peace Army (WPA) took their message into the halls and streets of Brisbane.[15]

In early February 1918, the APA, led by Alex Gorman, a Queen Street tobacconist, conducted a well-attended rally at the Brisbane Exhibition Hall. Here, Joseph Silver Collings, militant labour propagandist and Central Political Executive (CPE) organiser, and radical Labor Senator, Myles Ferricks, spoke as peace advocates alongside Percy Mandeno and Jim Quinton (local IWW supporters who had both served prison sentences for anti-war activities), Margaret Thorp, the English-born Quaker secretary of the WPA, as well as interstate visitors, the celebrated feminist, Vida Goldstein and Kathleen Hotson. Hotson, a radical pacifist engaged to imprisoned IWW activist, John Rudolph, was known to Military Intelligence as the 'South Australian firebrand', due to the effectiveness of her public performances. As Hotson inspired the large, sympathetic audience with the message that 'the power of the people must stop wars', matters seemed to have altered considerably from a mere four months before, when she had narrowly escaped being stoned by a hostile western Queensland crowd at a railway siding. A month later, Hotson appeared at the Brisbane Domain, an inner-city 'free speech' area, sharing the platform this time with State Labor parliamentarians, Edgar Free, MLA for South Brisbane, and William Bertram, the Chairman of Committees, demonstrating once more that the 'tacit coalition of socialists and competent liberals', which the anti-conscription struggles had recently forged, still existed. That evening, at Trades Hall, the ebullient IWW supporter, Gordon Brown, lectured a substantial gathering upon 'British Hun Atrocities' in Ireland, and again called for universal brotherhood and peace.[16]

Such insistent demands and a heightened public receptivity to them were inducing anxious glances from military authorities as 1918 began. Gordon Brown's Trades Hall meeting was nothing more than 'a hotbed of disloyalty', reported Military Intelligence agent, Thomas Walker. One 'encouraging' sign was that the participants were still 'split up into factions with different ideals: some favour getting redress for their grievances through Parliament; others believe in doing away with politicians and wiping out all laws'. Nevertheless, he concluded ominously, 'All are united in the desire to sweep away the moneyed class'. Local representatives of Military Censorship read less ambiguous revolutionary signs into these demonstrations. Assistant Censor, J. Botten from Cairns, who attended the Exhibition peace rally, emphasised in his report the revolutionary sentiments of Myles Ferricks, which were 'certainly calculated to cause disaffection – to create public alarm – to interfere with the success of His Majesty's forces'. Similarly, the Censor himself, Queensland University's languages specialist, J.J. Stable, in assessing the BIC's snub to Captain Cottam, commented pointedly:

> This is the first public expression of antagonism to the British war aims by the Industrial Council, but evidence of the growth of the inimical spirit has not been wanting. The taint of IWWism is disaffecting unionism throughout Queensland. There is no question of its growing influence in Brisbane, while Northern Districts – Cairns, Cloncurry, Townsville – are riddled with it . . . [17]

This interlinking of the anti-war mood with a precise revolutionary spirit owed its inspiration to loyalist qualms about several matters. First, the recent conscription referendum furore, which had been most intense in Queensland; secondly, the persistence of IWW action there, after a federal axe had been applied to its roots elsewhere; and, lastly, the Bolshevik Revolution itself, perceived by loyalists as a mad act which local radicals would try to emulate. Due to Queensland Labor's anti-conscriptionist stance, the 'foul weed' of disloyalty was said to be flourishing most luxuriantly in Queensland, with Premier T.J. Ryan as one of its principal cultivators. Wild talk about imminent rebellion or secession had infused Queensland government circles in late 1917, and equally wild solutions about counteracting this had been proposed by the commonwealth.[18]

In August 1917, Military Intelligence, under the control of

Commandant Godfrey George Irving, had begun compiling a list of local IWW members for possible prosecution. Irving, a towering physical presence, had already earned a reputation for martinet qualities, returning from the Palestine front under a cloud, after ordering a disastrous desert march of battle-weary troops. In Queensland, he was to prove an indefatigable scourge upon what was officially construed as 'the anarchist and most ignorant section of society'. With the aid of his secret informant, 'Agent 77', his initial listing netted thirty-four IWW activists operating in Brisbane under the guise of a Universal Freedom League (UFL), as well as a dozen more metropolitan radicals, regarded as fellow-travellers. 'Most of these men are birds of passage, having no stated address', Irving commented. 'They gather in the Parks and the Botanical Gardens is their favourite haunt. As may be expected, they are few, idle and on the vag.' Yet, during 1918, this modest register of the disaffected would be considerably expanded. From 1 September 1917, George Frederick Ainsworth, businessman and former Antarctic explorer, began adding to the roll call by compiling a card index of the potentially subversive for the Special Intelligence Bureau (SIB).[19]

The SIB had developed from the Counter Espionage Bureau, a child of the war under the guardianship of the 'domineering' Major George Steward, the Governor-General's secretary, acting in liaison with MI5 in London. In July 1917, Steward had appointed Ainsworth to its newly formed Brisbane branch, under the camouflaged title of 'Traffic Inspector'. As his official diary reveals, Ainsworth set about establishing an information network, involving Military Command, Intelligence and Censorship, as well as the state police, various leading loyalist citizens and several paid agents — with himself at the centre of the surveillance web. The beginning of 1918 found him busily attending Domain and Trades Hall gatherings, perusing 'invisible ink documents' from headquarters in Melbourne, and receiving weekly reports from his own secret agent on suspect radicals, Russians and Germans. By March, his card index contained only twenty new names, with attached biographical details; but, during the year, it would be expanded to 312 entries — only forty-three less than the total number of 'dangerous' individuals identified by the SIB in all the other states.[20]

Out of the much sensationalised Warwick referendum debacle, involving Irish egg-hurling larrikins and Prime Minister Hughes on 29 November 1917, a commonwealth police force had also been conjured in a manner described by the Governor-General as one of indecent haste. Just four days later, 'without the Governor-General's knowledge', an Executive meeting was summarily called in Sydney by Hughes and Sir Robert Garran, the Solicitor-General, to deal specifically with 'latent rebellion' in Queensland. The idea of counteracting this with a federal force, soon to be dubbed by the left as 'the Commonwealth Fusiliers', had originally come from George Steward of the SIB. At the Executive rump meeting on 3 December 1917, which endorsed its formation, Senator E.D. Millen, former Vice-President of the Executive Council, quite irregularly 'designated himself as deputy Governor-General — an office he does not hold' to authorise the gathering. Significantly, Hughes, Millen and Postmaster General William Webster, who was also present at the 'hustled proceedings', had all been subjected recently to humiliating personal assaults by Queensland anti-conscriptionists. 'I have seen Sir Robert Garran [who acted as Clerk at the gathering] and pointed out the questionable nature of the procedure', the Governor-General reported angrily to the British Colonial Office. 'I told him that in future no business of such importance should be dealt with at an Executive unless its nature has been communicated to me and I have been given an opportunity of expressing an opinion.'[21]

After these shaky beginnings, W.J. Anderson, an elderly New South Wales police inspector, formerly associated with strike control, was appointed as Commissioner, and embryo groups of constabulary were formed at Brisbane, Warwick, Rockhampton, Townsville and Cairns under Sergeants Short, Curtis, Marshall, Cooper and Browne respectively, by January 1918. Most of the constables initially appointed were returned soldiers, many of whom were directly recommended for the positions by W.A. Fisher, State Organiser of the Returned Sailors and Soldiers Imperial League of Australia (RSSILA). Throughout the various urban centres, these constables conscientiously combed the streets and public gatherings for hard evidence of prevailing disloyalty. For instance, on 8 January, Constable W. MacGregor-Davies overheard a group of men outside a South Brisbane hotel shouting such sentiments as: 'To hell with King George and England. I would not fight for anyone but the Irish Republic and will shoot Billy Hughes if I see him.' A fortnight later, he detailed a wildcat strike at a Brisbane engineering works which had been prompted by the dismissal of union delegate, Alex Hildreth, an anti-war activist and self-proclaimed IWW member, for 'disloyal statements'. The workers' support for Hildreth finally resulted in his reinstatement. Then, on 10 February, MacGregor-Davies, along with three other constables, mingled among the listeners at the Brisbane Domain, and reported speakers Charles Collins, Labor MLA for Bowen, and Vida Goldstein for statements supporting Bolshevism and Internationalism.[22]

Thus, to all appearances, Queensland, with the only surviving Labor government in Australia, was being singled out by the four major surveillance organisations (the SIB, the Commonwealth Police, Military Intelligence and Censorship) as the 'most disloyal' state. Ainsworth, Anderson, Irving and Stable, it seems, all shared similar convictions about this. Their conspiratorial analysis, which interlaced the state socialist policies of Labor with the anarcho-syndicalist strategies of the surviving IWW, persistently overlooked the fundamental dissonance between reformers and revolutionaries, between pragmatists and visionaries, and between those who inhabited the corridors of power and those who were 'battling for a hold' from the periphery. By combining the often-competing interests of 'labour extremists', anarchists, pacifists and Quakers, Irish Roman Catholics and German 'enemy agents' into a co-ordinated disloyal assault (as Captain Stable was prone to do), the official view was inspired more by a war-enhanced sense of paranoia than any objective assessment of socio-political and ideological realities.[23]

Yet such phantom fears seemed to attain substantive form on the night of 1 May 1918. On that evening, as the *Daily Standard* had earlier forecast, Queensland was at last to celebrate "The Real May Day" as, in concert with many European nations, it went "a'maying in real continental style" in protest "against the continuation of the present upheaval". Although the Censor attempted to have commonwealth police suppress the celebration, it went ahead at the Brisbane Centennial Hall, before an audience of some four hundred people. Spread throughout that meeting, carefully surveying the proceedings, sat Captain Ainsworth of the SIB, Commandant Irving's 'Agent 77', a junior Assistant Censor, Mr De Tournouer, and an interpreter, A.B. Gibson, and no fewer than four sergeants and six constables of the commonwealth police. These fourteen surveillance officers watched closely as speaker after speaker called for 'this bloody madness' to end. Gordon Brown and Ted 'Darkie' Stewart of the UFL spoke of the imprisoned IWW twelve (recently convicted for arson attempts in Sydney) and of their own interstate exploits with police, as another member, George 'Curly' Johnston, sang 'Should I be a Soldier?' Alex Gorman and Kathleen Hotson appeared briefly for the peace organisations, and Jennie Scott Griffiths, secretary of the New Socialist Party, ventured, 'As long as there was solidarity among the workers, all hell could not make you put on a uniform.'[24]

Although neither Labor parliamentarians nor trade union representatives appeared among this 'platform talent', the federal agents were still able to associate the assembly with the mainstream labour movement through the presence of Joseph Silver Collings of the CPE, whom they dubbed 'a well known red-ragger'. Additionally, they were not slow to relate Labor's absence to the fact that, the same evening, these parliamentarians were attending their own packed protest rally at the Exhibition Hall against 'Conscription in Ireland'. Here, along with numerous Catholic bishops and clergy, they were rising to their feet to sing 'God Save Ireland', even as the radicals at Centennial Hall intoned 'The International'. Furthermore, the state government's complicity with the radicals was sealed, in the minds of the commonwealth officers, by Collings' announcement that the Home Secretary, John Huxham, had just approved the granting of five 'free speech areas' in the City, Fortitude Valley and South Brisbane where public forums could be legally held, exempted from the Traffic Regulations. 'I believe', wrote Sergeant McCullum, 'this will give an opening to the Sinn Feiners, IWW and UFL people to get into street speaking again.'[25]

Yet to these agents – as well as to the *Brisbane Courier* and *Daily Mail* the following day – the most disturbing feature of the rally emerged when a rough head count was taken of the various nationalities present in the hall. Apart from eighty or so Anglo- and Irish Australians among the four hundred participants, Agent 77 estimated, there were some two hundred Russians, forty Greeks, thirty Germans, twenty Poles and fifteen Finns. Speeches were delivered in Russian, French, Greek, Polish, Finnish and Esperanto. Indeed, it had been the local Union of Russian Workers (URW) which had organised the rally. The Russian anarchist, Nicholai Lagutin, who had been most active in arranging the event, spoke in halting English of the history of May Day in Russia, while a group of Russian actors presented a revolutionary tableau entitled 'Breaking the Chains of Bondage'. Although Agent 77 dogmatically dismissed this performance as a 'most ludicrous' spectacle, the Russians were certainly no slouches at dramatic production, having earlier been involved, along with the Jewish Workers Association (JWA), in the staging of several successful Yiddish and Russian plays.[26]

Before a darkened hall, the stage was bathed in a red glow as Comrade H. Ruzki spoke of the Russian Revolution and the fall of Nicholas II, 'this scarecrow with a crown on'. Since that time, he narrated, two political groupings had fallen into 'sharp antagonism' in Russia — Bolsheviks and Maximalists on the one hand and Mensheviks and Social Revolutionaries on the other. The Bolshevik Revolution — 'the best of friends to the working classes' — had succeeded but, under the threat of counter-revolution and Allied invasion, now faced 'danger . . . on every side'. For that revolution to survive, it must have the active support of workers of other countries. Working men and women should realise that capitalists controlled not only their 'muscular strength', but also much of their ability to think rationally about their 'own helplessness and economic slavery', by manipulating 'the strings' of educational and parliamentary institutions and the press. Australian workers must now learn to cast off these shackles. At the close of his narration, two actors, who had stood transfixed with upraised hammers throughout, broke the chains of a third, as a loud explosion of flashlight powder brought the performance to a close. Members of the cosmopolitan audience then rose to their feet and lustily sang 'The Red Flag'.[27]

The evening's 'distinctly disloyal' proceedings seemed to encapsulate those features which loyalists feared threatened the maintenance of their social world and its values. The 'polyglot' nature of the affair carried its own affront to the 'essentially British' character of Queensland society, as much as its sentiments of peace and internationalism challenged war commitment and imperial duty. Lastly, its revolutionary symbolism, heralding an overthrow of capitalism, conveyed an unequivocal message. 'This meeting is just a starter here', warned commonwealth policeman, Alex King. 'We shall see and hear more of this kind of thing in the near future and possibly much stronger will be the language and more bolder [sic] their efforts to establish IWWism and Sinn Feinism.' The following morning witnessed the start of a loyalist outcry in the conservative press and among returned soldiers of the RSSILA against this 'anticapitalistic anti-militaristic' demonstration. As questions were asked in the House of Representatives by John Chanter, the Chairman of Committees, the Crown Solicitor began to compile a case against the Centennial Hall speakers. Yet as none of the surveillance personnel present had been able to take verbatim notes, the chance of sweeping prosecutions was missed. Only one of the speakers, the bizarre Bjelke Boesen (alias Dr Xarus Sphynx), an eccentric freelance lecturer on 'physical culture', birth control and eugenics, was singled out for special attention. Boesen, born in Liège, Belgium, of Danish parents, had spoken in French against 'effete Capitalism' and 'senseless slaughter', ending his talk with a stentorian cry of 'Vive l'Internationale!' Why, he wondered aloud, had French and Belgian troops not shot their officers in the trenches and scrambled out to fraternize with their German comrades, instead of being 'slaughtered like a crowd of sheep'? For such frank speculations, Dr Sphynx was to be seized and interned by the military in June.[28]

Although this jumble of leftwing groups may have been moving into a rough anti-war alignment – much as they had colluded against conscription – neither tactically nor ideologically were they the united front feared by federal surveillance. Yet who, for instance, were these Russians who had organised the May Day rally and who claimed in their publication, *Workers Life*, that they could now 'see the peace cloud coming'? They were, in short, conspicuous strangers in a strange land, and their alliance with the Anglo-Australian left was at best an uneasy one. Even when they were fêted, particularly by the local IWW, as representatives of those who had so dramatically overthrown Western-style Provisional Government (Kerensky's regime) in the third largest country in the world, language barriers, cultural stances and political differences all conspired to keep them distinctly apart from Australian labour's mainstream. And it was not merely their intense revolutionary commitment which emphasised their distinctiveness. Their ethnic origins played as large a part in singling them out. It had, indeed, been their obvious 'Russian-ness' which had first marked them as unique, odd and suspect.[29]

The Queensland Russian community, a minority of some three to four thousand residents, was composed of groups of many political persuasions – Monarchists, liberal reformists, Mensheviks, Bolsheviks and Maximalists – although their main political allegiance had increasingly emerged as a Bolshevik one. Most of these Russians were already anti-Tsarist. They had settled in Queensland almost by default — it was a Western outpost at the end of a tortuous escape route from political imprisonment, principally in Siberia. Between 1909 and 1915, a stream of these haggard exiles and escapees had entered a society which played host to non-Britishers only reluctantly. Stigmatised as unsavoury and diseased, criminal and potentially subversive, they experienced great difficulty in establishing a foothold in a suspiciously Anglocentric, antipodean world. As four of them later explained:

> the Russian workers . . . were subjected to an unconstant employment because of unstable development of industry and partly through unequal treatment of . . . foreign workers . . . The opposite psychology of the masses here and its characteristic British antagonism to the other nationalities (especially to the Russians) . . . always kept us in the position of a class of workers being able to depend only on the casual employment which affords one just a bare living and no chances of any savings . . . [30]

In their search for scarce employment, their migrants had been scattered statewide, but many congregated in the seedy boarding houses of South Brisbane (parts of which had become virtually a Russian ghetto), in the sugar districts of north Queensland, at Townsville, where they laboured on the wharves and at the meatworks, and on the Cloncurry mining fields. In a diary purporting to describe his experiences in 'a free country', one Russian related how, soon after arrival, he had hoped to become an Australian 'gentleman'. He had even aped their ways 'by putting on a straw hat and white boots' and repudiating his nationality. Yet social acceptance had avoided him. With the outbreak of war, however, these assimilationist gestures were abandoned; 'his political convictions were roused to life and he became the same Russian revolutionary as when he landed'.[31]

The war had not been the only catalyst to political activism. Even prior to its outbreak, the revolutionary awareness of the Russian migrant had crystallised in the URW, 'formed . . . for the purpose of self-education and general advancement of social thought in the spirit of . . . International Socialism'. A 'handful of Russians' had initially carried the organisation in this leftist direction under the inspiration of 'Tom' Sergeev (alias Artem), a confidante of Lenin who had taken part in the 1905 uprising at Kharkov. Subsequently imprisoned in Siberia, he had escaped via Korea, arriving in Brisbane during 1911. Early in 1912, he had transformed the Union of Russian Immigrants, a self-help organisation, into the URW, giving it a political orientation which embraced both Social Democrats and Social Revolutionaries hostile to the Tsarist regime. Returning to Russia following the February Revolution of 1917, 'F.A. Sergeev' had become, in August, one of the fifteen members of the Bolshevik Central Committee which planned the October coup. Meanwhile, in Queensland, the URW, too, had become more homogeneously Bolshevik, as numerous Menshevik supporters of the Russian Provisional Government had also headed homewards. The enormous pride which members felt for the increasingly embattled URW is captured in the following statement of seven of its adherents:

> A great deal of sacrifice, time and money were put into this organization in order to build it up. The great devotion with which the group started it was not in vain. The organization soon embraced Russians throughout Australia by the system of branches in every State. Its library is better than a good many Australian working class libraries. The Russian worker often refused his dinner and subscribed the shilling to enrich the library. Sweat and toil built it up! It has its history, traditions. It has sub-organizations of 'self-assistance' and 'relief' to the political prisoners in Siberia and other places . . . The RWA had even a 'Field Naturalists Club'. Yes, it had a great deal in which the Australian working organizations are deficient, in the manner of self-education.[32]

Its organisational centre — the Russian club rooms, situated in the Atlas Buildings, Stanley Street, South Brisbane — was constantly the hub of spirited meetings, lectures and social occasions. Daylong debates on 'world-wide questions' were waged there; a series of Russian newspapers was planned and produced, while the rooms also housed the prized workers' library of more than one thousand 'precious volumes'. Yet what stood as a source of dignity for some was clearly a cause for mounting concern to others. Sergeant A.M. Short of the commonwealth police, later in 1918, reported the presence of 'strong Bolshevik branches' in Queensland at Ipswich, Townsville and Cairns, and less developed ones at Rockhampton and Toowoomba. Overall, there were twenty-eight known Bolshevik branches throughout Australia. To Sergeant Short, as to the Censor, J.J. Stable, 'IWWism' and Bolshevism were simply 'one and the same thing'. 'The Russians are the real IWW', Captain Stable asserted; 'they are the real live agents of the doctrine. They never permit anything to take prior place in their thoughts to IWWism — they live and move and have their being in its revolutionary atmosphere — it is their very existence.'[33]

Although, in making such claims, these commonwealth officers displayed considerable ignorance about the doctrinal contrasts between Bolshevism and Syndicalism (the former concentrating upon a politically conscious vanguard seizing the state apparatus and the latter organising industrially towards widescale revolutionary unionism) their prognosis did carry some hint of truth. For the URW and the IWW were both fully committed revolutionary bodies and, of the two, the Russians were clearly the most zealous. As Peter Perfileff, a Russian canecutter at Halifax, north Queensland, complained, the English IWW members in his work gang were 'much too quiet'. 'We Russians always every hour discuss the Labour movement', he wrote. Anglo-Australian workers, however, merely paid some attention "when we start to converse with them in English . . . but that is the only time they give the matter a thought . . . I asked them how they are getting on with the Revolution . . . they told me the people are not ready yet . . . The question arises — when *will* the world be ready?"[34]

Yet, of all the Australian radical organisations, the IWW was the only one for which the Russian revolutionaries had any serious time. The refurbished Queensland Socialist League (QSL) positioned itself too close to the Labor party for their liking; the pacifist groups, although uncompromisingly anti-war, short-sightedly lacked an acceptable anti-capitalist critique. The other parties were only 'followers', the URW executive later reasoned. 'With those parties we can be on the best of terms, but all our active assistance we must give to the parties which do not recognise the Bourgeois Parliament and which stands for the Socialistic Republic. This party is IWW . . . ' For the parliamentary Labor party and for the trade unions, however, the Russians registered little more than contempt. The Labor politicians were merely 'Cabinet fighters' continuously urging war involvement, they argued, whilst the parliamentary system itself stifled the manifestation of every revolutionary thought and prevented people from taking 'any direct or immediate part in Government'. Similarly, Australian unionism was condemned as 'useless, timeworn and crumbling . . . an organisation which is far behind the labor movement of Europe', delivering nothing more sustaining than 'bread and butter' into the workers' hands.[35]

In mid-1918, three URW members, led by Konstantin Klushin (alias Orlov), a Russian intellectual, refused to pay a customary workers' levy to labour's *Daily Standard* because the newspaper did not endorse their ideals. Subsequently, they were sacked from their jobs at the Eagle Farm meat freezing plant, apparently after Meat Union officials (AMIEU) pressured its management for their dismissal. A heated clash between Russian and BIC delegates resulted at Trades Hall, inducing Klushin to warn other workers angrily against union leaders who gave lip service to 'One Big Union' principles, yet failed practically to support 'Direct Action'. Do not trust Mr MacDonald [Editor of the *Daily Standard*]', Klushin urged. "He, by his policy of adaptation . . . is more harmful than the *Courier*, because the *Courier* is well known to you as a capitalist paper; while the *Daily Standard* is today for you, tomorrow against you. Today it defends Craft Unionism, tomorrow the OBU. Take care what you are fed with . . . "[36]

Thus, discord between the URW and the bulk of the labour movement was deep-seated; it remained concealed rather than healed by any likemindedness on such matters as conscription and war prosecution. Russian workers had originally been to the forefront of the anti-conscription movement, calling 'A Conference of Citizens of the World' in Brisbane to fight militarism as early as December 1915. Yet, during 1916, they had been deflected from greater commitment to the struggle by problems of their own. For, even before the first conscription referendum campaign had begun, D'Abaza, the Imperial Russian Consul, had virtually imposed military service upon his erstwhile countrymen, without any apparent murmurs of dissent from Australian workers. In fact, the Hughes Labor Government had tacitly complied with the Czarist regime's wishes, forcing Russians in Australia 'to go into the Volunteer Armies and either enlist or get . . . exemption papers in order to be allowed to look for work outside the Military enterprises; any Russian that had no such papers to show him . . . unfit . . . was refused employment in . . . civilian life.'[37]

Labor's relationship with the IWW movement was just as contradictory and capricious as it was with the URW, despite the claims of federal agents. Labor's Treasurer, E.G. Theodore, had made his first public condemnation of the syndicalists, as early as mid-1916, branding them a 'great danger'. Yet the exigencies of the long conscription struggle had brought the Queensland government and the revolutionaries into an uneasy, temporary alliance. Labor's commitment to the anti-conscription cause had been cemented by a curious combination of fears. Although genuinely alarmed by the creeping autocracy of Hughes's Nationalists after 1916, they were equally perturbed, Queensland's Governor, Hamilton Goold Adams claimed in December 1917, about the local radicals' enhanced capacity for mischief, should the conscription referendum succeed. Goold Adams, a warm admirer of both Ryan and Theodore, regarded this latter concern as their main reason for opposing the military compulsionists. Cabinet ministers, via 'secret channels of information', he reported to the Colonial Office, had nervously anticipated what the militant factions intended if 'Yes' proponents won the plebiscites. 'It was understood by them', he revealed, . . . that if conscription was adopted, the extremists would by acts of violence and sabotage upset the whole social and industrial life of Australia . . . It was, I believe, a real fear of a crisis of this description that influenced my Premier and his colleagues . . . to oppose the enforcement of conscription.'[38]

Viewed from this perspective, Labor's alliance with the IWW and other radicals on the Anti-Conscription Coordinating Committees had been less an exercise in leftwing consolidation than a strategical holding operation to curb threateningly rebellious excesses. In late 1917, state police were used to suppress IWW street meetings, and Premier Ryan informed Hughes that the 'evil' was also being contained by 'unions . . . expelling members . . . and discouraging their propaganda'. His government favoured 'police surveillance' and union expulsion, Ryan added, rather than the 'precipitate action' of political imprisonment employed in several non-Labor states. To accommodate the leftwing of their own broad-based movement, the Cabinet therefore steered an uneasy course, between the Scylla of Nationalist 'tyranny' and the Charybdis of radical 'extremism'.[39]

During 1918, however, the Queensland government seemed to be increasingly rudderless against the rising tide of 'disloyalty'. To 'Win the War' zealots, 'disloyalty' represented the rankest treachery to the Empire, whereas to 'Stop the War' converts, it had increasingly come to represent the ultimate in sanity and human decency. And so, during the final year of warfare, certain Labor parliamentarians were sometimes to be found sharing public podiums with peace advocates. The failure of a 'last ditch' recruiting conference organized by the Governor-General in April was followed by the militancy of the Perth ALP Federal Conference in June. Delegates roundly condemned 'the policy . . . of war frenzied jingoism, which has bled Australia white'. The war was simply being prolonged by 'financial and commercial greed, land hunger, militaristic ambition and a spurious public opinion . . . sustained by an unscrupulous press', many argued, as they came within two votes of opposing any more men leaving Australia for military service abroad. Instead, it was agreed the issue be put to a national poll of union members, which was still being conducted when the war ended.[40]

Meanwhile, in Queensland, an anti-recruiting campaign gathered momentum. As early as June 1917, the BIC, representing most of the metropolitan unions, had begun an attack on 'worms in khaki' haranguing workers at recruiting rallies. By the following May, it was openly calling for an armistice on all fronts and 'peace on the basis of "no indemnities and no annexations".' This statement, dubbed 'The White Flag Manifesto' by the conservative press, went on to assert that any labour leader advocating enlistment had failed lamentably to interpret the views of workers upon the matter. Campaigning outside the capital for the Returned Soldiers Employment Bureau, Thomas O'Hagan, an old warrior who had no time for 'shirkers', found that in the west the desire for a permanent peace was uppermost. 'The *Brisbane Courier* west of Charleville or Rockhampton is not read or seen', he wrote. Here militant labour views held sway. At eight centres he visited, the voluntary recruiting movement was distinctly hampered. Recruiting sergeants tended to agree, one of them later recollecting that the position 'was one of the toughest jobs I've ever pulled on'. Another, writing from the central west in September 1918, reported forlornly:

I have been astonished at the marked disloyalty of the labouring class in Emerald and Jericho. The eligible men are in the habit of making gross disloyal statements. Posters pasted up on the walls of public buildings are torn down immediately. As I was delivering handbills on the station at Emerald, I was publicly insulted by both men and women on the Railway staff. Complaints to the Station Master were treated with indifference. I was even advised not to speak at a recruiting meeting as the police informed me there would be trouble from the disloyal element. I was unsupported in these outside districts as the residents are afraid to give any help or information regarding the Voluntary ballot because they have been threatened with boycott.[41]

Even the 'snowball' recruiting marches, often covering enormous distances and picking up volunteers en route, no longer enthused rural populations as they had done in 1915. A spectacular 'March for Freedom' enlistment drive, co-ordinated throughout southern Queensland by loyalists between June and November 1918, witnessed country crowds still turning out to applaud, yet precious few 'eligibles' were offered for the firing line. In some centres, the columns found the going much tougher. At Barcaldine, for instance, recruits were stoned by twenty 'disloyalists' (who were all subsequently gaoled), and at Mount Larcom, they were met by a Red Flag demonstration. Further altercations with pacifists occurred at Bogantungan, Bundaberg and Maryborough.[42]

Although Premier Ryan attempted to bolster languishing enthusiasm by sponsoring a 'Ryan's Thousand' for the Front, following upon the May recruiting conference, disdain and abuse from both pro- and anti-war advocates supplanted the enthusiasm and support he expected. After the Perth Conference, Ryan abandoned the exercise entirely, still almost 550 recruits short of his target. Instead, the Labor party now found itself drawn into a series of conflicts with the federal government which only aggravated the estrangements born of the conscription wrangles. An anti-internment campaign mounted by the party in July was quickly followed by an attempt to thwart the deportation of Italian reservists for overseas conscription in September. Then, in October, a renewed protest was directed against the impact of official war propaganda in Queensland state schools. So altered seemed Labor's emphases that W.H. Barnes, Opposition MLA for Bulimba, asked at parliamentary question time in August whether the government now proposed flying the Red Flag 'from Parliament House and other public buildings'. Corporal H.E. Sizer, Conservative MLA for Nundah, was also moved to speculate whether, under Labor rule, they were sitting 'in a British or an alien parliament'. To loud applause from a Loyalty League gathering, he charged that 'what was at the back of the whole thing was . . . what had had such an effect in Russia — the doctrines of Bolshevism'.[43]

Thus, following upon the Perth Conference, the red flag, as a symbol of irreverence and rebellion, had become a new target for loyalist rage. At that conference, delegates had re-endorsed it as the flag of the Australian labour movement. 'The Red Flag', stated the *Daily Standard* proudly, 'has ever stood for freedom as against tyranny. From time immemorial, it has symbolized the discontent of the downtrodden, the revolt of the discontented, . . . the affirmations of brotherhood, of comradeship [and] . . . of life . . . ' Yet the meanings attached to this emblem varied significantly amongst its many supporters. To some, the 'blood-coloured' banner was simply 'the workers' flag' and to others 'the flag of the Trade Unions', or even of the Labor Government itself. To many, it represented 'reform more than revolution', whilst to Melbourne socialists, H. Scott Bennett and R.S. Ross, it was comprehensively 'the race flag . . . Humanity's flag'. What was there about it which should alarm any decent man or woman, asked the Brisbane *Truth* in early August. It was the standard of 'international fraternity and social republicanism', and those who sang its praises or raised it asked for 'nothing but justice'. Yet, to both local Wobblies and Bolsheviks, the significance of the flag was clearly insurrectionary. 'This is the only flag worth fighting for — every other flag should be trampl-ed underfoot', claimed IWW advocate, Norman Jeffery. 'The Red Flag stands for . . . revolution. The Revolution must come; Bolshevism will never be stopped in Australia.'[44]

Such polemics were clearly alarming, and to Empire loyalists the flag represented only one thing — the overthrow of society. As a *Brisbane Courier* correspondent concluded in September, it denoted nothing more than 'blood, fire, destruction and devil worship'. It was the flag the Bolsheviks carried, and did they not represent — as the conservative press disclosed almost daily — 'the worst terror in the history of revolutions'? Flying this flag expressed 'a direct challenge to . . . patriotic sentiment', stated Acting Prime Minister, W.A. Watt, for was not the only emblem Australia needed, symbolic of humanity and fair-play, the Union Jack?[45]

The 'Tory' press had suddenly become prone to 'epileptic attacks . . . whenever anything red is mentioned', jibed the Brisbane *Truth*, while the *Daily Standard* prescribed ice-cold baths for those taking such fits. Yet the vigorous Perth resolu-tions had added a new tone of defiance to the commitment of the left, which loyalists now felt constrained to heed. Their anti-war message needed to be pushed 'as far as . . . humanly possible', wrote APA secretary, Alex Gorman, as he prepared a 'Monster Peace Rally' for Ipswich in July. Hopefully, he added, such ef-forts might soon mean 'the only fight that will be waged will be the one on the present insane system of society which makes it possible for such wars to take place'. In response to the Perth example, red flags were now being unfurled elsewhere – one was raised first over the Melbourne Trades Hall, then Brisbane and Sydney quickly followed suit. Red flags were also appearing above workers' homes. Throughout northern and western Queensland, the red flag anthem invariably opened and closed every workers' meeting and, as early as February 1918, a red flag procession had marched through the streets of Cloncurry.[46]

The large red banner which flew over Brisbane Trades Hall, located in upper Turbot Street and overlooking the city, was soon to lead to heated debate and violent confrontation. On Sunday afternoon, 29 July, George 'Gunner' Taylour, a radical returned soldier addressed a crowd of 1,500 at the Brisbane Domain. His continued references to peace, revolution and the red flag led to a minor riot. Taylour was physically attacked by six other returned soldiers, led by W.A. Fisher, Queensland's RSSILA organiser, knocked from his makeshift platform and assaulted. As police intervened, radicals in the audience sang 'The Red Flag', only to be countered with the soldiers' rendition of 'Rule Britannia' and 'Australia Will Be There'. That evening at the Albert Street Methodist Church, the Reverend Dr G.E. Rowe, an ardent loyalist spokesperson, turned a sermon entitled 'What the War has done for Harry Lauder' (the famous Scottish entertainer) towards matters closer to home. Nodding in the direction of the red flag flying conspicuously upon the nearby hill, he charged: 'Why do you men here in Brisbane allow the red flag to be flown over your city? There is that flag at the Trades Hall, a menace to the Union Jack. There is the enemy behind much that is going on in this State . . . It is part of . . . the work of the great Hun spy system. Men of Queensland, awake! Awake! . . . Why don't you rise as one man – as did Oliver Cromwell and his men of old – and sweep out this 'House of Parliament'?'[47]

Rowe's words of incitement, amplified in the conservative press over subsequent days, were soon to be taken quite literally. During the first week of August, certain officials of the Queensland Protestant League, an avidly Anglophile, pro-conscription body, in association with a number of recruiting sergeants, approached returned soldiers, requesting them to demonstrate at Trades Hall that weekend. 'Those circularized', claimed the *Daily Standard*, 'were given to understand that . . . their mission would be fruitless if the Trades Hall were not stormed and the Red Flag on the roof torn down'. That Saturday afternoon, therefore, a raiding party of a dozen returned soldiers, selected at the YMCA club rooms by recruiting sergeant, De Lacy Evans, approached the Trades Hall building. The unionists, however, were forewarned of the assault and a score of men, led by 'Gunner' Taylour, had strongly defended the entrances as well as the stairs leading to its tower. After some scuffling and altercation, the soldiers' invasion was thwarted by the arrival of a dozen police.[48]

Just five days later, the first March for Freedom recruiting column was heading across the Darling Downs from the Stanthorpe district towards Brisbane. At Darra, a small working-class settlement on its outskirts, the 110 recruits were welcomed by local patriots, led by A.C. Elphinstone, the newly elected State Nationalist member for Oxley and President of the Royal Society of St George, as well as Federal MHRs, Hugh Sinclair, an Ipswich factory manager, and J.G. Bayley, Nationalist member for Brisbane. Over lunch, provided at the local school by Red Cross 'ladies', the volunteers' attention was drawn to a workers' Victory Hall, still under construction some distance down the road. For several weeks, the soldiers were told, meatworkers, who were building the hall each weekend, had flown a red flag from the structure, much to the chagrin of local loyalists. Thereupon, the March for Freedom rapidly reconstituted itself and headed for the hall. Labor Shire Councillor, A.A. Elliott, witnessed the column approaching at 2 p.m. and the soldiers' agitated search through the half-completed building for the flag. At last they detected it beneath a pile of timber — a piece of red rag little more than one-foot square. Before a swelling crowd of onlookers, the square of material was mangled, torn, attacked with an axe and finally burned. A Union Jack was then raised above the hall on a sapling flag-pole, as the soldiers, now soberly back in formation, saluted it and the civilian bystanders cheered.[49]

The Darra 'Red Flag incident', as it came to be known, was merely a moment of fury and patriotic ritual, conducted haphazardly in a small Queensland settlement. Yet its implications were both alarming and far-reaching. The spontaneous rage of the soldiers and the approbation of the watching civilians were portents of the far graver conflicts which lay ahead. For, if a mere rag could evoke such blind passion, it was worth asking, what painful destiny lay in store for the flesh and blood advocates of revolution at the hands of Queensland loyalists?

[W.A. Watt]: Losing his head (*Worker*, 23 January 1918)

Darra's startling little 'incident' was publicised Australia-wide, while the local press reaction once more revealed the chasm between left and rightwing advocates. What, to the *Daily Standard*, appeared as a clear case of 'vandalism' and 'cowardice', comparable to the Zabern incident (a 1913 assault by German officers upon citizens of a small Alsatian town) was to the *Brisbane Courier* 'an exciting and thrilling scene' of patriotic inspiration. Federal politicians applauded the soldiers' performance, and only one week later the Acting Prime Minister announced that Commonwealth action would now be taken to lower all red flags flying across Australia. Thus, on 19 September, a federal prohibition against any public display of Sinn Fein colours, issued in March, was extended to include the Red Flag, which was now depicted as the emblem of an 'enemy country'.[50]

Twelve days later, two Military Intelligence officers arrived at Brisbane Trades Hall with a federal order to have its offending red flag removed. The huge flag was so securely fastened to its rooftop pole, however, that the military men could not budge it. Nor would any Trades Hall member agree to help. Finally, someone from the curious street crowd was paid ten shillings to scale the flagstaff and laboriously dislodge the illicit standard. Thus, for only a small bribe, the red flag in Brisbane came down — after little more resistance than a few granny knots — as loyalists roared and unionists looked helplessly on. In the months ahead, however, the ongoing cost of suppressing that flag — and the fractious spirit it embodied — was to prove a far more daunting proposition.[51]

Chapter 2

The Tory Mob

If I were boss of the land, I'd soon
   Have things put straight.
I'd find an island, and there maroon
   And leave to their fate . . .
Men who'll do any old thing save fight;
Men who prate for "a Social State";
Men who for peace would "negotiate" . . .[1]

Lionel Lindsay (1918)

By the beginning of October 1918, victory on the Western Front seemed almost a *fait accompli*. The infusion of fresh American divisions into the firing line since mid-year, the Australian and Canadian advances near Amiens in August and the storming of the Hindenberg Line in late September all pointed to one inescapable conclusion. By the close of September, Bulgaria had surrendered and Allenby's cavalry units had driven the Turks from Damascus. 'The last two weeks', wrote Hughes on 28 September to the Governor-General, '. . . bring us to the very threshold of the Promised Land'. Within six more days, the German Chancellor had been dismissed and the Central Powers were suing for peace. Two days later, on 5 October, Australian troops at Montbrehain fought their last campaign of the war.[2]

From Brisbane, T.J. Ryan wrote to the Colonial Office of great jubilation throughout Queensland at the impending 'overthrow of Prussian despotism'. In the city, church bells had rung out and factory hooters blasted incessantly. Business premises had been gaily decorated and employers had magnanimously released their workers for fifteen minutes to congregate in Queen Street and sing the national anthem. 'With almost startling suddenness', the *Brisbane Courier* noted, 'the [war] situation has changed from one charged with gloomy possibility to one irradiated with confident hopes'. Loyalists, sensing the sweet smell of military success, encapsulated their emotions in one striking phrase: 'Rejoice: we conquer!'[3]

"And the old chariot rolls on" (*Worker*, 10 August 1916)

Yet such rejoicing was not the prerogative of all, certainly not of a socialist Premier. When Ryan attempted to speak at a 'victory demonstration' arranged outside the GPO the following day he was quickly reduced to silence by a barrage of hooting and interjection. To the glee of returned soldiers leading the protest, he became 'furiously angry' as the din of opposition mounted. Even the intercession of Brisbane's conservative Lord Mayor proved to no avail. As the indignant Premier left the podium, and the strains of 'God Save the King' rang out, loyalist women knocked the hats from the heads of 'disloyal' males in the audience.[4]

To those for whom 'peace by negotiation' had represented a peace without honour, the scent of outright victory over 'hordes of atrocious Huns, Turks and other barbarians' was intoxicating. Triumph over warfront opponents seemed a vindication of every loyalist ideal, and must surely now be matched, it was argued, by a 'fight . . . to the death' with the enemy at home. 'The Red Flag element is more conspicuous in Queensland than in any other State', wrote a *Courier* correspondent on 2 October: 'America stood no socialistic nonsense when she entered the big campaign, but took prompt action by deporting the revolutionary section . . . we should similarly treat the Trades Hall parasites who are alone responsible for the prevailing unrest and turbulence in Queensland . . .'[5]

Such an appeal to the United States' example is an instructive one. For, in her official suppression of radicalism and dissent, Australia had already matched — and to some degree surpassed — the American response. The US *Espionage Act* of June 1917 paralleled the censorship intentions of the Australian *War Precautions Act* of October 1914. Yet wartime censorship in Australia had certainly proceeded longer and, apparently, been far more intrusive, with less resistance, than in the United States. Similarly, America's *Sedition Act* of May 1918 performed a function, in combatting leftists, equal to the Australian *Unlawful Associations Acts* of December 1916 and July 1917. Yet, official repression of the IWW in the USA did not begin until the government raids of September 1917 — a year after Hughes had struck in New South Wales and Western Australia. With the exception of the gaoling of the Sydney Twelve, sentencing in the United States, which began in April 1918, had been far more draconic in terms of the length of imprisonment imposed. Yet,

whereas 200 Wobblies were gaoled in America, the commonwealth, with only a small fraction of that country's population,
had already incarcerated as many as 120. Between February
1917 and November 1919 some sixty unwanted aliens were
deported from America, yet in that same period the federal
government would deport at least fifteen IWW supporters,
almost a dozen Russian Bolsheviks as well as several hundred
Italian reservists and thousands of interned German residents.[6]

There was one area of response, however, where the United
States clearly outflanked Australia in its vigour and ruthlessness.
Its popular vigilantism — the phenomenon of night-riders and
lynch-law — had become virtually an American institution. 'A
GERMAN LYNCHED: HOW THEY TREAT THEM IN
AMERICA', the *Croydon Mining News* of north-western
Queensland had headlined in April 1918, as though the kind of
mob action which had despatched Robert Prager of St Louis
might provide a precedent worthy of local emulation.
'Queensland must be purged clean of all skunks and curs', wrote
a returned soldier in October 1918, as he related how a Brisbane
Domain orator had libelled his comrades. 'I was amazed to find
that the man was not immediately lynched', he exclaimed.
'However, this is Queensland. They do things better in America.'

Yet, despite public innocence of the fact, an attempt to coordinate Australian responses with American vigilantism had
already been made. During the spring of 1917, the government-
sponsored American Protective League (APL) had been launched
after Albert Briggs, a Chicago advertising executive, had approached the Bureau of Investigation with the idea. This officially funded loyalist organisation, which eventually recruited some
250,000 citizens, operated, according to historian David
Kennedy, as

> a rambunctious, unruly *posse comitatus* on an unprecedented scale.
> Its "agents" bugged, burglarized, slandered and illegally arrested other
> Americans. They opened mail, intercepted telegrams, served as
> *agents provocateurs* and were the chief commandos in a series of
> extra-legal and often violent "slacker raids" against supposed draft
> evaders in 1918 . . . The League sometimes counselled its members to
> commit outright physical assault on dissenters. It was, in one author-
> ity's summary view, "a force for outrageous vigilantism blessed with
> the seal and sanction of the federal government".[7]

Soon after the APL's inception, Washington was visited by a
former Australian Intelligence agent, R.C.D. Elliott, a
Melbourne businessman and country newspaper proprietor.

Here he examined the organisation's activities and format and its methods of official propaganda dissemination. Elliott's report, submitted to the Minister for Defence, Senator George Pearce, upon his return to Australia, resulted during 1918 in two inter-related developments. First, a Directorate of War Propaganda was established by the commonwealth with branches in all state capitals to counteract disloyal 'outpourings'. In Brisbane, its contact was the subsequently prolific amateur historian, Malcolm H. Ellis, who had established links already with the SIB. Secondly, and more covertly, a private meeting between Acting Prime Minister, W.A. Watt, and Herbert Brookes, a business associate of Elliott, took place on 28 May 1918. They discussed the formation of an Australian Protective League to operate along the same lines as the American prototype.

Herbert Robinson Brookes was a leading member of the Melbourne establishment and, in 1918, was probably one of the most influential public figures in Australia. With a family for-tune accumulated through mining and manufacturing ventures in Victoria and large-scale pastoral activities in Queensland, he had been prominent in the foundation of the Liberal Party and had married Alfred Deakin's eldest daughter in 1905. As Presi-dent of the Victorian Chamber of Manufacturers, he had become involved in a series of wartime committees, particularly muni-tions, and as a fervent conscriptionist, had apparently developed close relationships with Hughes, Pearce and Watt. Militantly Protestant and Anglophile, as well as increasingly politically conservative in outlook, Brookes had directly influenced both Hughes and Watt in the banning of the Sinn Fein flag and the red flag during 1918. Yet he believed that something more systematic than symbolic suppression was necessary to counter the impact of 'insidious, subversive propaganda' in Australia. Elliott's suggestion of a vigilant Protective League seemed to fulfil this need.

The preliminary, secret discussions about an APL are not clearly documented; but during 1918 these seem to have involv-ed – along with Watt and Brookes – Pearce, George Steward of the SIB and Major E.L. Piesse, Director of Military Intelligence. In August–September, too, Brookes had visited Brisbane in con-nection with the superintendence of his Central Downs pastoral properties and there contacted Frederick Charles Urquhart, the Queensland Commissioner of Police. From one perspective, it may seem startling that the putative organizer of an extra-legal, vigilante force should now approach the official fount of law and order in Queensland for support and validation of his intentions. Yet, clearly, such a move is no more remarkable than the fact that some of the nation's leading politicians and civil servants were already embroiled in a plan to unleash the watchdogs of loyalty with their official blessing — 'to effect drastic measures without . . . assuming the full formal authority to do so'.[8]

Urquhart possessed the same impeccable credentials as Brookes. Indeed, he was the beneficiary of a far longer loyalist pedigree. For Urquhart could trace a direct line of descent from Sir Thomas Urquhart of Cromarty, in northernmost Scotland. Sir Thomas, the eccentric translator of Rabelais, had been a fervent Royalist supporter during the Civil War period and had taken part in an abortive rising at Aberdeen upon Charles I's execution. He had reputedly died in 1660 after an apoplectic fit, caused by a bout of 'uncontrollable mirth' after hearing of Charles II's restoration. Another notable member of the 'Clan D'Urquhart of Cromarty' was David Urquhart, a Tory publicist and obsessive Russophobe who, in the late 1830s, had become convinced that Chartist agitation in the British Isles was being 'fermented by Russian agents'. Police Commissioner Urquhart's role in the prelude to, and aftermath of, the Brisbane Red Flag riots, was destined to become a curiously accurate reflection of his predecessor's extravagant convictions. As David Urquhart himself had pertinently commented in 1850, 'Race is not easily rubbed out'.[9]

The loyalist and military traditions of the Urquhart line had been reinforced by the career of Urquhart's father, a major in the Bengal Artillery, and had been further drilled into young Urquhart at the Felstead Military College in Essex. After joining the Queensland Native Police force in 1882, Urquhart saw eighteen years frontier service in the far north and west of Queensland, suppressing Aboriginal resistance and rising to the rank of first class inspector in the process. Emulating his father's soldierly activities among a preponderantly 'native' military force in India, Urquhart had reputedly drilled his native troopers 'with all the vehemence of a Prussian Sergeant Major'. Ultimately, in 1884, he led the bloody charges of black police and white posses which routed the mighty Aboriginal confederation of Kalkadoons of the Cloncurry district. During various punitive sorties, he had been twice wounded by Aboriginal warriors — in the thigh and in the groin.

Posted to Brisbane in 1896, he had assumed control of the Criminal Investigation Bureau (CIB) for eight years before being promoted to Chief Inspector in 1905. Eulogised in the conservative press as a man of forcefulness, with 'the rare gift of commanding obedience and respect', he had also earned the enmity of the labour movement. During the 1912 Brisbane General Strike, he had patrolled the city's streets like 'a very Napoleon . . . [on] a sturdy charger' and led the vicious police charges of 'Black Friday'. War's outbreak in 1914 had witnessed scenes predicted by Urquhart in a poem he had written earlier, published in *Camp Canzonettes* (1891): 'Australia's "boys" ' took their place in 'Britannia's Army . . . To front the world in arms'; his prediction was fondly recalled in 1914. This Imperial commitment remained all-consuming as Urquhart advanced to the position of Commissioner of Police in January 1917. He took particular pride in the achievements of his only son, Lieutenant Colonel W.J. Urquhart, a Duntroon graduate, serving with the Anzac Mounted Division in Palestine as one of the few Australian commanders upon the general staff there.[10]

Herbert Brookes had little to fear, therefore; in the person of the Police Commissioner he would meet a likeminded ally. Soon after assuming this position, Urquhart had attended a secret SIB conference in Melbourne on 19 February 1917 which had discussed 'alien enemy agents and suspects', espionage and a new system of recording surveillance information 'on the lines laid down in the Imperial Most Secret Memo on the subject'. Later that year, he requested that the Premier's Department take action 'to decrease the influx of an undesirable class of Russian' into the state. By this time, his liaison with the SIB was virtually a constant one as, from September 1917, he was meeting Captain Ainsworth twice and sometimes three times weekly to discuss the problems of Domain disloyalty, German and Russian aliens and the IWW threat. Hence Brookes, in August 1918, found him receptive to the suggestion that he, Urquhart, should now act as 'permanent formal head' of an Australian Protective League 'in charge of Queensland and New South Wales'. Writing to Brookes in Melbourne on 9 September, the Commissioner indicated that he was prepared to serve in this capacity if 'the embryo' developed. There were at least '20 well-known agitators' in Brisbane, he estimated, who could be rapidly suppressed by a firm enforcement of the *Unlawful Associations Act*. Unofficially too, Urquhart now began making the rounds of the extant patriotic organizations in Brisbane, dropping 'various hints' about the possibility of a more formidable coordination of loyalist forces.[11]

Loyalist organization at this time was rudimentary and confined mainly to the capital. In late August 1918, the Returned Sailors, Soldiers and Citizens Loyalty League (RSSCLL) had been launched at the Brisbane Domain. Its principal members were C.J. Peiniger (President), a returned soldier who had enlisted in August 1914 and had been 'smashed up on two occasions by the enemy', T.G. Mills (Secretary), another war veteran, and E.R. Jenyns, a local manufacturer of women's corsetry and member of a long-established Brisbane family. At their inaugural meeting, these three vowed to crush the growing element of 'disloyalists, traitors and the scum of Australia' – whom they believed were being financed by 'a great deal of German money' – and 'to keep the Union Jack flying over Australia, the flag that stood for liberty, progress, civilization and Christianity'. 'If the Union Jack were taken down and the red flag or any other flag hoisted in its stead,' warned Peiniger, 'it would be God help the workers of Australia.' The following Sunday, the RSSCLL experienced a rough baptism when its Domain meeting was overrun by radicals, led by George 'Gunner' Taylour, and forced to close.[12]

Considering itself under siege, the new Loyalty League called upon all Britishers to band together, ready for any eventuality. Yet its formation was invading ground already pegged out by other loyalist groups in operation since late 1916. The Returned Soldiers and Patriots National League (RSPNL), for instance, had been formed on the eve of the first conscription campaign with a strong anti-alien, anti-radical platform. Through its mouthpiece, the weekly *National Leader*, under the editorship of E.S. Emerson, a former *Brisbane Courier* sub-editor and a descendent of Ralph Waldo Emerson, it had mounted an ongoing campaign against the Hun, the Wobbly and the Bolshevik. Despite a massive Labor majority in the March 1918 state election, the reactionary RSPNL had returned three members to parliament from among eight candidates fielded. These three military officers – Corporal Hubert Sizer (Nundah), Sergeant Richard Warren (Murrumba) and Major James Fry (Kurilpa) – had all recently seen service abroad. Sizer, a former *Daily Mail* journalist, had been among the first Australians landed at Gallipoli, whilst Warren, of the 26th Battalion, had been wounded there.

Telephone—Central, 1222.   Box 423, G.P.O.

Returned Soldiers & Patriots
National League

DARRAGH'S BUILDINGS, 331 Queen St. Brisbane, Q'ld.
Opp. Union Bank.

Secretary:
G. S. BARTLETT

General
Organising
Secretary:
ROBT. WELLS

OUR MOTTO

The above National League has been formed, having in view the following IMMEDIATE OBJECTS —

1. To do all in our power to win and bring the war to an early and successful conclusion.
2. To protect the interests of all Soldiers, Sailors and their dependents.
3. To deport all interned alien enemies at the close of the war.
4. To foster, encourage and develop all Australian resources, industries and productions.
5. To form a National Policy for a Progressive Australia at the conclusion of the War.

If you are prepared to support this league, help us by becoming a member AT ONCE. The membership fee is **1/-** Members can however give any further financial support they wish.

Additional information and particulars will be furnished on application to the Secretary.

Issued by the Authority of the Committee of the above league

Returned Soldiers and Patriots National League (dodger from the *National Leader*)

Major Fry, in turn, had served with the 9th Battalion in France. Sizer, the most politically promising of the three (and subsequently, Secretary for Labour and Industry in the Country National Moore ministry of 1929), was regarded as a stirring platform speaker and had opened the second conscription campaign in Queensland for the compulsionists. Major Fry, though not so outspoken, remained in close contact with commonwealth surveillance, paying several visits to Ainsworth's SIB office during 1918. Overall, the RSPNL claimed a membership of 14,000, as well as an electoral influence over another 50,000 voters. 'We too are forming "One Big Union", warned Andrew Grant, a local businessman and amateur historian, in the *National Leader* in September 1918: ' . . . and its members are the men who are described by the advocates of the other movement as "repressive parasitical scabs on the workers". Our union is one which draws the color line; it is open only to men of the one color, and that color is khaki.'[13]

The third major loyalist group at this time — and the one which, during 1919, was to seize the initiative in the mobilization of returned soldiers — was the Returned Sailors and Soldiers Imperial League (RSSILA). Yet, by late 1918, its membership was still comparatively small and its Queensland movement marked by internecine struggle. Its early Brisbane gatherings, noted the *National Leader*, were tumultuous affairs, where general disorder often turned the meeting into 'a bear garden'. By late 1918, as the Censor would later report, the RSSILA was clearly passing through a crisis: 'There appears to be a considerable amount of friction between those who belong to the rank and file and the ex-officers', he noted, ' . . . an atmosphere of discontent and rowdyism' exists.[14]

Thus, from a loyalist standpoint, Urquhart's suggestions about a closer coordination of its patriotic forces seemed most apposite. Although the numbers existed for an impressive mobilization, and were indeed growing as more and more fighting men headed homeward, its energies remained scattered, unfocussed and unnecessarily replicated. In reference to Queensland, the Governor-General had written worriedly in late August 1918, 'The extreme elements of the Labor Party are rampant. Other elements of the community seem to be ineffective and unable to combine.' Yet there was evidence of a drive towards a more militant, combative unity which, behind the scenes, was being encouraged by influential voices, additional to

A slump in business (*Worker*, 23 January 1919)

that of the Police Commissioner. 'There is an extremist element in the National Party, uncompromisingly hostile to Labour', reported the Censor, J.J. Stable, in late September 1918:

> . . . an element which, in Queensland at least is deliberately working to precipitate a crisis on the assumption that as trouble must come, the sooner it comes the better as:
> (a) a general strike in Queensland would have the same effect now as it did in 1912 [i.e. a workers' rout].
> (b) that the collapse of the general strike in New South Wales last year would be repeated here.

Fired by their sense of an imminent Bolshevik threat, these organizers appeared merely to be awaiting the appropriate moment to strike – and to strike hard.[15]

Once more, it seemed as though the American example might provide the necessary cue, not only for loyalist organization itself, but for an outbreak of concerted vigilante activism. Between July and September 1917, local businessmen of Jerome and Bisbee, Arizona, had organised armed posses of 2,000 or more citizens to corral almost 1,300 purported enemy aliens and IWW followers, force them into cattle trucks with little food or water and deport them into the blistering deserts of New Mexico. Likewise, in early 1918, vigilantes in Seattle, Washington, led by Spanish-American War veterans, had mounted an organization of Minute Men to root out 'disloyal individuals and spies'. With the tacit support of local federal officers and the Seattle Chamber of Commerce, they had tracked down and harassed several hundred alleged Wobblies by the close of January. And, most recently, in September–October 1918, troops, police, as well as Anaconda Copper Company agents and gunmen, organised by Major Omar Bradley, had conducted a veritable reign of terror against radicals in Butte, Montana – arresting copper miners without due cause and beating workers on the city's streets – to thwart a possible onset of strike activity there.[16]

Yet were Queensland's loyalists – patriotic business and professional leaders, returned military officers and federal agents – so obsessed with 'The Thing called Bolshevism' that they were prepared to resort to similar mob tactics? Were they willing, in short, to attack radical dissenters physically with the vehemence displayed against the red flag in August? In early October, Brisbane loyalists still seemed content to compile lists of prominent, 'dangerous' radicals and forward these to military authorities, with a demand for decisive action from the federal government against those named. Yet even as they hesitated, a dramatic response to the insistent quandary of loyalist escalation burst upon them from a rather unexpected quarter.[17]

Late in September in the small pastoral town of Hughenden in central Queensland, twenty-five female domestics, working at seven of the local hotels, met to air their grievances. Hotel owners, they argued, were denying them retrospective pay for a half-holiday award won in December 1917. Thus they had decided upon strike action to gain the increase. The outstanding sum in question totalled only £50, but the hoteliers remained obdurate. On 30 September, Hughenden railway men and shearers from the surrounding Redcliffe, Ballindallock and Hughenden sheds met at the Labour Hall and declared the delinquent hotels 'black' until the women received their payment. Only the Hughenden Hotel, named by the Censor as a habitat for 'undesirables', had acceded to the women's requests and remained in full operation.[18]

A fortnight later, the dispute intensified with the arrival of James Durkin, the northern AWU organiser, Mick Kelly of the newly formed Townsville Industrial Council and Archie Eastcrabb, northern secretary of the QRU. Both Kelly and Eastcrabb were well known for their militancy. Indeed, Eastcrabb, according to the Censor, was 'one of the worst' IWW advocates in Queensland. Along with local industrial organisers, William Huxley and George Bellamy of the AWU, and Labor Aldermen, A.H. Bartholemew and J. Minogue Green, the three visitors arranged street meetings to publicise the position of the female domestics. Both Bellamy and Bartholemew, it would be also alleged, were strong IWW sympathisers.[19]

Yet what was essentially a local dispute over a relatively minor industrial issue was soon to assume far more awesome proportions, as pastoralists and local businessmen began organizing vigorous counter-measures. On the evening of 16 October, as the first street meeting of the strike commenced, a gang of 'thugs' hired by the hoteliers physically attacked the speakers and a wild riot resulted. The disrupters were led by pastoralists, James and Tom Penny, brothers who had lost two other family members in the war. From this point onwards what was soon to become a major loyalist mobilisation continued to escalate along both class and military lines. Over the next two days, according to Captain Wills of Military Intelligence (Townsville), 'pastoralists, hotel proprietors, professional and commercial men of the town' organised a force of some 150 returned soldiers from surrounding districts 'to smash up' any future meetings, by concocting a tale that an injured veteran had been brutally assaulted by the protesters. From some centres, motor vehicles were arranged to transport the soldiers into Hughenden. On Thursday, 17 October, Sergeant Major Furay and Lieutenant W.S. Byrne of the RSSILA were cabled at Charters Towers to assume leadership of the loyalist forces. Significantly, Byrne was himself acting as a Military Intelligence agent at this time, collecting information about western Queensland's disloyalists for Captain Wills at Townsville. The following day, Byrne and Furay were met at Torrens Creek by Mr Croxon, a station owner and Mr Hamilton, a local solicitor, who informed them that Hughenden was in 'a state of chaos' with 'seditious' meetings being held thrice weekly.

When Byrne and Furay arrived in Hughenden just after 7 p.m. that evening, a 'beer boycott' meeting had already begun in the main street. Inside the Central Hotel, several hundred returned soldiers and other loyalists were awaiting their direction. After hurried consultations, the mob spilled through the hotel entrance-way and, yelling abuse, charged the speakers' platform. 'It would take a war correspondent to describe the subsequent happenings as it was one big mêlée', Byrne afterwards admitted; 'loyalists could no longer restrain themselves [&] I do not wonder at any man . . . worthy of the name of Britisher trying to show those IWW men that they . . . would no longer tolerate their actions'.[20]

The violence continued until almost midnight as enraged 'packs' of loyalist vigilantes hunted strike supporters throughout the town. There was very little police intervention during this time. 'Blood they wanted and blood they must have', wrote a Hughenden Hotel employee, as he described witnessing 'the most cold-blooded atrocities'. Dozens of men were 'kicked . . . nearly to death' as loyalist 'bloodhounds, half drunk with grog supplied by the squatters and publicans . . . hunted in packs of from 20 to 30 in search of unionists from house to house'. Such assaults continued intermittently over the weekend, as homes were broken into and men attacked on their way to work and savagely bashed. One by one, the union leaders were singled out for attention — mobbed, beaten and driven from the town.

Doping the returned men (*Worker*, 15 May 1918)

Furay, Byrne and another returned soldier named Kimmorney took a leading role in these disturbances. At the Hughenden railway station, railway workers were brutally beaten by a group of men, led by the Penny brothers. A ganger, Tom Black, was helping a fellow employee named Lennox whose ankle had been broken by the mob when he too was set upon. He finally escaped the town with broken ribs, several teeth missing and severe lacerations to most of his body. P.J. McSharry was similarly aiding an injured workmate named Tefler when he was so savagely beaten and kicked that doubts were expressed about his recovery. On Sunday afternoon, 20 October, Archie Eastcrabb and an associate were surrounded by a dozen men in the main street, robbed, then 'knocked down and kicked about the head and body'. Pursued by a mob to the railway station, the badly injured Eastcrabb was next ordered to quit the town. Only the arrival of more than a score of police reinforcements that evening, with instructions to use their firearms if the violence continued, finally restored some semblance of order.[21]

Although in trying to exonerate his own behaviour, Byrne subsequently reported that he had attempted in vain to control the mob, other reports told a different story. Byrne, with no clear perception of the local situation, simplistically believed that IWW members were 'emissaries of the Hun' and his Hughenden harangues, along with those of Furay and Lieutenant Webb of the Townsville RSSILA, had more likely inflamed the mob than pacified it. All the strikers and their supporters were indiscriminately branded 'IWW-ites' and execrated as enemies, scum and scorpions. 'We have given the IWW one of the biggest keel-haulings yet given here', stated Byrne at a noisy loyalist meeting on 20 October. 'They are the enemy in our midst . . . a lot of reptiles poisoning the minds of others.' Writing from Townsville some time later, however, Captain Wills seemed far less enamoured of the actions of his fellow Intelligence officer. There was no evidence whatever that a direct attack was made on returned men by labour agitators, Wills concluded. 'I certainly think that Lieut. Byrne and Serg. Major Furay were ill advised in proceeding to Hughenden in uniform on a matter which in no way concerned the Defence Department, as it has been repeatedly said that the Military intervened.'[22]

The Hughenden fracas, therefore, possessed many characteristics of the illegal IWW expulsions occurring in towns and cities across the United States, a fact was was not lost upon the *Daily Standard* when it wrote of the 'American methods' and 'Prussianist tactics' of these mid-western loyalists. And, as the jubilant Hughenden defenders gathered under the leadership of their Mayor (and aggrieved hotelier), Alderman O'Neill, to draw up a list of agitators to be deported from the district, the analogy was once more accentuated. 'The IWW were kicked out of America', asserted Lieutenant Crawford. 'And we are doing it here too!', came answering cries from the crowd.

The mob violence at Hughenden ultimately failed to break the beer strike which struggled gamely onwards. Clashes and demonstrations would continue sporadically for several months before it collapsed. Yet the Hughenden 'purge' marked a decisive break with loyalist activism of the past. For here, without any apparent qualms, loyalist advocacy and passion had been skilfully converted into unrestrained loyalist action of a most determined kind. Certainly, loyalists elsewhere had previously attacked socialists, pacifists and anti-conscriptionists throughout the war period; but such physical assaults had usually been of a more spontaneous and erratic kind. Yet Hughenden, quite unexpectedly, had hosted the emergence of a precise pattern of loyalist coordination, orchestrated by elite citizens, fuelled by the anger of carefully manipulated returned soldiers and led by a headstrong Military Intelligence agent and officers of the RSSILA. It was this particular military/civilian coordination which was to provide the precedent for future activism, as the anti-radical hysteria of one township was now given a statewide projection. 'The so-called loyalists had started something far bigger than they realised', observed the *Daily Standard* prophetically; it was 'a political movement' which was already underway in Brisbane and elsewhere to attack the forces of labour.[23]

Among loyalist spokespersons, there was a deal of dissembling over the amount of lawlessness and brutality of Hughenden. Although the Adjutant General reported to military command that Byrne, Furay and Webb had considerably encouraged the disorderly element, others preferred to dismiss this. Instead, these officers had restored order, Captain Wills finally concluded. Commissioner Urquhart stated that there was no evidence showing returned soldiers involved at all. Strike supporters were simply guilty of lying and 'mendacity' added Captain Stable; he observed nevertheless that Eastcrabb still 'carried the signs' of his assault a week later, and trusted the beating had 'done him good'. In selectively accepting such reports, the Acting Prime

Minister concluded that Byrne and others had been the means of preventing further disorder and 'possibly personal violence to the speakers'. In any case, none was an employee of the commonwealth government. Yet, behind this camouflage of denial, it was clear that an important tactical lesson was being absorbed. The diggers' 'dinkum stoush', as the *Brisbane Courier* termed it, was henceforth to serve as a spearhead for loyalist activism elsewhere.[24]

Less than a week later, at Toowoomba, another fracas erupted. Local pacifists and others attempted to celebrate the first anti-conscription victory, in order to draw attention to the continuation of 'boy conscription' in Australia. Advocating 'Hughenden-style action' loyalists besieged the Town Hall on 24 October, preventing its use by anti-conscriptionists later that evening. Speakers for the proposed rally were accosted in the vestibule and a brawl finally erupted in the main street. Gloating anti-conscriptionists, who would now flaunt their victories in the faces of widows and orphans of dead soldiers, stated Alderman Crisp, were no better than 'the Huns themselves who, when they got a man down, kicked out his brains'. Following the fracas, an agitated band of loyalists immediately formed an impromptu 'Loyal Vigilance Committee of Toowoomba' (LVC). 'We must see if we can move out some of the disloyalty', stated Alderman Hamwood. 'You know what has been happening at Hughenden . . . ' With so much Bolshevism rampant, claimed another, a lot of people were 'getting down to the Hunnish level' and he was personally prepared to shoulder a rifle tomorrow to eradicate such influences.

Plans were laid for preparing 'LVC' badges so that 'members could recognise each other'; Job Stone, a former Mayor and owner of a large printing concern, was chosen to lead the Vigilants. If anti-conscriptionists attempted any open-air rally that evening, it was suggested, the LVC should turn out in force and 'bring all they could'. Then they might all enjoy 'a lively and interesting meeting in the middle of the street (laughter)'. Intimidated by this militancy, anti-conscriptionists largely failed to appear at their celebration that night. At their hastily reconvened gathering in the Eight Hour Day rooms, the Quaker pacifist F. Lister Hopkins presided over an audience of only twenty-six subdued men, women and children as returned soldiers, accompanied by 'the jingoes of Toowoomba', demonstrated loudly outside. He had just opened the meeting when a group of soldiers, led by Warrant Officer Lewis Kimber, local president of the RSSILA, entered the hall. When challenged, Kimber presented Hopkins with 'credentials to prove he was a secret service man [!]' and stated he had come in this official capacity to oversee the meeting. 'Was the nation now under Martial Law?' he was challenged; as police intervened, Kimber and his associates withdrew.[25]

Meanwhile, at a large rally convened at the Town Hall, Mr F. Bernays, local president of the conservative National Political Council, told a packed audience that loyalists were at the end of their tether. Queensland, added Job Stone, was absolutely the most disloyal state and all now must show unflinching determination to protect their children, who were 'the future Empire builders' from this threat. Further tactics for extending the vigilance movement across the Darling Downs were then discussed. The Toowoomba patriots had had 'an absolute triumph', Kimber reported to his superior, Captain Woods of Military Intelligence, the following morning. Local radicals had been humbled and visiting agitators, 'Gunner' Taylour, Joseph Silver Collings and the Reverend J.H. MacDougall, a Christian socialist, had been warned, 'Get back to Brisbane. It is the safest place for you.'[26]

In the light of what was about to occur in that capital, however, such advice was of dubious value. The outbreak of 'Hughenden fever' was imminent. As the Returned Sailors, Soldiers and Citizens Loyalty League (RSSCLL) congratulated Hughenden's direct actionists on 'narrowly avoiding bloodshed', and vowed to support Job Stone's Vigilants, they escalated pressure upon the Defence Department to 'order the exit' from Brisbane of certain 'conspicuously disloyal' persons. Lists of these individuals had already been posted to Military Intelligence. Then, on 4 November – only ten days after the Toowoomba conflict – another flashpoint for loyalist activism presented itself. That afternoon, according to an advertisement in the *Daily Standard*, the Russian organisers of the much maligned International May Day gathering earlier that year were planning a further celebration.

As the European war sped to its close, the first anniversary of the Russian Revolution was also looming. The URW had decided to respond with a rally of commemoration on 8 November, with Russian music, songs, dances and speeches – in short, an evening of radical jubilation. As in Toowoomba, the Brisbane loyalists moved rapidly to quash this 'enemy celebration' to take place at Centennial Hall. On the afternoon of 8 November they succeeded, when Senator Pearce obligingly banned the 'obnoxious' Bolshevik gathering which he deemed 'prejudicial to public safety' under Para. 27(c) of the *War Precautions Act*. The Loyalty Leaguers then rapidly decided to mount their own Victory demonstration in the hall that same night — as the Toowoomba Vigilants had done a fortnight earlier.[27]

Passers-by in Adelaide Street would have witnessed confusing scenes that evening, as hundreds of exultant loyalists rubbed shoulders with several score of bewildered radicals in the Centennial Hall entrance-way. Finally, the 'bolsheviks' were either physically forced from the building or else left voluntarily when the strains of 'God Save the King' confirmed their worst suspicions. As they milled about in the street, they were addressed by E. Winbourne, a fruit hawker and IWW supporter, who suggested that they should perhaps try to secure another meeting place in South Brisbane. The crowd, now grown to three hundred, then formed ranks and, with the Russian men and women in the lead, marched up Adelaide and George Streets, in the direction of Victoria Bridge, singing 'The Red Flag' and 'Join the Army of the Toilers'. Meanwhile, inside Centennial Hall, wave upon wave of cheering greeted such loyalist spokespersons as Opposition Leader, E.H. Macartney, a prominent solicitor and company director, A.C. Elphinstone, business manager and Imperial patriot, O.E. Rees and Hedley Gelston of the RSSCLL, and Dr Ernest Sandford Jackson. This prosperous Brisbane medical practitioner, with a pastoral family background, was about to take a leading role in escalating loyalist mobilisation throughout Queensland. Each speaker re-emphasised the theme that Queensland was now 'divided into two camps — loyalty and disloyalty'. As loyalists, they had had enough of the 'internal enemies' of Australia, 'the intellectual parasites who lived on the hard labour and honest sweat of the workers'.[28]

As they spoke, the 'parasites' themselves were thronging at a far less auspicious venue — an unlighted vacant allotment in Grey Street, South Brisbane. The crowd, now one thousand strong, spilled out onto the roadway, delaying passing trams. Their dampened spirits were enlivened by the inimitable platform style of IWW organiser, William Jackson. The loyalists lately seemed to have become as agitated as 'celluloid dolls . . . chased through Hell by an asbestos cat', he told them, as he tried to raise a few laughs. At this point, word passed through the meeting of the approach of a large body of returned soldiers from a rallying point at North Quay, determined to 'break it up'. 'Hold firm and close round the speakers', Jackson advised them. Though they were ordinary citizens who did not want to use violence, 'if force was shown to them, force would be used in return'.

The soldiers, marching in military formation, had been organised by Private John Marsh of the Motor Transport Brigade, Kangaroo Point Military Hospital (where Sandford Jackson was senior surgeon). As they wheeled into the Council reserve and promptly burst into patriotic song, Kathleen Hotson brought the celebration to a close. Some Russians attempted to confront the soldiers physically, but Commissioner Urquhart had ordered out so many police — more than eighty, with the mounted corps on standby — that overt violence was avoided. Instead, a singing duel of patriotic airs versus revolutionary anthems persisted for twenty minutes, until the release of a concoction of garlic-smelling asafoedita gum dispersed the songsters. It has all ended very quickly for the radicals. Back at Centennial Hall, Sandford Jackson was still speaking when a breathless returned soldier entered the gallery and informed the delighted audience that his companions had routed the Brisbane Bolsheviks.[29]

Loyalist delight was enhanced when, three days later, the news of Armistice — 'Peace with Victory' — swept them and hundreds of thousands of other relieved citizens into a display of joy and thanksgiving. A Brisbane socialist, Stan O'Neill, with the racket of jubilation still ringing in his ears, wrote caustically to his brother in Innisfail: 'A few months ago it was a crime to talk peace. Now it is an established fact . . . of course, the Jingo is top dog now, but he will soon sicken everybody with the "God save" and stupid flag flapping, so his reign will soon be over . . . ' Yet, as it eventuated, O'Neill was being overly hopeful in his assessment. Much of this extended jubilation was tinged with an unmistakably vindictive tone. German Lutheran Churches were attacked by mobs or burned down at Toowoomba, Maryborough and Bundaberg; elsewhere, in dozens of towns, 'Kaiser burning' demonstrations were conducted. At Rockhampton, the local Trades Hall was raided by returned soldiers who raised a Union Jack upon its roof; in another part of that town, a mob attacked the business premises and home of a well-known Quaker pacifist, Edgar Foreman, who was forced into hiding.[30]

Meanwhile at Dalby on the Darling Downs, an organiser for the Printers Union, Charles White, who had drunkenly declared himself 'a rebel' outside a local hotel, was promptly set upon by a bunch of returned soldiers, led by John Braddock, the proprietor of the *Dalby Herald*. White was ordered either to sing the national anthem or be immediately tarred and feathered. After prudently cooperating, he was bundled out of town on the first train west. In this manner, the Dalby Loyalty League was instituted. Similarly, on Armistice night, in the sugar town of Ayr in north Queensland, hundreds of demonstrating loyalists converged on the Delta Hotel, the town's centre for IWW activism. The trouble which had been brewing in Ayr for months was now exacerbated when more than a score of IWW supporters, led by cane cutter, W.A. Shepherd, converged upon the hotel verandah and began singing 'The Red Flag'. They were immediately besieged by loyalists who forced them down into the street. Greatly outnumbered, they were violently set upon and 'hustled out of town'. As Captain Wills reported, 'After chasing them out . . . the loyalists paraded the streets until 3 a.m. to make sure they did not return'.[31]

Three nights later, it was Townville's turn to witness loyalist mob action. Rancour had been simmering there for some time. Following upon the Hughenden riots, a well-attended meeting of eight hundred Townsville unionists, convened by the Industrial Council at the Theatre Royal, had listened with mounting anger as the battered Archie Eastcrabb and Mick Kelly related details of their 'bludgeoning'. Consequently, it was agreed to recruit a 'Labour Volunteer Army' to defend unionists. Local carters also decided to place a boycott on the transport of all beer to Hughenden. In response, the North Queensland Employers Assocation, claiming that the carters' sympathetic action was 'the commencement of the One Big Union movement' in the north, had succeeded in having the sixty of them sacked. For a time, a general strike seemed to threaten. Concurrently, a strike by sanitary workers over victimization claims had begun to turn inner Townsville into a fetid cesspit. An unquestionably filthy application of the sabotage principle – upending nightsoil pans in Flinders Lane, on the City Hall steps and in front of the homes of prominent citizens – had led to a typhoid panic. The pseudonymous 'Secret Service' of Townsville (very likely Captain Wills himself) exploded:

> Townsville unionists are deliberately invoking pestilence and plague to assist them in their demands . . . 'Direct Action' is an American product. There it is fought with 'Direct Action'. If a town was smeared with filth in America, someone would dangle from the arm of the nearest lamp-post . . . the general resistance is likely to produce an active vigilance committee to prevent acts of lawlessness and patrols would be formed to see that property is not destroyed. There is nothing illegal in assisting the police to maintain order . . . success goes to the party that organises its forces and is at all times vigilant to see that it is not assaulted with impunity.[32]

By the time of the Armistice, the dispute had been solved by Government intervention. The men had been reinstated and the refuse cleared. Yet the bitterness still rankled, and Townsville was compared in the conservative *Daily Bulletin* to a little Petrograd or Moscow. Thus on Thursday 14 November, when Townsville patriots and returned soldiers gathered in their thousands for a seven kilometre victory procession, the seeds of conflict once more began to sprout. Though some fighting between loyalists and radicals singing 'The Red Flag' occurred that afternoon, most of the violence was confined to the evening. A large number of radicals had gathered at their traditional drinking place, Cassidy's Palace Hotel at the far end of Flinders Street to carouse and sing revolutionary songs. At 8.30 p.m., a group of fifteen or so of their younger fellows, walking along Flinders Street en route to this pub, broke into a chorus of 'The Red Flag'. Furthermore, as they passed hotels where returned soldiers were drinking, they produced red handkerchiefs and waved them defiantly. In response, scores of veterans burst from hotel bars and chased the youths towards Cassidy's. 'And how the soldiers rose to the occasion', the *Daily Mail* enthused the following morning: 'They charged up the lane on the side of the hotel in massed formation. The lady in the bar slammed some of the doors, but the Anzacs broke through such weak defences and the singing quickly ceased.'

A widescale riot accompanied by broken bottles, chairs, table legs and fence palings resulted, as general fighting spread into the street. 'The hotel . . . appeared as if it had been bombarded by Germans', observed the *Daily Mail*. In the meantime, a group of boy scouts 'who at all times dog the foot-steps of returned soldiers rushed to all parts of the town with the news that returned soldiers were being ill-treated by IWW men'. Running into nearby picture palaces, they shouted to startled audiences, 'Diggers to the rescue at Cassidy's Hotel!' Soon, hundreds more were converging upon the scene. As police tried unsuccessfully to disperse the brawling men, watching women and children added to the din – their vigorous rendition of 'Rule Britannia' marked by constant repetition of the line, 'Britons NEVER, NEVER, NEVER shall be slaves'. Finally, six soldiers, one policeman and an undisclosed number of 'disloyalists' received medical treatment, mainly for head injuries. 'The red element got rather a bad time of it', reported Lieutenant Colonel James Walker; and, as wounded radicals were taken into custody for their own protection, an angry mob continued to surge and yell outside the police station. Later that night, a similar debacle occurred outside the Queensland Hotel.[33]

The following night, a force of some four hundred loyalists was recruited to break up the usual weekly workers' meeting in Flinders Street and to hunt 'these alleged IWW men . . . from the town'. Thousands of citizens patrolled the streets, but a coup against the radicals was thwarted when their gathering was wisely cancelled. With all hotels closed, matters remained quiet over the weekend – although a riot developed at Ayr over the screening of a propaganda film, 'Four Years in Germany'. On Monday, as news reached Townsville that meat employees at Ross River and Alligator Creek had begun a strike, fresh vigilante action occurred. A gang of forty soldiers and civilians, armed with fence palings and followed by a large, excited crowd, chased alleged Wobblies along Flinders Street, stopping outward-bound buses and searching among passengers for 'disloyalists', as well as raiding hotels at Hermit Park and Aitkinvale.[34]

While the loyalist mob action accompanying Armistice celebrations exploded in urban centres along the Queensland coastline and in the hinterland, it seemed that American vigilante solutions were becoming common in rightwing circles. 'Let us uproot disloyalty and establish sanity' was a theme reiterated in conservative press correspondence:

> The civilized nations have now to combat and destroy another enemy which threatens civilization . . . The sooner the American example is followed in rooting out and deporting this menacing class of undesirables, the better . . . Why does the Commonwealth not take direct action in dealing with the enemy within our gates?

Matters, however, were moving to 'fruition', promised the Reverend G.E. Rowe of the Loyalty League on 25 November, and 'it behoved the loyalists to be prepared'. Increasing alarm at their own contrived Bolshevik stereotype, presentiments of local revolution and a conviction that a 'radical-coddling' Labor Government could not deal effectively with the problem spurred the loyalists on. Nevertheless, in late November, Commissioner Urquhart was complaining that 'an inbred horror of such things as surveillance . . . espionage or censorship' tended to frustrate the smooth workings of official intelligence organisations. This was accompanied, he added 'by a sheeplike tendency on the part of Australian crowds to unthinkingly assent to the vile doctrine of glib-tongued agitators — as, for instance, many people, especially young people will cheer the red flag without the least real understanding of what the symbol stands for . . . ' Yet, by February 1919, he was able to report that 'Things are looking better' and that the hints he had circulated earlier among leading loyalists had at last'. . .fruitified (sic) in a wonderful way'.[35]

Indeed, during this period, it is clear that loyalist organisation had become considerably more sophisticated. Urquhart was informed from Melbourne in December that the SIB was now contemplating launching an Australian Defensive League (ADL) as the commonwealth's answer to America's APL. In January, Acting Prime Minister Watt and Major General J.G. Legge, the Chief of General Staff, met with Victorian and New South Wales Commissioners to discuss the coordination of state police with federal forces in the event of a Bolshevik outbreak. Lists of 'suitable' citizens ready to serve as special constables were to be compiled in every police district and stockpiles of military arms and ammunition gathered to be supplied to Police Commissioners when the occasion warranted it. Legge went so far as to suggest the use of 'small groups of picked men with machine guns and a few aeroplanes with improvised bombs'; but Cabinet, three days later, failed to endorse this.[36]

Throughout these preparations Queensland remained the *bête noire* of the zealously organising officials. On 20 November 1918, a physically ailing George Steward reported to Watt that Queensland was now 'undoubtedly . . . a hotbed of disloyalty, both to the Empire and Australia', due to the unchecked dissemination of Bolshevik propaganda there. He recommended 'imprisonment . . . deportation or both' for the ringleaders at the earliest possible moment. Major Harold Edward Jones, Steward's understudy and the man about to succeed him as SIB Director, consequently left for Queensland to contact Captain Ainsworth, with a view to connecting the leaders and their principal followings 'with revolutionary statements and activities'. According to Ainsworth's diary, the new director arrived on 29 November and collaborated with him on 'Aliens Procedure' and other matters until he departed again for Melbourne on 6 December, with a revised list of Queensland 'troublemakers' in his possession.[37]

Meanwhile, Ainsworth had continued to expand his Brisbane surveillance network. For instance, he was now conferring regularly with representatives of the conservative press upon undisclosed matters. Between 14 October and 12 December, John Henry Crowthers Sleeman of the *Daily Mail* (and later, editor of the Brisbane *Sun*) was briefed by Ainsworth no less than nineteen times. On 15 October, for instance, Ainsworth noted, 'Saw Sleeman and received copy of his report', while ten days later, after three further solo contacts, Sleeman was interviewed in the company of opposition leader, E.H. Macartney and Colonel A.J. Thynne, both of whom were now active in forming an anti-Bolshevik phalanx among the untidy Nationalist ranks. Concurrently, James A. Philp, ex-*Bulletin* luminary and commercial editor of the *Brisbane Courier*, had also become a regular visitor. Philp, a super-patriot, was later to write *Songs of the Australian Fascisti*, a publication which openly recommended a Fascist antidote to the 'apparently overwhelming wave of Bolshevism' threatening Australia. Such cooperation by Tory press men with the SIB no doubt served to cement the partisan alliance with the loyalists which the *Daily Mail* and *Brisbane Courier* subsequently would exhibit during the Red Flag riots.[38]

By the close of 1918, Ainsworth had also planted among the Russian community several named informants who reported back to him on URW activities. One was Leo Berk, a Russian returned soldier, who wrote to the *Daily Mail* of the 'animalism' purportedly displayed by the Red Army as it fought off Allied invasion into Russia. Another closer contact was Anton von Mendrin, a shady personage alleged to have formerly been a Russian magistrate involved in sentencing dissidents to death or to Siberia. Indeed, according to documents published in the Soviet organ, *Isvestia*, and ventilated by Mick Considine in the Commonwealth House of Representatives in December 1918, Mendrin had operated as an agent for a section of the Okrana — the Tsar's secret police — at Vladivostok and Harbin before he was 'unmasked' and forced to flee Russia. By late 1918, he was active in contraband trading, selling stores originally bound for Russia from Britain on the Australian black market. He was roundly condemned by Brisbane businessmen as 'an utter rogue' and 'immoral in every way'. Yet Ainsworth continued to receive information from him which he no doubt counted as worthwhile. Ainsworth's unnamed secret agent, too, was especially active in this period, attending Domain, Trades Hall and URW gatherings. Between October and December 1918, he met with his superior fifty times, receiving orders and dispensing information. Simultaneously, Commissioner Urquhart had also placed his agent, Richard James Brown, among Trades Hall radicals, whilst a Russian named Dolyenko relayed internal information on the URW to commonwealth police. General Irving's 'Agent 77' seems to have been the most successfully integrated of all these spies; in mid-1918, he was reported as actually chairing the IWW meetings at Trades Hall![39]

Concurrent with this successful penetration of the radical sects, Ainsworth had recruited Malcolm Ellis to prepare a special report on disloyalty in Queensland and its connections with the Ryan Labor Government. Ellis was now also working as secretary to Opposition Leader E.H. Macartney and had compiled a *Handbook for Nationalists* — a litany of Labor's sins and omissions — for use by conservative candidates in the March 1918 state election. His lengthy 'Summary of Ryan's Disloyal Associations' was an outgrowth of the biassed preoccupations of the *Handbook*. Ellis (later to become an established amateur historian) had been introduced to Ainsworth in late October 1917 by a Mr Moodie of the commonwealth legal firm of Chambers and McNab which would later handle the Red Flag prosecutions. Subsequently, he had prepared reports for the Directorate of War Propaganda, established by the commonwealth government in May 1918.[40]

Ellis's secret 'Summary', compiled for use by the Defence Department in November 1918, displayed a convoluted and obsessive tracking, over more than sixty pages of typescript, after the worm of disloyalty eating into the heart of the labour movement. As his later writings reveal, Ellis was a dedicated anti-radical and his zeal can best be assessed by allowing his dossier to speak for itself. 'Ryan has all along cunningly refrained from actually making disloyal statements himself', he wrote:

but he must be judged by the company he has kept in his Cabinet and his political organizations . . . Ryan himself is an Irishman, married to Lily Kuch, daughter of a German father and Irish mother. Theodore . . . is the son of a Bulgarian (the latter born in Rumanian territory). [He] . . . is married to an Irishwoman. Theodore was previously a Union Secretary and prior to that ran "two up schools" on the mining fields. "Two up" being the lowest form of gambling surreptitiously conducted in this country. McCormack, the SPEAKER OF PARLIAMENT was also a union secretary and prior to that ran two-up schools and also travelled the Shows and Racecourses in the Far North of the State WITH A PERFORMING GOOSE! He is nicknamed in some places "Goosey McCormack". McCormack of course is an Irish Roman Catholic . . .

And so the strange report continued, trailing the disloyal 'conspiracy' through the peace movement, the IWW, the BIC and the Labor party machine.[41]

As Ellis prepared his pot-pourri of radical and alien intrigue for commonwealth delectation, Military Intelligence in Queensland was also escalating its own investigations. In December 1918, Lieutenant Colonel James Walker, who had been involved with Italian deportations in north Queensland, filed a report to the Adjutant General which described the state as 'the dumping ground for all the disloyal elements in the Commonwealth'. Subsequently, on 18 January 1919, the Acting Prime Minister called for a reliable and comprehensive review of Queensland's industrial and political situation from 'some discreet officer'. The 'level-headed' official eventually chosen was the Censor, J.J. Stable; influenza quarantine regulations had prevented use of an investigator from interstate. In a sixteen-page report completed in early February, Stable outlined the relative strengths and weaknesses of labour and conservative forces. The Labor Government, he concluded, which had extended its power base in the March 1918 election through the support of anti-conscriptionists, Roman Catholics, the German and Italian 'alien' vote, the liquor trade and civil servants, was 'in the hands of the more militant section' − 'Parliament by the Industrial Council'. It would not desist, Stable warned, until 'everything worth nationalising had been nationalised'.[42]

The Nationalists, on the other hand, were emerging from a state of chaos, induced by squabbles over the selection of candidates and their trouncing in the previous March election. The National Political Council [NPC], 'the most powerful party within the Nationalist body', was left in disarray. Yet E.H. Macartney had since taken a hand in regenerating conservative

Kidding themselves (*Worker*, 6 March 1919)

hopes. In December 1918, aided by Catholic millionaire, T.C. Bierne, and Macartney's legal partner, A.J. Thynne, a company director and ardent loyalist, the Opposition Leader launched the Australian Democratic Union (ADU). Promoted by the *Daily Mail* (controlled by Catholic entrepreneur, John Wren), the ADU had 'quickly absorbed the old National party' and secured the endorsement of conservative stalwarts, Sir Alfred Cowley and Sir Robert Philp, the sugar and shipping magnates. Significantly, the ADU had been 'publicly launched with but one plank – and a negative one at that – anti-Bolshevism'. The Nationalist 'extremists' Stable had first warned of in late September, it seems, were about to gain the upper hand. At a Toowong ADU meeting on 3 February, Macartney had called upon all 'loyalists – men and women, no matter of what class – to unite under one banner' against Bolshevik practices. Then, on 25 February, after much wrangling, the ADU and NPC finally combined to form the National Democratic Council (NDC) – 'a strong and undivided front' opposing the forces of 'Socialism and Bolshevism' in Queensland.[43]

Just as anti-Bolshevism formed the foundation stone for this new conservative party, Stable noted, another 'very strong movement' against revolutionaries had also surfaced – the United Loyalist Executive (ULE) headed by Dr Ernest Sandford Jackson. Jackson had recently led a vote of thanks at Macartney's ADU rally at Toowong. Like Herbert Brookes of Melbourne, he was one of Brisbane society's most prominent establishment figures. An acknowledged medical reformer and amateur historian, educated at Geelong Grammar, he was a former president of the Queensland Club and, as a leading surgical specialist, had also been president of the British Medical Association of Queensland and a founder of the Australasian College of Surgeons. Described by his biographer, Ross Patrick, as 'a strict disciplinarian', he was, additionally, a most influential anti-labour and anti-Catholic advocate. 'Tall and well built, with a moustache and clear blue eyes,' Patrick writes, 'Jackson had a magnificent presence, a fine speaking voice and a deep sense of honour.' Four of his five sons had enlisted in the AIF, two of them seeing action at Gallipoli. Early in the war period, Jackson too had served as a major in the first and second Australian General Hospitals in Cairo. Invalided home after contracting influenza in late 1915, he had become increasingly 'sick at heart'

— to employ his own phrase — to discover 'the trouble being caused by Bolshevism and IWWism' in Queensland. Attaining the rank of lieutenant colonel by the close of the war, Jackson was indeed to prove an inspiring loyalist leader. Succeeding where others before him had failed, he had managed, by February 1919, to coordinate a vast array of loyalist societies such as the Protestant League, the Royal Society of St George, the Navy League, the Returned Soldiers Associations, the Loyal Orange Lodges and the Loyalty League under the control of a Central Executive. He then mounted a concerted campaign against Bolshevism and disloyalty. By March, this Executive was claiming a statewide influence, with 60,000 members enrolled in its fighting ranks.[44]

It was the formation of this ultra-loyalist phalanx, in particular, which had so excited Commissioner Urquhart when he wrote to Herbert Brookes on 23 February. Brookes himself, however, had already been in correspondence with Sandford Jackson, sending him loyalist pamphlets and other instructions earlier in February. Thirty patriotic societies had now 'given their adhesion to a "Limited Loyal League"', Urquhart reported:

> and yesterday three of the leaders came along to ask my advice about joining problems and told me *inter alia* that they would have 60 societies joined up and expressed a wish that I might take a hand in the matter. I would [have] liked to be able to give them some idea of what was in contemplation [regarding the ADL] but felt that I was not free to do so. They wish to go pretty far — not only to uphold the constitution by peaceful means but to have *a formidable striking force ready if required*. If our organization were ready, these people would rally to it with enthusiasm but the Federal Government is slow about it . . . if they are not pretty prompt in the near future, the wind will be taken out of their hands [sic] and they will have to follow where they should have led.[45]

Grass roots vigilantism, flourishing in the largely protestant, middle class and ruling class sectors of Queensland society, had thereby stolen a march on government-sponsored mobilisations. Even as commonwealth officials prevaricated, the Tory mob — like an avalanche down a mountainside — now seemed prepared to let nothing stand in the path of their passionate resolve.

In contrast to Urquhart's ebullience over the ULE's formation, Constable Hubert Foote of the Commonwealth Police on 22 February sounded a chill note of warning. Preparations being made by Brisbane loyalist societies, he reported, included 'the supplying of arms to their members'. (In response, military authorities covertly attempted to stop supply of ammunition to rifle clubs in the Brisbane district.) A week later, Foote approached Captain Woods of Military Intelligence with his findings. To Foote's surprise, Woods curtly responded, 'Our work is only concerned with the disloyal associations. We do not worry ourselves about what the Loyal Societies are doing.' In any case, most of the members of 'the Grand Executive', already members of rifle clubs, would have no difficulty in getting a gun. 'Any man with a few pounds to spare could easily purchase one.' In terminating the interview, Woods left no doubt about where his own sentiments lay. 'If they form the . . . Grand Executive', he confided, as he ushered Foote to the door, 'all the more power to them'.[46]

Thus, by early March 1919, the situation had become extremely volatile. 'Some happening was imminent', reported Sergeant A.M. Short to his Commonwealth Commissioner. The ULE and NDC were clearly spoiling for a fight. The returned soldiers among their ranks, skilled 'functionaries of destruction' and directed by their ex-officers, would provide the necessary shock troops in any likely confrontation. The lesson of Hughenden — the same lesson which had been absorbed from the excesses of American vigilantism would be enforced by the loyalist network with either the tacit or overt approval of officialdom. The radicals had so far proven most unwilling listeners to the loyalist message. The lesson they must now learn, it was argued, would require something far more substantial than verbal persuasion or reprimand.

Chapter 3

A Bit of Revoluse

Australian workers . . . have gone from
the country to fight for the shadow.
Was it not right that they should now
fight for the substance?

Percy Mandeno[1]

At first sight, the city of Brisbane hardly seemed a likely place to
host a revolutionary outbreak. Life normally moved slowly in
this bush capital of some two hundred thousand souls. Its casual
pace was accentuated by the drawling speech patterns of its in-
habitants, a climatic emphasis upon persistent summer heat
which migrants found so enervating, drumming rain and hail,
chirruping cicadas and droning mosquitoes. There was even an
appearance of torpor about the place: shafts of strong sunlight
played on the dusty roads and glinted from the tin roofs of
weatherboard houses, set on their high wooden stumps with an
attitude of gawky permanency. It was at once a sprawling,
overgrown country town, with some outward pretensions of
municipal splendour, and a sub-tropical outpost, clinging
tenaciously to British ways and loyalties – more often aped than
studiously replicated. Scattered along a meandering river, span-
ned as yet by only one bridge or crossed by hand-rowed ferries,
it was still a town for casual strolling and horse-drawn transportation. The clatter of tramcars and the clangour of 'dunny carts'
periodically broke the suburban silence, whilst its night life
flickered haphazardly around a handful of picture shows, cafés
and popular theatres, as well as a host of pubs and a sprinkling of
brothels. Communications were slow, with few telephones, and
motor vehicles only beginning to make their appearance among
the possessions of the rich. In 1918, there were little more than
2,600 motor cars and cycles in the whole metropolis – all expected to observe a speed limit of only four miles per hour –
though this was poorly enforced. A rather rattled public servant

Hatched the wrong chick (*Worker*, 19 June 1919)

complained in August that year: 'I can assure you it is a tax on my nerves with the buzz of the motor cars . . . one is taking a big risk crossing roads. . . . The owners of cars seem to consider that it is no concern of theirs . . . that poorer people have to walk . . . tired men who after a hard day's work are necessarily slow in mind and movement.'[2]

Yet tranquil appearances could be rather deceptive. For instance, on the very day of the Bolshevik coup, as John Reed noted in *Ten Days That Shook the World*, there was an air of normalcy even in Petrograd. Streetcars on the Nevsky, packed with workers, were still running and most of the shops were briskly trading. 'All the complex routine of modern life – humdrum even in wartime – proceeded as usual.' The quiet town of Brisbane meanwhile – although no scene of revolution – had nevertheless witnessed in its time some stirring episodes. 'Bread or Blood' disturbances in the 1860s, anti-Chinese riots in the 1880s, the Maritime and Shearers' Strikes, unemployment agitations and Federation demonstrations of the 1890s, Boer War clashes of the 1900s and, in 1912, a massive general strike, somewhat erroneously touted as 'the first simultaneous strike in the world'. During the war, loyalist attacks by civilians and soldiers on pacifist and socialist speakers had escalated into the series of street battles which accompanied the conscription referenda; and, since then, the patriotic rancour exhibited against dissidents – particularly Wobblies and Bolsheviks – had erupted into overt conflict on several occasions.[3]

Although Brisbane's level of industrialisation was relatively low – with eighteen hundred factories employing forty-two thousand hands in 1919 – working class consciousness had been considerably sharpened by the rigours of warfare, especially the socio-economic hardships and civil restrictions it had imposed. Suburban segregation of wealth and poverty was also apparent, with the rich ensconced in their high-set 'villa' residences of Wickham Terrace and Highgate Hill, Hamilton, Clayfield and New Farm, Toowong and Indooroopilly, and the poor holding to the crowded river flats and valleys. They dwelt in rented rooms in the seedy boarding houses of South Brisbane, Woolloongabba and West End, the city's back streets or Fortitude Valley. Otherwise, they occupied the cramped workers' cottages in such areas as Petrie Terrace, the hollows around Spring Hill and Red Hill, as well as the shabby houses of Kangaroo Point, lower Paddington, Rosalie and Milton.[4]

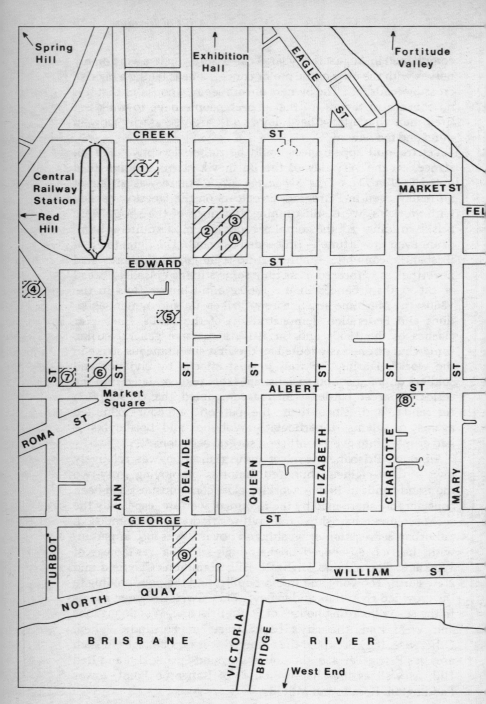

Brisbane venues 1919

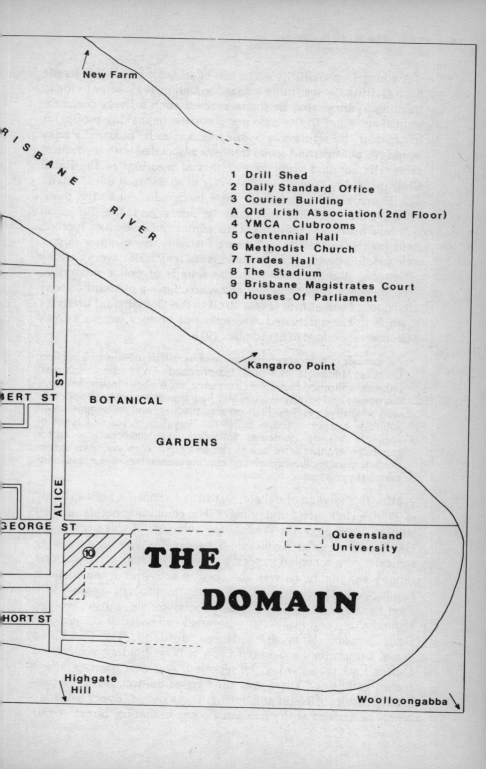

1 Drill Shed
2 Daily Standard Office
3 Courier Building
A Qld Irish Association (2nd Floor)
4 YMCA Clubrooms
5 Centennial Hall
6 Methodist Church
7 Trades Hall
8 The Stadium
9 Brisbane Magistrates Court
10 Houses Of Parliament

New Farm

BRISBANE RIVER

Kangaroo Point

BOTANICAL

GARDENS

ALBERT ST

ALICE ST

GEORGE ST

SHORT ST

⑩

Queensland
University

THE

DOMAIN

Highgate
Hill

Woolloongabba

A young Don Griffiths – the son of socialist journalist, Jennie Scott Griffiths – was quite amazed to find in 1918, after living in bustling Sydney, that Brisbane seemed such a lively place for radical activism. In the time not absorbed in 'making profits for my master', he wrote to a Sydney associate, he pursued a busy agenda of political and social interests associated with the radical sects. His Sundays were spent either at meetings of 'the Rebel Club' (probably the UFL) or listening to speakers at the Domain. The Domain was a patch of waste land, adjacent to the river, which bordered the university grounds and the Botanical Gardens near state parliament. In winter, it served as a football field for the university and, more furtively, on summer nights, as a 'saddling paddock' for casual lovers' trysts. But every Sunday afternoon, it came alive with the sounds of police-supervised 'free speech' activities. 'Being one who enjoys a pleasant Sunday afternoon, I sometimes take a stroll to the Domain and listen for a while to the variegated assortment of orators', wrote a *Daily Mail* correspondent in September 1918:

> All manner of subjects are in course of ventilation: Returned Soldiers Leagues, Industrial Council, imprisoned IWW men, interned citizens, unlimited paper note currency, six o'clock closing, religious discourses and loyalty leagues – I had almost forgotten the speaker who is always perched high on a stepladder, and harangues on all subjects, his pet aversion being the Salvation Army. Each set of speakers has its particular followers, the cosmopolitan visitor generally strolling from one to the other . . . With very few exceptions, the orators are earnest and confine themselves to the planks for which they appear.

After this farrago of debate, Griffiths attended a political rally at Trades Hall each Sunday night. His remaining nights seemed similarly occupied. On Wednesday evenings, it was back to the Hall for the regular 'Economic Speakers Class', where budding radicals were schooled in platform oratory. Then, after work on other week nights, he was absorbed in activities at the Socialist League or at the home of Ernie Lane, the utopian socialist William Lane's more radical brother. Social activities also revolved around these organisations, with weekend socialist picnics and *Daily Standard* fancy dress dances to attend. 'The Combined Social Committee and Rebel Club will be holding a picnic at Dutton Park on Saturday', he reported, 'and we expect to have a record gathering.' There was time set aside, too, for more personal pursuits of 'Night and Spring: Toots Lassie'. Every Saturday night, he arrived at the Russian Rooms in Stanley Street – 'our friend in blue teaches me how to handle my clumsy feet . . . I am beginning to get to be quite a dancer'. This 'friend in blue', he reminded his correspondent, was none other than 'Fanny' (Civa) Rosenberg, a lively Russian teenager whom they had both met at the Anniversary of the February Russian Revolution, held at the Alliance Hall, South Brisbane, earlier that year.[5]

Before the close of 1918, young Civa Rosenberg would find herself involved in more momentous activities than teaching the smitten Don Griffiths to waltz. For Civa was the daughter of Michael Rosenberg, a waterside worker and an executive officer of the Brisbane URW. Additionally, by late 1918, she was falling under the spell of Alexander Michael Zuzenko, a fitter and seaman by trade who had arrived in Brisbane during 1917 from cane cutting activities in Halifax, north Queensland. Zuzenko, described as a physical giant of a man, a fine writer and fluent public speaker, was passionately involved in revolutionary politics. As a confirmed Bolshevik with a charismatic presence, he had tended to assume the dominant role in the URW after its leading light, Peter Simonoff, an ex-miner from Broken Hill, left Brisbane in March 1918 for southern capitals, on becoming Australia's Soviet Consul.[6]

By September–October 1918, both Simonoff and Zuzenko had fallen under increased commonwealth surveillance. Simonoff was, by then, back in Brisbane publicising a campaign against Allied intervention into Soviet Russia, at such venues as the Third Queensland Trade Union Congress. According to three 'loyal Russian businessmen' who informed to commonwealth police, Simonoff had attacked the returned soldiers' badge as 'a disgrace'. 'This is the badge you should wear', he exclaimed, rolling back his sleeve to reveal an IWW emblem attached by a chain to his wrist. In late September, therefore, Simonoff was prevented by Captain Woods, under a newly gazetted Section 17(c) of the *Aliens Restriction Order*, from further public speaking in Queensland, despite vain appeals for some recognition of his diplomatic status. In the meantime, the Censor had been keeping close watch upon Zuzenko and was alarmed by his growing political effectiveness. After examining his intercepted correspondence, Captain Stable concluded worriedly that he was both 'very earnest' and a fine 'artistic' writer with an immense talent for leadership. Upon observing Zuzenko in action on the podium, Stable warned his superiors: 'At first one would put him down as a morose Russian serf, brooding over some trouble, but when he talks, he loses the repellent feature and one recognises the reader and thinker quite capable of leading men — a more dangerous man than Simonoff'.[7]

The censorship of Zuzenko's correspondence also revealed that he was now intent upon forming a Federation of Russian Groups, drawing all the smaller — and sometimes squabbling — Russian factions in Australia together into one grand organisation. It was 'a step towards the One Big Union', Stable cautioned. Thus, when Zuzenko approached the Censor for permission to publish a monthly magazine in Russian in mid-August, this was firmly denied. Instead, he too was prohibited under the *Aliens Restriction Order* 'from addressing or taking part in meetings . . . or any propaganda whatever'. It was in this way that Civa Rosenberg found herself drawn into the central activities of the URW. Although Zuzenko was to continue his political intrigues more covertly, Civa, with whom he had become romantically involved, was now granted nominal secretaryship of the organisation. Her father, who was living away from home, protested ineffectually that, as she was only seventeen, she was not 'a proper person for this responsible position'. Yet, after the supression of the November Bolshevik Celebration (which Zuzenko had organised), it was Civa's name which appeared upon a protest resolution sent to the Labor Government. 'In spite of the capitalist clique's lying Press', this document maintained: 'the Russian Revolution is being recognized to be one of good faith. But blind reaction seems not to have any limits . . . Our meetings have been broken up by force with the benevolent permission of the Military Authorities. The lying press pours out upon us its dirt and there is no right to freely reply to our detractors . . . '[8]

For the Russian language press in the meantime had also been savaged by censorship. *Knowledge and Unity*, the weekly URW newspaper, was suppressed by the Defense Department after an issue in mid-November announcing, 'Peace has been declared, so do not sleep, brothers. The time has come for work . . . We are all brothers fighting the one enemy, Capitalism, . . . fighting for liberty and for the Red Flag.' When Zuzenko, employing the pseudonym of 'Cane Mamena', attempted to launch a new paper entitled *The Ninth Wave*, it too was silenced by Commonwealth Police after only two issues. Again using Civa as a shield, Zuzenko therefore decided to resurrect *Knowledge and Unity* under her ostensible editorship — this time as an English publication. In its first issue of 31 December 1918, the new

'Editress' chidingly addressed her Anglo-Australian readers: 'You have not been strong and alert in the past, comrades of ours . . . Papers have been suppressed – you have not troubled to acknowledge the fact. Comrades have been gaoled – you have passed resolutions. Militant members of the working class have been deported . . . You have read the news uninterestedly and turned to the sporting page.' Commonwealth intervention, therefore, had actually spread Bolshevik propaganda further afield. It was now also available to interested members of the Australian proletariat. This move to involve 'the English working man' was a laudable one, wrote a Russian meatworker, particularly if the strategy was to 'close our ranks solid – both English and Russian'. The problem was, however, that for Russians with little or no grasp of English, *Knowledge and Unity* is absolutely useless'.[9]

As Zuzenko, with Civa's aid, circumvented his suppression order, Simonoff once more had left the First Military District of Queensland and embarked upon a lecture tour of Newcastle, Sydney and Melbourne, where he spoke throughout October to capacity audiences of socialists, trade unionists and pacifists on the subject of 'Russia Today'. A Newcastle activist who heard Simonoff at the Trades Hall interpreted his message as an endorsement of IWW methods. 'The Russian Consul is a great organizer,' he reported. 'He tells the workers that the politician is a hindrance . . . the only salvation is "go slow", sabotage and industrial organization.' Although Simonoff complained bitterly to Brisbane colleagues of financial duress and federal 'spirits at my heels', he reacted jauntily to his enthusiastic reception by militants at every venue. 'Let them accept me as I am – extreme revolutionist', he declared to Norman Freeburg of the Brisbane *Worker*; yet, to Zuzenko he confided: 'Tell the little ones that the slaves here [in Sydney] are alive and not sleeping. I simply can't get away from this place . . . they proposed to me that I should stay on another fortnight, so as to hold two or three more meetings.'[10]

However the 'spirits' at his heels were closing in. Captain Stable, intercepting all Simonoff's correspondence, expressed mounting concern at the 'tremendous reception' he was receiving. 'Simonoff's vanity has been tickled', Stable observed acidly on 29 October, 'and he will – given the opportunity – be more aggressive and dangerous than hitherto. If he is anxious to join the ranks of the internees, he is certainly going the right way about it.' At the Censor's instigation, therefore, a new restraining order was placed upon the Consul on 1 November. Simonoff, however, remained undaunted. 'I would prefer to hang myself on the first lamp-post than to stop my work, which is my duty to humanity', he responded. By this time, he was in Melbourne, where he addressed both the annual Australian Peace Alliance (APA) conference and socialist gatherings on the Yarra Bank. But his luck was running out. On Sunday, 3 November, with 'only 6d' in his pocket, he was arrested while walking in the street after a rally and eventually interned at Darlinghurst in Sydney – 'the worst gaol in Australasia'.[11]

The targeting of Zuzenko and Simonoff for gagging or intern-ment was significant. In a country where reliable press reports of Soviet developments had been effectively stifled, it was a recognition by federal authorities of the key position which Rus-sian propagandists now held as authentic interpreters of the Revolution. This was a reputation which the Russians themselves did much to cultivate. Workers 'can understand that us Russians, a handful only, represent the glorious Bolshevism', declared Nicholas Blinoff (alias Pamnuskin) in February 1919. 'It looks as if smoke is beginning to rise. There cannot be any smoke without fire. Great fire is unavoidable.'[12]

In retrospect, it seems as though Antipodean radicals – Russians and Anglo-Australians alike – were drawing unwarranted in-spiration from such wisps of 'smoke' as the Great War ended. Revolution was in the air, they believed – they could almost smell it – drifting their way across the Russian Steppes and the ravaged nations of Europe. Had not a mere 'handful' of revolu-tionaries directed the Bolshevik coup in November 1917? And did not the Kiel mutiny and the Sparticist revolts in Germany signal the likelihood of the first proletarian revolution in a highly industrialised country? All across Europe – in Poland, Hungary and Bavaria – the ruling order faltered as crowned heads fell and socialist republics were proclaimed. Disturbances throughout Britain, Canada, South Africa and the United States; great strikes in India, Japan and Argentina and incipient na-tionalist uprisings in Ireland, Egypt, Fiji and British Honduras, all seemed portents of one inescapable outcome. 'The impatient world will wait no longer', wrote Australia's Frank Anstey in *Red Europe*. 'Capitalism listens with quaking soul to the drumbeats of the Armies of Revolution. Those beats grow louder and louder — they draw nearer and nearer.'[13]

In Brisbane, Captain Stable wrote with concern of the preoccupation with revolution he observed around him. 'Every second man in the street will prophesy trouble,' he warned; 'some talk as if revolution is a certainty'. In the north, added the *Daily Mail*, Townsville was 'like a boy sitting on a powder barrel smoking a cigarette'. Certainly, talk of revolution was rife in the letters the Censor confiscated and in the galley proofs of the *Daily Standard* and *Knowledge and Unity* he so diligently vetted. 'Things promise to be startling throughout the Commonwealth in the very near future,' wrote an Irish socialist on Armistice day:

> The workers at last look as though they are waking up and realize they can do without Capitalism . . . Things are far different in Russia than the Tory press would have us believe . . . the workers there are a d---d sight better off now than they have ever been before . . . the European workers know what is the right thing . . . so we read that industrial upheavals in the Central Powers all have marked Bolshevik tendencies . . .

A Toowoomba syndicalist shared his optimism: 'If Holland and Switzerland follow suit, and Spain follows in a year or so, the Socialist movement will spread over the world in one form or another.' A week earlier, Randolph Bedford, the redoubtable Labor publicist, had caused a storm in that conservative bastion, the Queensland Legislative Council, when he suggested that a war which had relegated kingships into obscurity and enthroned 'Bolshevism and Universal Republicanism' as 'the political system of the world' may not, after all, have been fought in vain.[14]

In the final analysis, however, these local revolutionary cries can be viewed as little more than a kind of romantic wish-fulfillment in the wake of four harrowing years of war's torments. The response was visceral and intoxicating, but there appears to have been little consideration of practicalities, of hard-headed socio-economic, political or ideological assessments about revolution's possibility in the Antipodes. Instead, revolution was naively depicted by both its supporters and adversaries as some kind of geographical progression, swallowing up old regimes as it flowed lava-like across the globe. Its Australian opponents believed it necessary to staunch that flow by determined repression; its advocates believed it equally essential to open the floodgates to revolution by constant publicity. Euro-

pean Bolshevism, it was either hoped or feared, would capture
Australia by a process of political osmosis — percolating into
working class consciousness.

Yet the very advocates of a socialist millenium, whenever
pressed, seemed equally perturbed about the comparatively low
level of working class consciousness in Australia. Although
clearly enhanced by war-induced privation, it seemed a pale
reflection of its European counterpart. 'That we are far too sub-
missive is shown by the long lapses of time between our disputes
in any single avocation', wrote a *Daily Standard* correspondent in
late 1918. 'This timidity of the worker is due to his want of
knowledge and must be overcome,' added Broken Hill's
charismatic Percy Brookfield in a letter to Townsville syndicalist, Cliff Barrett. To the revolutionary, the evidence of class
oppression seemed self-proclaiming: long-term exploitation and
profit extraction, exacerbated by the more recent impositions of
warfront slaughter, wartime inflation, profiteering and
unemployment. Yet, frustratingly, many workers viewed such
problems as unrelated encumbrances, as individual or temporary difficulties. Awareness of themselves as a separate class
remained largely elusive or ill-defined, like a view of the world
through a grimy window that they were usually too weary to
polish.[15]

'Thinking hurts, you know,' admits a Brisbane worker in Jack
Lindsay's *The Blood Vote*, set in late 1917: 'It's damned hard to get
out of a rut and face up to things. It hurts like hell. A man gets
tired out, slogging away all day. It's easier to cuddle a girl or
drink a pint of beer. Who can blame him? Thinking hurts like
teething . . . ' The 'servile virtues' encouraged by the ruling class
pressed as heavily upon the working class as fatigue, argued an
IWW placard, pasted up on railway station walls in December
1918: ' . . . patience, humility, contentment, loyalty, reverence,
obedience, respect for law, the hope for reward after death . . .
Each one is a dastardly betrayal of every interest, whether of
person or class which the worker can possess.' In the main, Jerry
Cahill lectured an IWW Domain gathering a month later: ' . . .
the great trouble with the workers was that their want of being
class conscious and their general apathy made them a prey for
the Master Class, who were ever-ready with their newspapers,
Bibles and churches to delude and fool the [m] . . . '[16] How then
could this considerable gap between the workers' poorly
developed class consciousness and the goal of successful insur-

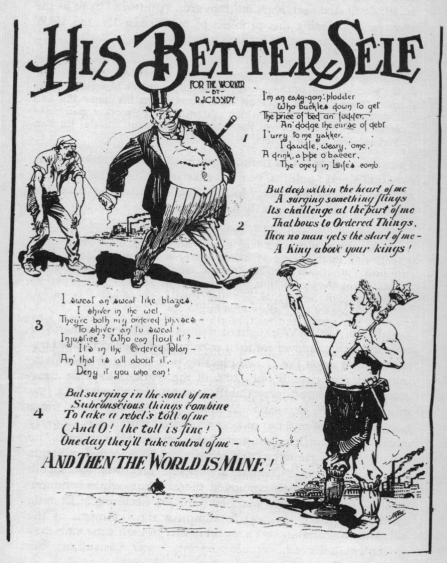

HIS BETTER SELF

FOR THE WORKER
— BY —
R.J.CASSIDY.

1

I'm an easy-goin' plodder
 Who buckles down to get
The price of bed an' fodder,
 An' dodge the curse of debt.
I 'urry to me yakker,
 I dawdle, weary, 'ome,
A drink, a pipe o' baceer,
 The 'oney in Loife's comb.

But deep within the heart of me
 A surging something flings
Its challenge at the part of me
 That bows to Ordered Things,
Then no man gets the start of me —
 A King above your kings!

2

3

I sweat an' sweat like blazes,
 I shiver in the wet,
They're both my ordered phases —
 To shiver an' to sweat!
Injustice? Who can flout it? —
 It's in the Ordered Plan —
An' that is all about it,
 Deny it you who can!

4

But surging in the soul of me
 Subconscious things combine
To take a rebel's toll of me
 (And O! the toll is fine!)
One day they'll take control of me —

AND THEN THE WORLD IS MINE!

His better-self (*Worker*, 4 May 1919)

rection be closed? With the imperturbable confidence of the small, dedicated sect, each militant group preferred itself as the answer. Addressing this problem of mass passivity, the URW intellectual, Konstantin Klushin reasoned:

> we approach the solution . . . very simply and with mathematical exactness — we ask: which form of government is of more benefit to the working class or the people? Which organization of society brings more happiness to the individual, strengthens his inner life and creates harmony? Under which system does the worker gain more economically? Of course, the answer is so plain . . . the Russian Federal Republic of Soviets.

Thus, it was argued, 'a definite group' of the enlightened must eventually seize political power in the interests of the majority, and the mass would simply follow. For, in Klushin's estimation, 'the crowd' was an eminently malleable entity:

> The crowd was and still is only the canvas upon which the artist creates the picture according to his will. The masses are capable of believing in the Great Preacher and of worshipping Caesar; they follow Luther and burn Savonarola; they kill Marat with the same interest as they guillotine Robespierre. The Hero — with a perfect knowledge of the psychology of the crowd . . . becomes all powerful, is worshipped and . . . does what he pleases.[17]

Although the IWW vanguard painted a different scenario of revolutionary takeover for their own 'heroes', they too placed immense faith upon the crowd-pleasing potential of the compact, informed minority. 'If only 20% of the workers became class-conscious', declared Jerry Cahill, 'it would be all over in a few minutes.' IWW organiser, William Jackson was even more hopeful. 'Only 4 or 5 out of every hundred workers, if properly educated was sufficient to control the actions of the majority,' he calculated in November 1918: Why, 'only 10 educated militants were in the Alligator Creek meatworks . . . and these 10 controlled the 990 other men employed there!' Thus, while commonwealth officials happily watched numbers declining at Domain meetings, nothing seemed to diminish the optimism of the militants. Revolution was a world reality in their time and, they fervently believed, would become an Australian fact eventually.[18]

Further encouragement could be drawn from the fact that increasing — though statistically indeterminable — numbers of workers were paying more heed to the revolutionary message. 'Revolutionary ideas are spreading in the unions', noted Captain

Stable, even if Domain numbers were low. This was particularly true of the Brisbane Industrial Council, the railway and meat-workers, and even some sectors of the Australian Workers' Union, all attempting to 'form the vanguard of socialistic activities within the State'. Significant numbers of unionists who, at the commencement of global hostilities were merely loyal, were 'now identified with the revolutionary section and have, in most cases allowed that section to take full control of their organization'. Calculating along similar lines, but with evident relish rather than dismay, W.A. Shepherd, a syndicalist organiser at Ayr declared, 'I tell you, we have the grand spirit of IWWism in every centre and branch of industry in Queensland.'[19]

IWW ascendancy in Queensland in 1918–19 was still an important political and industrial fact, setting the state apart from the rest of the commonwealth. For, whereas the imprisonment of over one hundred militants in 1916–17 and the deportations of more than a dozen in 1918 in the southern states and Western Australia had either muted or crushed this once powerful move-ment, the temporising approach of the more libertarian Ryan regime had allowed it to survive and largely prosper. Edward Shannessy, a northern meatworker, claimed that the Sydney IWW trials made him 'begin to think and I became an IWW'. At the Ross River meatworks near Townsville, he con-tended, 'When I talk IWW to anyone it is to get a few more sym-pathisers and members to join . . . We have a continual progress and that progress is growing daily.' Furthermore, suppression in the south had contributed to this late efflorescence. Groups of militants from interstate had infiltrated the relative sanctuary of Queensland and attempted to rally their forces once more among Brisbane workers – or, with greater success, in the radical strongholds of north and western Queensland. The townships of the sugar coast, the wharves and meatworks of Townsville and Cairns, the metal mines of Mt Morgan and Cloncurry and the shearing sheds of the central west all experienced their stirring impact in these later war years. In towns such as 'Ayr, Proser-pine, Hughenden, Cloncurry, Longreach and others', Captain Wills reported in November 1918, IWW propaganda was preached openly and consistently.[20]

Among a list of fifty-two IWW activists at the Townsville meat-works, compiled by Wills in December, only seven were described as local men. Fifteen were recorded as New South Wales imports, and another twenty-eight as arriving from places 'unknown'. Prominent among them was Norman Rancie, former Sydney editor of *Direct Action*, working with the AMIEU at Ross River and sowing the seeds of the One Big Union scheme there. Another was Pat Hickie, a well-known New Zealand activist and organiser of the pre-war Waihi miners strike. In late 1918, he had toured Queensland, financed by the QRU, lecturing on OBU methods and finally arriving at Townsville in November. IWW strategies – 'the Irritation Strike, the Lightning Strike and the Slow Down policy' – were openly preached in Townsville's main streets, at Alligator Creek Meatworks and at Gordon Vale, near Cairns, Captain Reginald Hayes reported in late 1918. Some workers at Alligator Creek were even wearing "red jersies with the word 'REVOLUTION' woven across them" and greeting each other as fellow "WOBBELIES" [sic].[21]

The IWW presence was particularly pronounced on the Cloncurry fields at Selwyn, Dobbyn, Dolomite and Mt Cuthbert, Wills noted. A considerable number of IWW followers had migrated there from the New South Wales mining districts of Broken Hill and Cobar during 1917. 'It was a haven of rest for them from the clutches of the police who were hunting them down', he reported. 'Many of the most prominent agitators amongst the newcomers were men who had to steal away across the border . . . for fear of arrest.' Around Cloncurry, they had engaged in 'Go Slow and Sabotage' tactics, influencing a large 'alien' population of workers (estimated at sixty per cent of the miners in some areas). According to Wills, most of these 'aliens' were radical Russian émigrés, led by a compatriot named Ker Broft. The syndicalists' impact upon 'many young fellows' was especially effective, he contended, encouraging them 'to recognize all wage slaves as brothers, and all rich people as their arch enemies'. So successful were their efforts that mineral production had fallen as much as fifty per cent in a short space of time. By the end of 1918, IWW leaders from each mining camp were holding regular, secret meetings 'in secluded spots on the banks of the copper creeks' to plan further industrial action.[22]

Among a hard-core group of twenty-one IWW leaders, whom Wills enumerated, he highlighted the activism of John Morrison, 'The Murrumbidgee Cod', John O'Brien and his female partner, May Ranchie, a Spanish-born leftist, from Sydney and Broken Hill respectively, and Fred Anderson (alias Henderson), a fiery Swiss orator from Cobar. Especially prominent in fomenting 'many industrial troubles' (according to Wills) was Paul Freeman, a German–American activist, originally from Mt Vernon in the United States. During late 1916, Freeman had travelled from Broken Hill to Cloncurry and soon became IWW organiser for the Dobbyn area. From early 1918, he was under close police surveillance as an enemy alien and his public speeches were carefully vetted. Finally, at the connivance of Cloncurry mine managers with Commissioner Urquhart and Captain Woods of Military Intelligence, a damning report was compiled against Freeman and his deportation to the United States was ordered on Christmas Eve, 1918. In early January 1919, several police arrested Freeman in a night-time swoop on his Dobbyn camp and he was swiftly removed to Darlinghurst for early deportation on the *Sonoma*. As it eventuated, however, the commonwealth was not to be rid of him so easily. A long saga of failed deportation attempts, hunger strikes, supportive political strikes by Australian workers, and violent clashes between demonstrators, armed police and marines stretched ahead, throughout most of 1919.[23]

Southern IWW influences were also apparent along the sugar coast, particularly at such centres as Innisfail, Proserpine, Ingham, Ayr and Childers, described as 'a nursery of IWW propaganda' by the Censor. Indeed, as IWW involvement in the sugar strikes of 1917–18 reveals, Wobbly agitators made their iconoclastic presence constantly felt. Syndicalists such as George Henry, Ben Noy, Ted Healy, Dave Kidd, Charles O'Malley, James Kelly, Richard Jones and James Driscoll kept contact alive with the Industrial Labor Party (ILP), run by Betsy Hamilton Matthais as a moderate survival of the suppressed Sydney 'local', and sold scores of its newspaper, *Solidarity*. W.A. Shepherd wrote to Sydney that his band of IWW followers at Ayr now felt the time was ripe — 'in fact, rotten-ripe' — for forming 'an international union . . . open to any legitimate worker, male or female, black, white or brindle', as the AWU seemed of such little benefit to manual workers. Then, in February 1919 came news that the Sydney ILP executive had been overthrown and a more radical organisation, the International Industrial Workers (IIW) established to replace it. 'Here is the first genuine effort made since our defeat to revive the old thing', wrote Denis Foley, formerly of Townsville, to his north Queensland contacts: 'It is identical in structure and policy with the Wobs with one exception that we cannot openly advocate scabs to go [ie. dismissal of strikebreakers]. All the old crowd of any importance are attach-

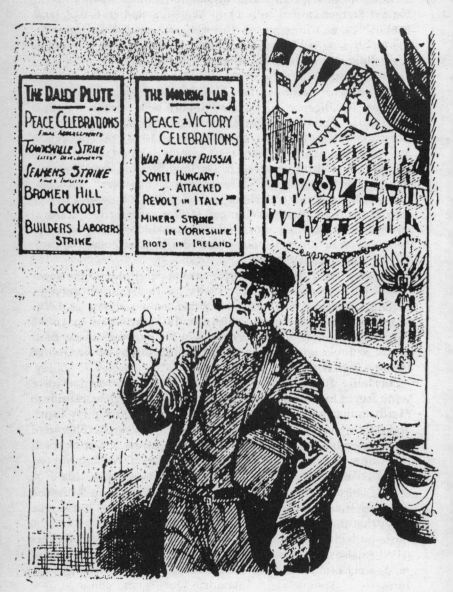

Peace! When there is no peace (*Worker*, 24 July 1919)

ed to it, so we hope to revive quickly. We have a paper called *The Proletarian*, edited by a chap named Callanan . . . try and establish locals wherever possible . . . ' As a direct consequence, a One Big Union Propaganda League (OBUPL) was formed in Townsville during the meatworkers strike, and *The Proletarian* was soon under surveillance by federal agents in Queensland as a more radical version of either *Solidarity* or *Direct Action*.[24]

In the capital, an OBUPL had already been in existence for some time. The old Woolloongabba IWW local had run a chequered course since the 1917 suppressions, but nevertheless could trace a virtually unbroken line of descent through the Defense and Release Committee of 1916–17 and the Universal Freedom League (UFL) of 1917–18. In mid-September 1918, the UFL had revamped itself as the OBUPL, under the leadership of Jack Burke, the former IWW secretary, and Norman Jeffery, a Sydney import, advocating 'industrial unionism of a revolutionary kind'. A 'new anarchist organisation' had been spawned in the metropolis, the Loyalty League warned Military Intelligence. The Brisbane OBUPL carried its message to anyone willing to listen, from a large platform, erected each Sunday evening at North Quay; earlier in the afternoon, their propaganda was ventilated at the Domain from the splashboard of a 'Red Van' – a horse-drawn vehicle owned by George 'Curly' Johnston, a local Wobbly who led the crowd in the singing of 'Pie in the Sky' and 'Put the Bosses on their Backs'.

Constable Foote of the commonwealth police was trudging home from Domain duty on Sunday, 20 October, when the Red Van trundled past him in Queen Street, filled with Wobblies "singing their 'Liberty' songs". A little earlier, he reported, Gordon Brown had spoken from the van in praise of Bolshevism. The Union Jack was attacked as an emblem of 'robbery and exploitation' and finally 'The Red Flag' was sung by a crowd of several hundred, most of whom bared their heads. At the same time, the Censor learned that the van was intended literally as the vehicle for spreading the revolutionary word through Brisbane suburbs and beyond. Flying a red flag, the van was soon to attract complaints from the citizens of Breakfast Creek as its Wobbly occupants harangued passers-by in the streets. Furthermore, a 'Red Flag Crusade' was being planned for southeastern Queensland by Johnston and Jim Quinton, a veteran activist from Great Britain. 'Advertisement is what's needed,' Quinton wrote to Johnston:

just refer to yourself as the 'Vanner' and myself as anything. But get the *Standard* talking . . . You are wanted out at Killarney to assist in organizing timber-workers . . . Killarney is three miles from Tanymorel where 100 coal miners are awaiting your coming eagerly. They will give financial and other support. Tanymorel is seventeen miles from Warwick where I have been arranging things. Appropriate Irish songs are wanted for this place. The WPO will arrange all our meetings and pay advertising. We shall get a good many members . . . Directly the Van is really on the road the work will bear fruit.[25]

Yet, at the Brisbane Domain each Sunday, attendance figures continued to fall, making a mockery of both revolutionary optimism and the exaggerated fears of commonwealth surveillance. Although the activists themselves spoke buoyantly of good crowds and 'real ding dong songs', they were actually caught in the backwash of a euphoric loyalist tide welcoming peace with victory. Whereas crowds of fifty to sixty thousand Brisbaneites turned out for chaotic peace celebrations in mid-November, only a pitiful assemblage of a one hundred or so gathered in showery weather to hear Domain orators celebrate the global spread of Bolshevism. Yet federal officers remained ever vigilant. After the Centennial Hall fiasco of 8 November, two commonwealth constables overheard 'Bolshevik sympathizers' on Victoria Bridge vowing revenge against returned soldiers who had broken up their meeting. There was also talk in the *Daily Standard* of workers forming a 'protective organization' to defend their meetings, much like the Labor Volunteer Army of 1916 — although this seemingly came to nothing. As a consequence, however, William Jackson, who had advocated defensive retaliation on the night of 8 November, was now prohibited from further public speaking. Indeed, the federal authorities' unstated objective seemed to be the obliteration of all signs of Wobbly rhetoric from the city. Constable Foote was at an Ann Street public urinal when he saw printed on the wall before him:

Workers Organize
Direct Action. Sabotage
. . . and put the Boss on the back.
The End justifies the means.
– Industrial Workers of the World/
Bolsheviki.

Captain Ainsworth reported observing small and 'glaringly' red 'silent agitators' pasted over War Loan and Red Cross posters announcing:

> What about a FIVE hour day?
> SLOW DOWN on the job and SEE
> THE BOSS SMILE!

As a result, Jack Burke's boarding house rooms in South Brisbane were raided by Military officers and printing blocks, smuggled north by seamen from the Sydney IIW, were seized. Burke's deportation was strongly recommended.[26]

Despite these ongoing cat-and-mouse games, there were some indications, once November 1918, the month of loyalist jubilation, was over, that radical fortunes were modestly reviving. In December, more than two hundred gathered to commemorate the second anniversary of the IWW Twelve's conviction, defiantly pinning miniature red flags to their lapels, as they listened to Jennie Scott Griffiths and Jim McGuire, an associate of Red Clydeside's John MacLean (the Scottish revolutionary), denounce biased courts and police frame-ups. Like McGuire, the doughty old Eureka veteran, Monte Miller had also blown into Brisbane by this time for propaganda activities associated with the OBU. Although an octogenarian, Miller had remained an alert thinker who could still astonish audiences with his 'great vitality' and the example of his years of 'wonderful militancy'. Heralding his appearance, an IWW poster proclaimed in December: 'What we want are men who can rise to the same level as the men who stood for the cause of freedom at Eureka, men who know what they want and are determined to have it.' By January 1919, Miller's public appearances were credited with greatly increasing the size of radical audiences, as he was 'hailed with delight by every assemblage which he has addressed'.[27]

Another factor, born of desperate rather than inspirational circumstances, was also contributing to this modest January resurgence. A severe drought, a metal market collapse induced by the termination of war contracts, other trade dislocations caused by a sudden armistice and a glut of returned soldiers re-entering the labour market had all contributed to a rapid increase in unemployment, upon which fresh discontents could feed. Deputations by unemployed men had begun in early November; but, by January, their demonstrations had spread statewide. 'During the past three weeks', wrote Captain Wills on 20 January, 'unemployed agitations have sprung up in nearly every district . . . It is significant that the leaders . . . are reputedly men of the IWW type who seem to have arrived from the

South for the purpose of creating trouble.' Brisbane was described as being 'simply overrun with unemployed' and on 23 January
a crowd of two hundred, led by Jackson and William Dowd of
the OBUPL, marched on the State Executive building, besieging
the Home Secretary and Minister of Works in their offices.
Elsewhere, in the north and west, demonstrators sang and raised
the red flag, as their leaders spoke threateningly of 'direct action'
and 'revolution'.[28]

Unemployment problems were 'giving some trouble', Acting
Premier Theodore telegraphed T.J. Ryan, who had left the state
in December for a Privy Council appearance in London. Privately, however, Theodore was expressing more serious qualms. As
Ainsworth reported on 17 January, Commissioner Urquhart had
informed him that Theodore's Cabinet was 'very much concerned' about the agitations. Theodore was comparing them, it
seemed, to 'the Buenos Aires disturbances' and had become
'rather perturbed' in the process. In truth, however, the Argen-
tinian problems – a general strike ruthlessly suppressed by the
military – bore little relation to the Queensland situation. Yet
the local conservative press was presenting that strike as mob
rule fomented by Russian agents – and Theodore apparently
gave credence to such reports. Renewing an earlier assault upon
'labour extremists', he now attacked IWW agitators as
'troglodytes' and 'barnacles', and called upon moderate unionists
'to boot the loudmouthed disturbers out of the labour
movement'. At the same time, he issued instructions to Commissioner Urquhart to begin suppressing radical meetings and ap-
prehending their leaders – a virtual volte-face upon Labor's
prior policy of cautious rapprochement with the leftists and the
granting of free speech areas.[29]

A fortnight later, a ham-fisted attempt at political satire
by the left drove a further wedge into labour's ranks. On 30
January, an article, ostensibly from 'The Daily Liar' and entitled 'BOLSHEVISM HAS BROKEN OUT IN HEAVEN – GOD
ABDICATES', raised a storm of protest when it appeared in the
Brisbane *Worker*. The piece was intended as a parody of the
daily anti-Bolshevik propaganda, published in the conservative
press under such headlines as 'BOLSHEVISM'S TERRIBLE
RAVAGES . . . CHINESE EXECUTIONERS USED'. Yet the
heavy-handed approach of its author, Wobbly propagandist W.S.
Woods: 'The Almighty has been arrested and is now being tried
before the Soviet for being a despot . . . It is rumoured that Jesus

Theodore: 'You'll do a lot of good old man, by throwing that into your own building. Don't you think so.' (*Worker*, 13 July 1916)

Christ and Mohamet have combined forces to stir up a counter-revolution . . . ' caused the joke to backfire miserably. The Methodist Conference expressed its 'abhorrence of such rank blasphemy' and many Catholic Labor supporters signalled that they had now had enough. 'This paper', raged the Catholic-influenced *Daily Mail*: 'standing apparently for Bolshevism is preparing the ground for the local Bolsheviki to cast out priests and ministers from the churches throughout Queensland and convert to their own profane and secular uses the sacred temples of God.' A salvo of anti-Bolshevik statements, fired by Brisbane's Archbishop Duhig, now reached a crescendo. 'Extremists' in the labour movement were 'anything but comforting to Catholics', Duhig warned, as he heralded a mass desertion of such voters from Labor's ranks. By February 1919, Captain Stable recorded that this rank and file repudiation was well in progress as 'the menace of Bolshevism' drove growing numbers of Roman Catholics into the Nationalist fold.[30]

At the same time, Stable noted, the AWU executive was doing everything possible to thwart the ambitions of the OBUPL by suppressing its propaganda and granting 'Preference for Return-ed Soldiers' within its large membership. The Brisbane branch of the Waterside Workers Union (WWU), despite its relatively militant reputation, also was refusing membership to all known Wobblies. In fact, its secretary, Dawson, was cooperating direct-ly with commonwealth police to oust them. As Constable Foote reported:

> Mr. Dawson . . . in the course of a lengthy conversation told me that they had received applications for membership from Jackson, Winbourne and others of the IWW persuasion but they had been turned down . . . He said . . . if any information reached him regard-ing any of the known IWW clique . . . he would communicate same to me at once . . . Mr. Dawson strikes me as being perfectly genuine in his attitude against the IWW and this can . . . be accounted for by the fact that the IWW fraternity here are speaking directly against the organization and control of the Craft Unions and vilifying the officials (especially the AWU) who will not support their propaganda . . .[31]

Among craft unionists affiliated with the BIC, in particular, op-position to the OBU's 'subversive' intentions was quickening. Unions such as the Engineers, Carters and Printers, Stable observed, had become 'openly antagonistic'. Early in February, the Master Painters and Decorators Association attacked 'extremists' and foreigners who 'in the Domain on lorries, in the streets on fruit cases, or in conference' advocated direct action and opposed arbitration courts. These 'Bolshevists', they charged, were encouraging the 'Russianising of Australia . . . a product of the Hun'. A fortnight later, the Printers Industry Union met to end its affiliation with the BIC, which, it believed, was packed with Bolshevik and IWW representatives. At a violent and stormy annual assembly, which resembled more of 'a free fight' than a union meeting, this aim was accomplished.[32]

Elsewhere in Queensland, too, moderate workers were combining to expel the radical and the foreigner. Unemployment, it seemed, could cut both ways, increasing immediate agitation for jobs or rations on the one hand, yet scapegoating certain aliens and dissenters with blame on the other. At Townsville, for instance, the unemployed dismissed their Dutch syndicalist leader, Barend Meyer, explaining irrationally that 'a drift had set in against foreigners'. As hard times hit the mining industry, workers at Mt Cuthbert and Cloncurry turned upon Russians and IWW supporters amongst them. At the Biboohra Meatworks, Cairns, Bolshevism was decried and ten 'extremists' forced to quit the workplace. Finally, at Gladstone in late February, a claim was made that a group of Wobblies had attempted to burn down the local meatworks, valued at £300,000. The incendiarism was allegedly foiled when an alert nightwatchman discovered a smouldering rag lodged in an airduct of the freezer room. At a subsequent meeting of angry AMIEU members, 'the IWW crowd was badly stoushed' and several 'extremists', led by Dan and Leo Brophy, were 'warned off for life' and forced to quit the town. At the Gladstone Roman Catholic church, Father Ginsbach preached a fiery sermon to his proletarian flock, denouncing revolutionaries as 'parasites of the first water'. 'In the interests of civilization', he thundered, 'they must be rooted out of the country.'[33]

This mounting disaffection by craft unionists against both radicals and aliens, together with the vast and violent middle-class mobilisations underway, seemed to point to only one outcome. Despite the inflated hopes and conscientious designs of the OBUPL and the URW, the drift of events and opinions was undeniably turning against them. Despite the inspiring vision of the Bolshevik Revolution and the rhetoric which enshrined it; despite a modest infusion of qualified support from disaffected workers and the unemployed; and despite the efforts made by the revolutionary movement among militant miners, railway-

men, canecutters, shearers and meatworkers, it was the anti-
revolutionary crusade which was gathering in the huge army of
converts.

Acting Premier Theodore, lacking T.J. Ryan's libertarian
scruples, had made it clear that any toleration of revolutionary
initiatives by Labor had ended. And, in unison, moderate union
leaders were now responding to his example. As the AWU
representative at Mt Cuthbert stated bluntly, 'Mr. Theodore had
openly asserted that these undesirables must be got rid of, and
when Mr. Theodore said that, he meant it'. Such workers, it
seemed, were not prepared to risk the reforms and arbitration
concessions granted by 'the only working class government in
the world', outside Russia, for the utopian destiny vaguely promised by persuasive revolutionaries. Although they had suffered
great privations during the war, they believed that better times
of peace now lay ahead – and that an elected Labor Government
would guarantee these. A female Labor supporter presented the
reformist case in simple 'bread and butter' terms in late 1918:

> The conditions of the toiling masses are better today than ever
> before:

Tories	Labor
Past	Present
Bread and Dripping,	Bread and Butter,
Very little meat,	Cheap meat,
Twelve hours a day,	Eight hours a day,
Five shillings per day.	Ten to fifteen shillings per day.

> Which are you going to choose?

Clearly, to many workers, such basic material computations
overshadowed any dreams about a future socialist millenium. A
choice between the existing parliamentary forces seemed to
them the only choice which made sense. Labor in power, it was
strongly enjoined, was the only 'socialist vanguard' which
Queensland workers should ever need. Indeed, its ideals were
'almost the religion of the many thousands of Labor men and
women throughout the land'.[34]

Theodore's threats received more substance on 11 March 1919,
when the Central Executive of the ALP met to thrash out a
'Solidarity or Disruption' Manifesto, directed against 'the IWW
. . . and all similar propaganda'. In this formulation, the small
number of radicals on the CPE were outvoted almost four to one,
and the resultant document reflected such odds. The IWW, the

Manifesto asserted, represented only 'Nihilism' and 'a definite programme of destruction', in contrast with the reformist and educational advances of the labour movement. Its philosophy of Industrial Unionism was: 'not a doctrine, not a programme, not a movement, nor even a definite tendency. *It is simply a turbulent and a fractious state of mind.* It has no consistency of belief, and no uniformity of method. It carps and cavils and denounces and, where possible, it disrupts.' Whilst Labor welcomed legitimate and honest criticism, it was argued, it must now discriminate between this and the presence of 'treacherous antagonists', who had 'insinuated their way into the ranks and are seeking to spread a crafty and disruptive propaganda into the working class movement'.[35]

In the cause of 'solidarity' and 'discipline', all those who failed to conform to 'the policy laid down by the Labor Convention' must now be repudiated. Thus, as all unions and Workers Political Organisations (WPO) were regimented to drive out 'avowed or covert supporters' of the IWW, its street orators found that they too were being muzzled. As Norman Jeffery observed in *The Proletarian* of 8 March, the Brisbane rebels' accelerated programme of propaganda, which now included three meetings a week, was being forcefully impeded by state police. 'Judging by the attention being devoted to us by the Authorities, it is clear that they have something "up their sleeves" which will be disclosed shortly', Jeffery prophesied:

> A fortnight ago we were forbidden to speak at Market Square by a Sub-Inspector of Police, who had quite a detachment of cops and detectives with him. On the Sunday following, we were told to refrain from selling our literature and papers ... This move was countered by distributing the paper gratis, afterwards taking up a collection to cover costs ... The net result of this manifestation of "law and order" is the intensified activity of the local industrialists ... determined to maintain our right of free speech and to sell literature in this stronghold of Queensland capitalism.[36]

The Russians responded to escalating loyalist repression and reformist antagonism with 'intensified activity' as well. As Civa Rosenberg wrote in *Knowledge and Unity* during February: 'If you see the luxurious comfort, the wonderful mansions, the rich food, the motor cars, the yachts of the rich; if you catch the picture of suffering and want and that other picture of the few rioting in plenty, you will know you cannot remain neutral.' Following Simonoff's internment and the suppression of their

Centennial Hall celebrations, it was reported in December 1918 that the URW were holding 'very secret' meetings to plan further strategies. Their target was a twofold one: first, the repeal of the *War Precautions Act* and *Aliens Restriction Order* now that the war was over; secondly, a provision of passports to Russians eager to be repatriated to their revolutionary homeland.

On a superficial reading of events — with loyalists urgently demanding their removal and Bolsheviks in many cases anxious to leave — this latter demand might appear the easier one to grant. As a perplexed federal agent pleaded in mid-January, 'Why are these people not allowed to go? To my mind, every facility should be given them to get out of the country and none should be permitted to come in.' Yet this mutually advantageous outcome was not to be so easily accomplished. For, in accord with Britain's anti-Soviet policies, particularly its various naval and military forays into Soviet territory and the establishment of Allied 'zones of operation' there in December 1918, Russian Bolsheviks in Australia were now to be restrained by passport denials, rather than encouraged to depart. Repatriated Bolsheviks, it was logically argued, could only hamper counter-revolutionary forces in Russia. And, by January 1919, these counter-revolutionaries included Australian personnel. Since June 1918, at least nine Australian military 'advisers' had been secretly engaged with the White Army in North Russia. Several hundred other Australian volunteers were also covertly in training with British forces for invasion activities there. Thus, the perceptive cry of local Russians, that they were being kept 'in an off-hand manner . . . as war prisoners' in Australia, was greeted by an official wall of silence.[37]

The URW's position was therefore a most frustrating one, with their energies divided between local agitation and the taxing problem of getting home. Their characteristic answer to this dual dilemma was to move once more onto the offensive. Early in January 1919, Commissioner Urquhart learned from Agent Brown that the URW was planning to hold a red flag march through Brisbane streets before the end of the month to publicise their plight. Urquhart's Russophobic fears were immediately aroused. 'These Russians are of an undesirable class', he reported to Labor's Home Secretary, John Huxham:

> their aims and proceedings are deliberately intended to be subversive
> to law and order and . . . they cherish the intention of destroying the
> constitution of this State . . . the[ir] presence . . . in view of their

anarchical doctrines . . . constitutes a menace to the peace and well-being of this City. Steps should be taken, as recommended by Inspector Ferguson for the deportation or internment of these dangerous people.[38]

Within several days, Agent Brown was submitting new and more alarming accounts. On 19 and 20 January, he disclosed, he had attended meetings at the Russian rooms chaired by Zuzenko. Jerry Cahill and William Jackson of the OBUPL were also there, along with a large number of Russians. Here it was decided to mount a composite protest, with the BIC, the Socialist League and the Wobblies all joining the URW in a procession to the Domain, led by the Labour Band playing 'Keep the Red Flag Flying'. No traffic permit was to be sought. Red flags were to be carried, but in order to circumvent the prohibition, it was decided to place white lettering across the banners declaring, 'Down with Allied Intervention in Russia', 'Down with the War Precautions Act'. According to the agent, the Russians and Wobblies seemed fanatically committed. "Remarks such as 'The Flames only require fanning', 'Things are ripe for immediate action and fight', 'We must if necessary carry out a campaign of robbery and destruction' were made by the speakers during the course of the meeting", he alleged.[39]

An apprehensive Police Commissioner prevailed upon the Home Secretary to have the march banned, but Huxham replied that this decision was a federal matter. Thus on Sunday, 26 January, the procession went ahead, although in the wake of the police agent's extravagant claims, it must have appeared an anticlimax. Even the *Brisbane Courier* had to admit that the entire demonstration was 'most orderly'. Led by singing Russian men, women and children, more than fifteen hundred paraded, including 'a small sprinkling of returned soldiers'. The entire procession seemed festooned in red. Crimson sashes, ribbons and banners were much in evidence, although no red flags as such were carried. 'War Debts are Our Burden', read the sashes worn by the youthful members of the Children's Peace Army, while the larger banners were inscribed with such messages as 'Free Speech is a Crime in Australia', 'Our Fighters in Gaol — Is this Freedom?' and 'Abolish the Censorship'. At the Domain, a host of speakers, including William Finlayson, Federal Labor Member for Brisbane, 'Gunner' Taylour and Monte Miller, denounced internment, anti-Bolshevik press reports and the passport system, as well as praising Lenin, Trotsky and the red flag. After raising three cheers for the Revolution, the processionists then marched to North Quay, where they quietly dispersed.[40]

To all accounts, it seemed as though these January protestors had successfully flouted the regulations, without police or military interference. Yet, if they had triumphantly foiled federal authorities, the latter were quick to make amends. Several days later, Military Intelligence raided the Russian rooms and the homes of several Russians, including the anarchist, Nicholai Lagutin. The protest banners of 26 January, a large amount of revolutionary material, part of the Russians' printing press and other belongings were seized. Lists of 'dangerous Russians' were compiled and one of these, bearing the names of six Queensland URW members, was forwarded by the Governor-General to the Colonial Office in London. The military, it was intimated, should be called out immediately if the Russians attempted another such march.

Yet these moves triggered the very responses they were ostensibly intended to prevent. The angry Russians, surveying their wrecked Stanley Street rooms and smarting at their loss of expensive equipment, rapidly reconstituted the URW as a fully fledged Soviet Committee — the Southern Soviet of Russian Workers. A change of venue was also planned, from the debris of their Atlas building rooms to a leased, street-level hall in nearby Merivale Street. Arguing that the Military raid had 'interfered with the rights of citizenship', they vowed to hold another protest rally in the near future. On 17 February, the OBUPL voted to join them.[41]

The tiny clusters of Bolsheviks and Wobblies, with the wind of revolution at their backs, now moved swiftly towards their inevitable rendezvous with the united loyalists. Presentiments of conflict echoed from all sides. It a passionate hour-long speech before a North Quay crowd of three hundred gathered in stormy weather on 9 March, Jim Quinton vaingloriously depicted himself dying behind a street barricade 'in the Red Army'. Commonwealth police had anticipated a clash on Saturday, 1 March, but nothing eventuated. Military Intelligence set a date for the Russian demonstration a fortnight later, but again nothing happened. Yet, on Friday evening 7 March, at a socialist rally in Albert Square, violent scuffles erupted as loyalist soldiers attacked radical speakers and dragged them from the podium. 'The Bolsheviki are coming . . . You will see ammunition going off in Queen Street in a couple of months', forecast members of the crowd. There was not that long to wait. Scenes of mayhem lay directly ahead for 'sleepy Brisbane', as a small force which considered itself unstoppable sped unerringly towards a 'righteous' and immovable foe.[42]

Chapter Four

Days of the Pogrom

What was there in carrying the Red Flag or the Sinn Fein Flag? Practically little. But behind both there was *rebellion*.

W.H. Barnes[1]

If, at the end of the Great War, the Brisbane metropolis merited the adjective 'sleepy', then the nearby farming centre of Samsonvale, in the Brisbane Valley, could fairly be described as wellnigh comatose. Yet even here 'the dread spectre of Bolshevism' was sufficient to stir it violently from its slumbers. On Friday morning, 28 February 1919, a ballast train chugged its way towards Samsonvale railway station from Cedar Creek, on the Enoggera–Terrors Creek line. A small group of local farmers whose waggons had been commissioned to move the belongings of navvies to a new extension at Cobble Creek were enjoying an early lunch when they were startled to see a large red flag, flying brazenly from a carriage roof of the approaching train. As the train drew nearer, they heard with alarm the strains of the 'Red Flag' anthem issuing forth from the score of navvies on board. At the station, the singing workers were led onto the platform by Joe 'Nugget' Doyle, waving the flag before them on a pole almost two metres long. An immediate altercation broke out between Doyle and the station master, John Wilson, who grabbed the flag and threw it to the ground. The half dozen farmers, gathering around, then declared they would not cart the workers' belongings unless the offending flag was removed; and, as a consequence, Doyle propped it against the station wall and left it there while the loading proceeded.

Yet by the time the waggons were ready to leave, the navvies had reconsidered their position. 'The old flag' must now be flown from the leading waggon, Doyle informed an astonished farmer,

Apples of discord (*Worker*, 19 September 1919)

Fred Michael — all the way to Cobble Creek. A heated argument ensued; again the angry station master intervened, threatening to dismiss immediately any man who touched the flag. When Doyle ignored this direction and started towards Michael's waggon, Wilson grabbed at the flag to tear it from its pole, simultaneously calling upon the farmers to cut it loose with a knife. Within seconds, both farmers and station master were grappling with a dozen navvies in the dusty station yard. A ten-minute scuffle followed, during which blows were exchanged, before the outnumbered farmers finally ceded. Wilson was left to battle on alone in a futile tug-of-war until he too was exhausted. The cheering navvies — much like those military recruits who, six months earlier, had floated their Union Jack at Darra — next began an impromptu flag-raising ceremony. The flagstaff was secured in an open vertical pipe and the assembled workers sang several revolutionary 'hymns' before it. A Russian gang member — a militant named Faganoff — then delivered a rousing speech upon the red flag's meaning.

Yet the watching farmers remained unpersuaded and threatened to discard their load if a navvy climbed onto any waggon with the offending emblem. The work gang attempted to solve this impasse by marching ahead of the drays; but the farmers, whipping their horses, drove past the singing men with their red banner leaving them far behind. As Joe Doyle led the small red flag procession along the Cobble Creek Road, he called upon several speechless bystanders to salute the passing emblem. Soon the district was alive with the news that fifty men near Cobble Creek were all flying red flags; this was confirmed by a subsequent police visit. Thus at the official opening of the Enoggera–Terrors Creek line at Samsonvale on 3 March, the Reverend Thomas Leyden spoke of the urgent necessity to keep Queensland clean from all disease, not simply the pneumonic influenza pandemic now ravaging the southern states, but also 'the two germs known as IWWism and Bolshevism'. When William Lloyd, a Welsh schoolteacher and Labor member for Enoggera, attempted to interpose that IWW principles were similar to those of Christianity, he was rapidly silenced by the angry crowd.[2]

The Samsonvale red flag march was indeed a relatively small affair; but like the prior loyalist demonstrations at Darra and Hughenden, it served as a warning of the large-scale confrontations which lay ahead. The Lilliputian struggle of navvies and farmers over a flag in a station yard seemed an unlikely precursor to the savage Brisbane disturbances of some three weeks later. Yet that scuffle would raise enough dust eventually to send 'Nugget' Doyle into Brisbane gaol to share a cell with other red flag carriers, and place Faganoff, the Samsonvale orator, prominently upon one of General Irving's soon-to-be-compiled deportation lists. Furthermore, the Samsonvale incident — although remote and under-reported — was really the first occasion in Queensland on which the red flag had been successfully carried and displayed since it was hauled down from Brisbane Trades Hall in October 1918, five months earlier.[3]

When word of the incident reached Brisbane, it provided loyalist dossiers with yet another example of radical audacity and further goaded loyalist alarm. H.L. Hall of the anti-Bolshevik National Political Council (NPC) executive reported the matter to commonwealth police on 17 March and called for immediate action. In the same communication, from information supplied to him by a local dentist, he told of 'disloyalist' Russian Finns holding midnight meetings under 'a lonely railway bridge' near Nambour. The country seemed to be 'teeming' with such menacing elements, responded commonwealth police Sergeant, A.M. Short. Indeed, on the very day that Hall filed his report, the prohibited emblem of another 'rebel horde' was unfurled in the main streets of Brisbane. In the annual St Patrick's Day procession that afternoon, two Sinn Fein flags were carried by youths flanking three marching Roman Catholic priests. Simultaneously, the Sinn Fein colours of green, white and orange made their appearance in parades at Ipswich, Warwick, Bowen and Innisfail.[4]

It had originally been the banning of the Sinn Fein standard in 1918 which had set a precedent for the later suppression of the red flag. Yet, although the letter columns of the conservative press in March 1919 were enlivened by loyalists whose 'blood boiled . . . [with] humiliation and shame' at the defiant St Patrick's Day display, there was no corresponding street violence directed against Irish Catholics, in Brisbane or elsewhere. The Royal Orange Institute demanded retaliation for this War Precautions violation from Acting Prime Minister Watt, but no other loyalist organisations — the ULE, the NDC or the RSSILA for instance — forwarded a similar protest. And, from official sources, there were no instructions issued for the arrest,

The two flags (*Worker*, 29 August 1918)

fining, imprisonment or deportation of the flag-carrying miscreants. But if Brisbane radicals and local Russian Bolsheviks took this muted reaction to imply any slackening of loyalist resolve or tacit encouragement of their own red flag display, they were sorely misguided. For Sinn Fein, that shibboleth of the conscription campaigns, was no longer a target for patriotic attack. In fact, if the sectarian alliance forged by the merging of leading Catholics and Protestants in the anti-radical NDC was to hold, such an attack was to be studiously avoided. On the more pressing matter of anti-Bolshevism, the Roman Catholic prelate, Archbishop Duhig, stood staunchly beside the anti-Papist, Sandford Jackson.[5]

The Red Flag march at Samsonvale and the unchallenged display of the Sinn Fein tri-colour set the scene for a raucous Red Flag exhibition in Brisbane on 23 March, just six days later. The reasons for this pageant were more complex than a simple act of replication. Anger at the destruction and confiscation of property which accompanied military raids of 31 January on the Russian quarter was one significant spur. Furthermore, radicals generally considered it imperative to maintain a persistent campaign for the repeal of the *War Precautions Act* which effectively banned the revolutionary iconography essential to the socialist and syndicalist message.

In Melbourne, the elderly activist Jennie Baines, and rebel poet, Richard Long, had already been arrested for displaying red flags on the Yarra Bank on 23 February; and, on 18 March, they were sentenced to six months imprisonment for the offence. Two days later, Bob Carroll, militant secretary of the Engineers union, wrote to R.S. Ross in Melbourne that the BIC was now prepared to take supportive action. At a BIC executive meeting on 12 March, Carroll advised Ross, he had succeeded in having a motion carried – 'not unanimously worse luck . . that at all future demonstrations . . . the red flag be flown'. At this same meeting, the executive decided to support the February decision of the Brisbane 'Soviet' and the OBUPL to hold such a demonstration imminently; and, at a joint meeting of Bolsheviks, syndicalists and socialists held some days later, the date of Sunday, 23 March was chosen. The demonstration 'is set down for next Sunday afternoon', Carroll informed Ross, 'when we will hold a meeting of protest against the continuation of the WPA [War Precautions Act] and will then give THE FLAG an airing. Subsequent events should be interesting . . .'[6]

This militant resolve to flout the War Precautions regulation by mass civil disobedience was tempered by equivocation from other Anglo-Australian radicals. The BIC, as Carroll indicated, was not unanimous; and, when anti-conscriptionist, Cuthbert Butler, attempted to gain support from the Metropolitan District Council, he was rebuffed. Then, after the State Labor Cabinet agreed to grant a march permit only upon the proviso that no red flags be carried, the confrontational strategy seemed to become completely unstuck. 'The general feeling on Friday night and Saturday [21–22 March] was that the demonstration would be made without red flags', *Knowledge and Unity* later admitted. Such faltering commitment, however, was not to the liking of dedicated revolutionaries, particularly the Russians. Like the Wobblies, they saw little virtue in cooperating with the State apparatus upon any issue.

'The Labor party', *Knowledge and Unity* concluded in late March, 'has the soul of the bourgeois democrat, the little shop keeper and hard pressed lower middle class which envies the big fellow, but does not want to wipe out the system . . . ' Yet, every day, the social revolution was 'coming nearer' and it must be welcomed with iron in the soul rather than faintheartedness. The only legitimate tactic, therefore, was to make each day 'agitation day'. 'And let the rumblings come from the side streets, as well as from the main streets and the domains', *Knowledge and Unity* advocated on 22 March, the day prior to the Red Flag procession: "from the small towns as well as from the capitals; from the villages and the cabbage patch. Let there be agitation, ceaseless agitation. Agitate over the back fence, in your office, on the job and from the soapbox on all occasions. . . . AGITATE, EDUCATE, ORGANIZE!"[7]

The Russian Bolsheviks nursed a further motive for ignoring the mere proviso of a police permit. Their petitions to federal authorities, urging 'free passages' back to their native land, had so far been studiously ignored. Many therefore believed that something dramatic was necessary to 'have an influence on the Czars here'. Two days before the demonstration, Peter Petroff Kreslin, son of Russian peasants from Novo Troitzk, acting as secretary of the Brisbane 'Soviet', wired Acting Prime Minister Watt and demanded once more 'our release from here'. Simultaneously, he contacted Frank Tudor, the federal Labor leader, urging him to cable the European Peace Conference on the Russians' behalf. Increasingly desperate 'Soviet' members seem to have concluded that one possible recourse to their plight might lie in escalating agitation. For agitation, like an irritant thorn requiring urgent removal, might yet lead to the repatriation of troublesome Bolsheviks.[8] Thus, on the afternoon of the Red Flag march, Kreslin distributed dodgers demanding the release of Russian 'war prisoners' from their Australian thraldom. 'Comrades, demonstrate today and keep on demonstrating!' the leaflet urged. And, in the stormy wake of this demonstration, Kreslin was to deduce that street action had been quite 'successful' in stirring up a formerly 'stagnant pool' and beginning 'an agitation' for the deportation of the Bolsheviks. Intercepting Kreslin's letter to Russian contacts at Townsville, Cairns, Broken Hill and Sydney, Captain Stable remarked, 'The Soviet look upon [this] . . . as a lucky incident, hastening as they expect it will do, their deportation . . .'[9]

If Stable's conclusion is correct, and Kreslin's views are accepted as representative, the ironic convergence of design seems inescapable here. Those sworn enemies, the Anti-Bolshevik loyalists and the exiled Russians, even as they manoeuvred themselves into opposing battle positions, were seemingly intent upon securing a roughly identical outcome to the struggle of late March. The desire to initiate deportation proceedings, viewed by one side as sweet purgation and by the other as painful release, was a tenuous, unacknowledged bond they were both about to seal in blood, as well as fury. The catalyst to this confrontation lay in the hands of Alexander Zuzenko and Herman Bykov (alias Resanoff), a Bolshevik intellectual from Saratov, as they approached the demonstration that Sunday afternoon, 23 March, with three large flags, furled and concealed within newspaper wrappings.

At 2.30 p.m., a rather subdued assembly of four hundred — less than one third the number who had marched on 26 January — milled about in Turbot Street outside Trades Hall as the two Russians approached. The indecision of the crowd as to whether they would even march that afternoon, considering their numbers were so low, was great, *Knowledge and Unity* later claimed. Fifty of the would-be demonstrators were Russian and Anglo-Australian youngsters, belonging to the Children's Peace Army, and another fifty were women. Considerably more than half of the company were Russians, bedecked in red ribbons and sashes, and wearing red flag badges — attesting once more to the comparative reticence of Anglo-Australian radicals about participating that day. Represented among the non-Russian minority were a substantial OBUPL contingent, a group of Queensland Socialist League members, a scattering of militant trade unionists and a handful of radical returned soldiers, led by 'Gunner' Taylour. Eight state police stood complacently watching this small and seemingly ineffectual crowd, obviously expecting little trouble, whilst surveillance agents mingled among its sparse ranks as unobtrusively as they could.[10]

The crowd's indecision increased as William Wright, President of the BIC, appeared at a Trades Hall window and outlined Cabinet's refusal to allow any red flag displays. Yet the gathering's dejected mood suddenly swung to anger as he indicated the BIC's compliance with this directive and urged the demonstrators to 'loyally abide' by it as well. It was his unfortunate choice of the word 'loyally' in particular which had this electrifying effect. As he uttered it, the crowd spontaneously began to jeer, and Russian spokespersons, socialists and syndicalists began quarrelling with other trade unionists and BIC officials. (Whether the various 'secret agents' present also contributed to this clamour is impossible to say.) Hurried consultations continued inside the Trades Hall vestibule, until finally Zuzenko and Bykov strode from the squabbling throng and tore the newspaper wrappings away from their three large banners. As the red flags were 'raised on high and shaken out in the glorious sunlight', a cheer went up and Mrs Scott Griffiths, the Cahill brothers (Edward and Jerry), Monte Miller, George Taylour and others emerged from the Hall and began distributing a hundred handkerchief-sized red pennants throughout the throng, who were now marshalling themselves into processionist ranks.[11]

Civil disobedience thereupon adopted its own momentum, as Wright's cry of 'The procession is off, boys!' was lost amid the swelling hubub of the crowd. The eight police, startled by this sudden turn of events, now began to make their own moves. Sub-Inspector Brosnan argued with Mrs Scott Griffiths, warning her that the Children's Peace Army at the head of the column would not be allowed to march carrying red flags. Fearing for their safety, she withdrew these youngsters, as the Russian men similarly told their womenfolk to retire. Some women and children persisted in marching with the men, however, and police would later complain that it was their presence which prevented them from forcefully dispersing the demonstration. As the procession began to move off, seven of the eight police attempted to form a cordon across Turbot Street, as the other constable ran back to Roma Street to call out mounted police reinforcements. The three hundred or so determined marchers, however, quickly broke through this thin blue line. Brosnan struggled with Zuzenko for possession of his flag, but was easily overpowered by the physically superior Russian. Wielding their flagstaffs like lances to ward off other police, Zuzenko and Bykov led the jubilant marchers into Edward Street, singing 'Hold the Fort' and 'Solidarity Forever'. Here they were confronted by four galloping troopers, summoned from Roma Street; but as the horses charged the procession, the billowing red flags and the swinging banner poles caused them to falter and rear away.[12]

In Queen Street, several more unsuccessful attempts were made by the mounted and foot police to break up the procession, the horses slipping erratically on the trams rails each time the troopers wheeled to charge. Eighteen-year-old Don Griffiths remembered seeing a police helmet knocked off and sailing onto the roof of Lind's Umbrella Shop during one such scuffle. The constable who had run to Roma Street and back later reported:

> I again joined the Police endeavouring to stop the procession in Queen Street . . , and I saw Acting Sergeant Davis having a tussle with a man who appeared to be a Russian. Myself and others got in front of the procession and I sang out "Stop boys, somebody will get hurt". No notice was taken of my request, and George Taylour who was carrying a small red flag sang out to me "I can't stop them" . . .

After this confrontation, the singing marchers — now with a crowd of one thousand or so supporters and onlookers in train — were allowed to proceed along George and Alice Streets towards the Domain unmolested. 'When the processionists were not compelled to defend their flags from the police, they marched in a thoroughly orderly and peaceable manner', observed *Knowledge and Unity*. 'They sang, 'tis true, for the emblem of humanitarianism was aloft in the purifying sunlight and stood the test'. But at the locked Domain gates, they were brought to an abrupt halt by the four horsemen blocking the narrow entrance way. Norman Jeffery of the OBUPL thereupon climbed out onto the branch of an overhanging Moreton Bay fig tree and addressed the crowd. 'We have accomplished our purpose', Jeffery told them, 'and we are going to show that we will hold our

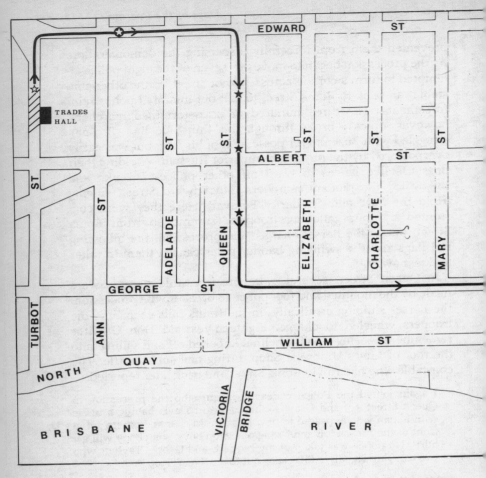

Not To Scale

demonstrations when we want them and not when other people want them. We as organized forces have had a display of solidarity this afternoon.' As Jeffery spoke, 'much shouting, threatening and arguing' continued between demonstrators and police, until Inspector Ferguson, nervously noticing 'a lot of road metal' lying about, withdrew his troopers and unlocked the gates. Vigorously singing and hooting the constables, the marchers then passed through into the Domain enclosure.[13]

Within the Domain, the speakers' rotunda was soon festooned with dozens of red flags, rapidly threaded through its iron lattice-work; and, as the orations began, Zuzenko placed himself beside

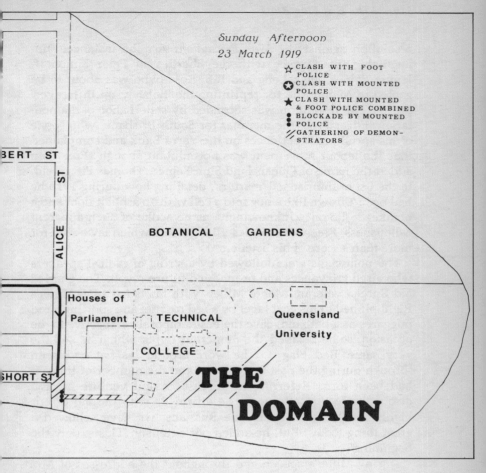

Sunday Afternoon
23 March 1919

☆ CLASH WITH FOOT POLICE
✪ CLASH WITH MOUNTED POLICE
★ CLASH WITH MOUNTED & FOOT POLICE COMBINED
⁝ BLOCKADE BY MOUNTED POLICE
// GATHERING OF DEMONSTRATORS

BERT ST

ALICE ST

BOTANICAL GARDENS

Houses of Parliament

TECHNICAL COLLEGE

Queensland University

SHORT ST

THE DOMAIN

The red flag march, Sunday afternoon, 23 March 1919

the platform, resolutely 'holding aloft the Red Banner'. As Edward Turner of the Socialist League introduced the first speaker, Senator Myles Ferricks, there were impatient cries of 'Cut out the politicians', but Ferricks was in no temporising mood. In a passionate and synoptic speech, he denounced censorship, internment and the curtailment of liberties, and examined such issues as soldiers' discontents and the commonwealth's suppression of the first Darwin rebellion against its official representatives in December 1918. 'The present Government of Australia is marching on its doom', he thundered, imposing conditions on its people calculated 'to bring about a state of revolt'. Moving a resolution against the *War Precautions Act*, he instanced 'unjustifiable interference with the liberties' of Peter Simonoff, Jennie Baines, Dick Long and R.S. Ross (who was about to be gaoled in Melbourne for reprinting the 'Bolshevism in Heaven' satire). The resolution was seconded by state Labor parliamentarian, Edgar Free, the member for South Brisbane, who spoke of his spruiking experiences on the Yarra Bank and complained that 'the labour movement was not militant enough'. Free then added the name of Queensland Sinn Feiner, Thomas Fitzgerald, to the list of imprisoned 'martyrs', detailing how during 1918 he had been 'thrown like a dog into a cell with an asphalt floor and a blanket to lie on'. Unknowingly, as he spoke of such apparent callousness, Free was also describing a fate which lay ahead for more than a score of his listeners.[14]

The politicians were followed by a string of radical speakers who aired grievances and prophesied future revolt. The gnarled old Eureka veteran, Monte Miller, with his faded 1856 Miner's Right pinned to his coat lapel by a red rosette, and sporting a red puggaree as a hatband, gave the best temporal perspective to the occasion, as he recalled 'the numerous fights' which he and the very same 'Red Flag . . . he wore around his hat had been through during the past forty years, and the number of times it had been torn'. Referring to their successful venture at civil disobedience that afternoon, he affirmed, 'with the aid of our highly intellectual friends, the Russians, we have achieved a great thing today'. But, he added portentously, 'This is only the beginning . . .'[15]

During Miller's speech and throughout the addresses of Mrs Scott Griffiths, Jim Quinton and Bob Carroll, intermittent fights erupted within the crowd, as Russians and others refused to provide their names to police, and returned soldiers and civilian loyalists sparred with exuberant radicals. Elation, frustration and outrage combined to keep the general atmosphere highly charged throughout the afternoon. As the meeting closed at 5.30 pm — thus ending three hours of radical pre-eminence in the public domain — 'The Red Flag' was sung and £4/15/6 collected 'for any prosecutions which may follow'. Clearly, none of the marchers had any real conception of the violent backlash which their actions that afternoon were about to unleash.[16]

Yet, once lit, the loyalist fuse was to prove a short and a fast-burning one. Even as the demonstrators quietly dispersed, the returned soldiers were marshalling their ranks. Within two hours, several thousand would descend upon the regular Sunday night OBUPL propaganda meeting at North Quay 'for the purpose of breaking it up'. The mechanics of this mobilisation can only be a matter for speculation. Evidence shows that even while the Domain speeches were proceeding, military officers associated with the RSSILA were circulating directives among war veterans and other loyalists in the audience to gather in William Street that evening. It may be inferred that a 'bush telegraph' then rapidly spread the word among other soldiers, congregated at venues such as the YMCA Hut, and that telephones of leading Brisbane loyalists rang constantly that evening. Loyalist spokesmen, such as Malcolm Ellis and AIF Captain E.R.B. Pike (who had consulted with the SIB on more than a score of occasions between January and March), were at the Domain taking notes, but the principal call for action seems to have originated amongst officials of the RSSILA. This, of course, was consistent with prior deliberations of United Loyalist Executive (ULE) leaders. For, when trouble began, they knew that it would be the trained, aggressive qualities of the returned soldiers within their ranks which they could depend upon to lead the attack. The examples of Hughenden, Townsville, Toowoomba, Dalby and elsewhere had already convincingly demonstrated this.[17]

North Quay that night was therefore the scene of immediate, purposive mob action. Scarcely had the open air OBUPL meeting begun when a large pack of infuriated soldiers rushed towards it from the opposite footpath yelling, 'Let us clear this scum out of Brisbane!' The small assembly was totally swamped. Bykov, Zuzenko and others were torn from the rostrum, and Wobblies and Russians in the audience violently assaulted. The huge OBUPL platform was lifted bodily into the air and hurled into the Brisbane River. The powerful Zuzenko broke away from his assailants and, sprinting onto Victoria Bridge, made for the rooms of the Russian Association in Merivale Street to alert members there. Bykov, a much slighter man, was not so fortunate, however. He was 'seized and mauled' by the mob, who were clearly in a lynching mood. Beaten across the head and back with staves and then stabbed with a knife, the small man was being hauled towards the steep river bank when police at last intervened to prevent the crowd pitching him into the river.[18]

As a number of the shaken radicals were being hustled onto

passing tramcars by police, it was next suggested that the crowd should follow in Zuzenko's wake across Victoria Bridge. A raid on the 'Bolshevik headquarters' was proposed, with the stated intention of 'burning it down and assaulting the Russians connected with it'. Two thousand men were soon marching across the bridge, singing patriotic songs and, as they approached the Russian club rooms, the leaders, calling 'Come on Diggers!', broke into a fast run. Zuzenko, however, had already alerted 'Soviet' members to prepare for their defence. When the loyalists were within two hundred and fifty metres of the hall, he and several others emerged from a side lane and fired three shots in quick succession above the heads of the charging mob, scattering them in panic. It was not until the soldiers had retreated further than a kilometre that more than a score of state police in attendance began to intervene. Commonwealth Intelligence Officers and military police who observed the action did nothing to curb the soldiers' volatility. In the words of Constable O'Driscoll:

> Plain clothes Constable Keefe and myself approached the building and said "We are police" . . . A voice answered loudly, "Anybody who comes near here will be shot". I said " . . . if you don't let us speak there will be trouble as the crowd will break in". One of the men then assumed an aggressive attitude towards Keefe and asked him to put up his hands . . . We could then see about 30 or 40 men, mostly Russians lined up inside a wooden gate; two or three had something in their hands which I could not discern . . . One of them said . . . "We intend to fight here until our bodies are lying on the ground". I said "There is no need for you to fight. We will see everything right if you keep cool." He said, "Send the mob away."[19]

O'Driscoll and Keefe then approached the soldiers and attempted to reason with them: 'You are not armed and if you expose yourself you will probably get shot and *do no good*. Leave these men to us and go home like good chaps.' The soldiers, however, paid no heed to these remonstrations until one of their officers interceded, suggesting that the assault had been insufficiently planned. They should withdraw to the YMCA Hut in the city, he argued, and approach Military Commandant Irving 'for ammunition and reinforcements to deal with the Russians'. As he spoke, heavy rain began to fall, and the drenched soldiers finally straggled back to William Street where an impromptu meeting vowed to return 'in full strength' the following evening to determine 'who owns Australia – Australians or the Bolsheviks'.

As the unfolding events of Sunday, 23 March 1919, are examined, it can be seen that from the time red flags were

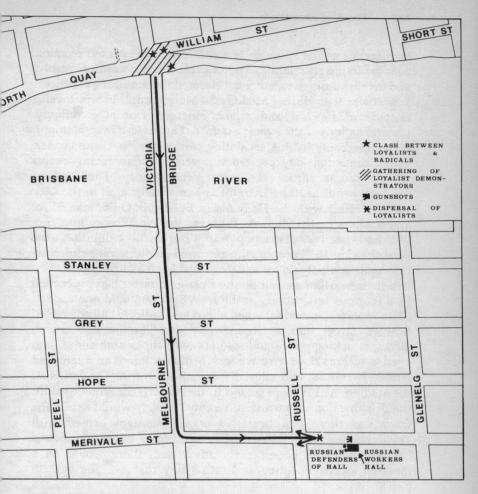

First assault on Merivale Street, Sunday evening, 23 March 1919

floated that afternoon until this final loyalist gathering, matters had proceeded in *ad hoc* fashion, with radicals, police and loyalist vigilantes each seemingly responding to the logic of the moment. This zigzag of alternating unplanned actions which began with the Russians jubilantly unfurling flags and ended with them defensively brandishing guns was to reveal, however, patterns of motivation which were far from haphazard. Civil disobedience carried its own clearly planned intentions; just as loyalist moblisation deliberately awaited an appropriate trigger. The red flag display was as much a symbol of this organised intransigence as the stimulus to a carefully orchestrated reaction. All else followed relentlessly from this point, as radical resolve and loyalist outrage together accelerated the mounting conflict.

So it was that, during Monday 24 March, a full-brown loyalist crusade of reprisal and attack emerged from the scrappy, visceral actions of the evening before. There were several important ingredients in this escalating campaign. First, the conservative press that day presented a version of foregoing events which was as partial as it was inflammatory. The *Brisbane Courier*'s headline, 'The Extremists Loose: Sensation in the City' vied for effect with the *Daily Mail*'s 'Bolshevik Outbreak: Police and Soldiers Badly Mauled'. Whereas the War Precautions protest had been a disgusting and disgraceful exhibition, the *Brisbane Courier* reported, the returned soldiers' vengeful reaction against 'a polyglot of agitators' had been a 'thrilling' display, and their 'warlike' assault on the Russian quarter had proceeded in 'a more or less orderly' fashion. What else could one expect, these reports demanded, when aliens and radicals had converted Edward Street into 'a Donnybrook' and 'Russianized' Queen Street, attacking police and soldiers with sticks and stones, and even 'a vicious dog'? 'Are we in a British colony?' an anguished female bystander had allegedly demanded during the fracas. If the soldiers had later persisted in their Merivale Street assault, the *Brisbane Courier* surmised, 'twenty or thirty would have gone down', as there had been '50 or 60' Russians armed with 'revolvers and small calibre rifles' waiting to shoot them. As a consequence, the paper freely advertised, there would be a massive loyalist meeting at North Quay that evening at 7.30 p.m.[20]

Such distortion and incitement crowned a conservative press campaign of more than a year's duration, in which the Russian Revolution had been consistently depicted as a pastiche of disorder, disease, immortality and atrocity. Bolshevism represented 'the worst terror in the history of revolution', the *Brisbane Courier* had calculated on 19 March, a compound of 'madness and undiluted savagery', torture and slaughter, misery, bankruptcy and the debasement of womanhood. 'Extremism whether it comes with notebooks or bombs in its hands', the paper warned, 'is out to destroy society and it is for society to get in the first blow.' Although Australian disciples of 'extremism' attempted to fool the people with 'a beautiful dream of peace, tranquility and happiness', the *Queenslander* added, they should

THERE is a higher object for effort than our one particular country, and that is the world — humanity.

THERE is a higher ideal than patriotism and that is Justice — righteousness.

Mr. Justice Higgins.

PRESIDENT:
Miss VIDA GOLDSTEIN

SECRETARY:
Miss CECILIA JOHN

LECTURER:
Miss ADELA PANKHURST

I CONFESS without shame that I am tired and sick of war. Its glory is all moonshine. Even success, the most brilliant, is over dead and mangled bodies, the anguish and lamentations of distant families, appealing to me for missing sons, husbands and fathers. It is only those who have not heard a shot, nor the shrieks and groans of the wounded, friend or foe, who cry aloud for more blood, more vengeance, more desolation. General Sherman.

The Women's Peace Army calendar for 1917, with its insistent anti-war quotations, presages a year of burgeoning radical activism in Queensland and Australia. (With thanks to Clarrie Beckingham)

With love to "Cosme"
all at Scott
Jennie Scott
Griffiths
Brisbane
May 1" 1920

Jennie Scott Griffiths, radical journalist, was a leading Queensland member of the Women's Peace Army and an organiser of the Children's Peace Army. As a pacifist, socialist and internationalist, she played a prominent role during the Red Flag crisis of 1919. (With thanks to Clarrie Beckingham)

Queensland's Police Commissioner, F.C. Urquhart, as he appeared during the Red Flag crisis of 1918-19, resolutely opposing radicals, Russians and revolutionaries.

Earlier, during the 1870s and 1880s, a much younger looking Urquhart is seen here drilling his Native Police troopers in North-Western Queensland. The combination of white vigilante posses with this official para-military force in the destruction of Aboriginal resistance may well have contributed significantly to Urquhart's attraction towards extra legal vigilante tactics, prior to the riots of March 1919. (With thanks to Ann McGrath)

Jeremiah Joseph Stable, languages lecturer and later English Professor at the University of Queensland was Chief Queensland Military Censor from January 1917 to May 1919. His enthusiastic surveillance activities did much to counter the impact of pacifism, syndicalism and Bolshevism in Queensland during these years. He returned to Intelligence work in World War II.

Escape of an Awkward Fact from the Press Censor's Office

This rare British cartoon humorously displays the obsessive concern for secrecy, suppression and surveillance which pervaded official activities on the home-front. Such preoccupations were as rigorously displayed at the Queensland Censor's offices, located at the Brisbane GPO, during and after the War years.

Herbert Brookes, the wealthy and highly influential businessman and pastoralist who campaigned forcefully for the suppression of all republican and revolutionary influences in Australia towards the end of World War I – photographed in later life.

Dr Ernest Sandford Jackson, poses here in his AIF uniform, had risen to the rank of Lieutenant-Colonel by the close of World War I. As the imperious and energetic organiser of the United Loyalist Executive and the King and Empire Alliance, Dr Jackson could well lay claim to the title of *Gauleiter* of the Queensland loyalist forces in this period.

Dr Jackson's dramatically opulent home, *Glenolive* was situated on extensive acreage upon a secluded reach of the Brisbane River at St Lucia. This imposing structure, surmounted by a firm atrium and containing a piazza, refreshment, drawing and playrooms, library and gymnasium, stables, coach-house and boat-landing undoubtedly provides some indication of how the wealthier Brisbane loyalist perceived the material world. (With thanks to Judith McKay)

Herbert Ebenezer Sizer, returned soldier, politician and loyalist polemicist can here be glimpsed in the back seat of his Rolls Royce (one of the few, and undoubtedly among the finest motor vehicles in the metropolis), returning home from a seaside excursion. (With thanks to Kay and Elizabeth Saunders)

Two candid photographs of crowds drawn to the Brisbane Domain, taken in late 1917. The size of this gathering (to express sympathetic support for the New South Wales General Strike) is probably atypical of the normal Sunday assemblages there. It is however, quite representative of the numbers who crowded the Domain on Sunday afternoon, 23 March 1919. (*Worker*, 13 September 1917)

In the aftermath of the Red Flag riots, aggressive Brisbane loyalists continued to display their anti-leftist and xenophobic prejudices. Here, acting-Premier Theodore struggles vainly to welcome home Victoria Cross holders on 28 March 1919, amid the catcalls of the crowd. Theodore, of Bulgarian origin, was assailed with cries of "You're no Australian!" and "Go Home!" as even the Governor's pleas for order were ignored. In the background, Major Taylor, an RSSILA organiser raises his hand to restore calm. (*Queenslander*, 5 April 1919)

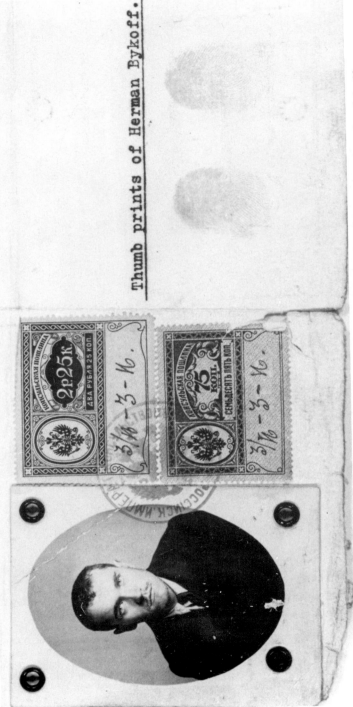

Thumb prints of Herman Bykoff.

Herman Bykov (alias Resanoff) was born at Saratov in June 1891 and arrived in Australia as a fireman aboard the SS *Mallina* in March 1916. Severely injured during the Red Flag riots, tried in Brisbane Magistrate's Court, imprisoned in Boggo Road gaol, and later interned at Darlinghurst and deported on the SS *Frankfurt* to Odessa, his case comprehensively reflects the scapegoating which accompanied the disturbances.

An artist's impression of eleven of the fifteen Queensland Red Flag prisoners:
Back row (from left): George "Gunner" Taylour, Jerome Cahill, Ludwik "Louis"
Roslan, Steve Tolstobroff. Middle row (from left): Edward Cahill, Gus Orance,
Herbert Huggot, William Elder. Front row (from left): Percival James, Mark
Ostapenko, Herman Bykov (alias Resanoff).

A passport photograph of Alexander Michael Zuzenko, born May 1885 at Riga in Russia. Zuzenko is described therein as being 6'2" in height and 12½ stone in weight, with a fresh complexion, light brown hair, brown eyes, a long face and a "lifebuoy, anchor and marlin spike" tattooed on his left forearm. (With thanks to Eric Fried)

Zuzenko (front centre) with a cane-cutting gang in North Queensland in 1916, before coming to Brisbane during 1917 to take up an executive post with the Union of Russian Workers (URW). (With thanks to Eric Fried)

A much altered Zuzenko on the bridge of a Russian vessel (the first of its kind built after the Revolution) in the early 1920s. His internment and deportation ordeals seem etched upon his face. (His deportation papers, significantly, now described him as having a broken nose, a badly scarred head and an indented jaw). Zuzenko however, returned to Australia on a secret mission to the Russian community in mid-1922, disguised as a Norwegian seaman. On leaving Australia once more in September 1922 on the *Hobson's Bay*, he suddenly produced a red flag from his coat and waved it jubilantly above his head, as the steamer pulled away from the Melbourne docks. (With thanks to Eric Fried)

THE CHALLENGE!

Returned Soldier: "This is Australia, and here is its flag. That one you wave at your peril!"

BOLSHEVISM

ANARCHY

B.E.Pike

The challenge! (*Daily Mail*, 26 March 1919)

never forget 'the throatcutting, the shooting, raping, looting and starvation which have so far marked in wide swathes' the path of revolution. Significantly, these same publications had never characterised World War I in this fashion. During March 1919, this anti-Bolshevik assault had been more rigorously pursued. In the fortnight preceding the Red Flag outburst Captain Ainsworth's diary reveals seven entries of memos which passed between SIB headquarters and the offices of the *Brisbane Courier*, the *Daily Mail* and the *Sun*. These communications culminated in contacts with the managers of all three conservative newspapers on Thursday, 20 March, three days prior to the civil liberties march.[21]

The impact of this crudely effective propaganda upon the soldiers' sensibilities was immediate and accelerative:

> The red rag germs are spreading far and wide
> Disease that's nourished soon is multiplied!

wrote one veteran versifier in the *Brisbane Courier*; whilst another ex-soldier, who had been fighting for four years in Turkey and France, added: 'One of the things that struck me on my return is the hold Bolshevism seems to be getting in this country . . . Is . . . this terrible thing to grow to the time no women would be safe in Queensland . . . If the Queensland Government . . . will not take action then it is up to the chaps who have been away at the war to step in . . . ' This male concern for women's 'safety' was a clear goad to direct action, long primed by sado-sexual propaganda about the ravishing proclivities of the Hun. Since late 1918, the same psychological responses had been carefully cultivated by a campaign against Bolshevik 'beastiality . . . and lust', based upon false rumours, eventually traced to Britain's Major General Poole at Archangel. Throughout Eastern Russia, Poole had asserted, each fertile female was to be converted into 'a breeding animal to be kept and owned by the State'. As the *Brisbane Courier* authoritatively embellished this: 'a system of promiscuity or free love had been officially set up, with a scale of penalties for its non-observance'. Predictably, a credulous wave of 'horror and disgust' greeted such news.[22]

This welter of propaganda, alarming as it was to civilians, was enough to drive returning soldiers into a frenzy of activity. Bouts of violence and terror, interspersed by the prolonged boredom, discomfort and alienation of trench warfare, had bred into these

The lying mirror (*Worker*, 6 March 1919)

men an unpredictable leaven of repressed anger and bitterness which demanded an appropriate outlet. An uncomprehending or unappreciative homefront population, excessive war 'profiteering', seemingly uncontrollable inflation and unemployment were all potentially easy targets for the veterans. Yet the easiest mark of all was an accessible and relatively powerless scapegoat group, against whom blame for all the system's failures could be stacked. The alien holding a job believed to be a returned man's due; the radical who had consistently opposed his arduous war effort; the revolutionary who would destroy the system he had volunteered to defend; and particularly those 'dirty, low-down dogs', the Bolsheviks, who had apparently deserted the Allies at Brest-Litovsk — all such groups, it seemed, were clustered, plotting, around the fount of discontent. Such 'extremists and cheap foreigners' — as the conservative press constantly depicted them — were 'strifemakers' and 'scum'; and, as such, an appropriate initial target for a social cleansing of post-war Australia. Those skilled warriors, the returned soldiers, must now lead this 'fight to the death for their hearth and home', it was urged, just as they had vanquished their Hunnish enemies.[23]

Throughout Monday, 24 March, press incitement was fortified by the pervasiveness of rumour. 'Rumours of trouble amongst Returned Men and the Bolsheviks continue to reach us', reported Sergeant Short of the commonwealth police that afternoon. The precise nature of such rumours can again merely be surmised, but they were conceivably an amalgam of well-primed anti-Communist and anti-foreigner rage. The Bolsheviks' resort to firearms against marauding soldiers the previous evening was especially resented, and the image of the Muscovite, armed, hiding and seemingly ready to pounce, was sufficient incitement for a correspondingly vicious reaction. Returned soldiers, meeting that day to plan their evening's activities, warned Inspector Ferguson, were asked by their officers to 'bring whatever they had with them' to the North Quay rally 'advertised' by the *Brisbane Courier*. 'This presumably means whatever weapons they had', Ferguson informed Commissioner Urquhart. 'Perhaps you will be pleased to get the military authorities to do whatever they can to prevent bloodshed.' Upon contacting Captain Binnie of Military Intelligence, Urquhart then learned: "that they had had their Inquiry Agents about all day among Returned Soldiers and from what they gathered the . . . Soldiers, as a body were resolute and determined to — as they put it themselves —

The new bogey (*Worker*, 19 December 1918)

'put down Bolshevism for good and all' by the use of the utmost force they could command."[24]

Perhaps the serious consequences of encouraging irresponsible vigilante action were now beginning to dawn upon the Police Commissioner. Armed loyalist vigilantes, he was soon to learn, need not necessarily act as a police auxiliary or a disciplined, avenging force of incensed 'gentlemen'. Indeed, the serious nature of the loyalist ferment, which Urquhart himself had helped release, was underlined when Military Commandant Irving informed him that a handpicked 'force of 40 Returned Soldiers' had now been 'armed with rifles' by civilian loyalists, and that these men intended attacking the Russian hall while the North Quay meeting was in progress. Police reinforcements in Brisbane had been considerably reduced, for a large number of men were absent at the border, patrolling there as a quarantine force to keep the influenza epidemic at bay. Consequently, the Commissioner ordered all available mounted and foot police to stand ready to counter a grave 'breach of the peace'; the men were issued with rifles, with bayonets fixed and loaded with ball cartridge. Within Enoggera Army Barracks, a military guard was placed upon the alert, manning two loaded machine guns.[25]

While these preparations were underway, a raid was already in progress upon 'Bolshevist headquarters' — a raid not organised by loyalists but by Military Intelligence itself. At 11 a.m., two Provost Marshals, Lieutenants Wearne and Morey, accompanied by twelve military police, had arrived at Merivale Street and began ransacking the Russian hall. The workers' library of '1,000 precious volumes' was plundered and scattered, and fifteen Russians present closely interrogated. A returned soldier, who later reported the outcome of this raid, admitted, 'I saw . . . smashed furniture and general disorder in the place. Thank God . . . that is not my dwelling.' Afterwards, the nearby homes of three 'Soviet' leaders were similarly 'searched' and from one residence all the Russian Association's official books and 'two bags of industrial literature' were appropriated. A deputation of Russians was preparing to protest against this invasion at Victoria Barracks that evening when rumours of a larger assault reached them, and they turned their energies instead towards seeking refuge for themselves and their families. Many Russians from adjacent boarding houses, homes and shops had already taken flight.[26]

As Monday evening fell, an impatient crowd had begun to

gather at North Quay, almost directly across the river from the Russian quarter. Well before the scheduled rally could commence, a succession of impromptu speakers exploited their emotions with such exhortations as 'Who let you down at the War? . . . Let's dig them out!' By 7 p.m., some half dozen orators were simultaneously attempting to make themselves heard above the tumult arising from the massed demonstrators — between seven and eight thousand strong — spilling back from the Quay into Queen and William Streets. Imposing order upon this densely packed assembly seemed virtually impossible, especially as it became clear that the crowd's central motivation was not to listen sympathetically to speeches, but to attack the South Brisbane Russian quarter. North Quay simply became a convenient staging ground for the assault. The only bridge linking the northern and southern banks of the river stood less than a stone's throw away from the loyalists' point of assembly.

Unaided by amplification, the voices of the struggling speakers could barely be heard above the din. Snatches of rhetoric, such as 'take the law into our own hands . . . ' and 'clear out of Queensland all the dirty Russian mongrels' merely accentuated the crowd's lawless resolve. In this combustible atmosphere, symbolic and purposeful action was likely to attract more attention than mere words. Such action gives physical expression and direction to the crowd's 'common vengeful or retributory purpose'. And once this lead is provided to 'the baiting crowd', as social psychologist, Elias Canetti shows, action follows action in rapid and logical succession. The impetus which drives the crowd from assembly formation into marching ranks, from a disorderly march into a charge, and from charge into riot, 'happens so quickly that people have to hurry to get there in time. The speed, elation and conviction of a baiting crowd is something uncanny.'

The catalyst on this wild evening was virtually the same as the one which had spurred the radicals into action the previous afternoon: the unfurling of a psychologically meaningful emblem — in this instance, a huge Australian flag. Lifted from its display point, high upon a William Street wall, it was carried by war veterans towards the portals of Victoria Bridge. The bulk of the crowd, speeches immediately forgotten, followed impulsively in its wake, as the wartime recruiting anthem, 'Australia Will Be There', rang out. Rank upon rank of the marchers took up the theme.

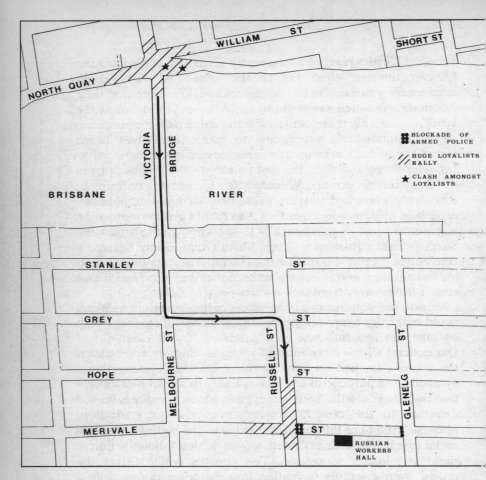

Second march to Merivale Street, Monday evening, 24 March 1919

As the chanting crowd surged across Victoria Bridge, intent upon its destination, it assumed a more perceptible organic unity. Its incentives were loudly proclaimed: 'Burn their meeting place down!', 'Hang them!' were the predominant cries, as others struck up an ironic refrain of 'Keep the Home Fires Burning'. Enveloped within the fortifying din of pounding feet, song and chant, participants merged their individual being into the orbit of the crowd's more immense social reality and power. 'The goal is known and clearly marked, and it is also near', writes Canetti, as though he were watching these very marchers: 'The crowd is out for killing and it knows whom it wants to kill. It heads for this goal with unique determination and cannot be cheated of it

. . . This concentration on killing is of a special kind and of unsurpassed intensity. Everyone wants to participate.' Soon, only a small, inactive group remained at North Quay to hear Provost Marshal Morey's futile appeal for order. The bulk of the crowd had crossed Victoria Bridge into Melbourne Street, wheeled left into Grey Street and then right into Russell Street — a distance well over a kilometre — breaking into a faster pace as they approached their ultimate goal, the Russian club house in Merivale Street.[27]

'The crowd was very excited, and was singing songs', stated Constable O'Driscoll who watched them approach. 'Several processionists shouted as they marched, 'We'll burn them out''. It was more of a mob than a procession, for some walked and others advanced at a slow trot.' Some carried guns and others were armed with the primitive 'jam-tin bomb which did good service at Gallipoli'. Certain of the demonstrators, however, seemed hazier about the exact purpose of their collective action. 'We intended to get all the Russians that were in the Russian club', a returned soldier, William Connellan later recalled:

> I don't know what they intended to do after that. I thought they were going to have a go at the Russians with their fists. I thought they would yank the Russians out and take them to Victoria Barracks, intern them and have them deported. We had enough legal officers there — men with stars on their shoulder. There was a major there pretty active . . .

Many veterans at Merivale Street, it would seem, were merely following a lead provided by 'officers of all ranks', as they had during warfront charges into the mire of no-man's-land.[28]

As the body of demonstrators sped towards the Russian hall, they were brought to an abrupt halt at the intersection of Russell and Merivale Streets by fifty police, stretched in two lines across the roadway with fixed bayonets at the ready. Another police line of ten armed men similarly guarded the entrance into Merivale Street from Glenelg Street, a block away. As one of these constables later wrote, many of the police were unhappy about protecting 'the dirty b_____ Russians'. 'I wish the soldiers could have lynched every b_____ of them', he added. It was also strongly rumoured amongst the force that their real task was to guard the Merivale Street tenement houses rented by Russians, but *owned* by Legislative Councillor, the Hon. Peter Murphy, a large scale real estate and commercial speculator and the father-in-law of John Fihelly, the Secretary for Railways. We were 'ordered to save the Hon. Murphy's buildings', wrote the constable, by employing whatever force was considered necessary. 'An ugly rumour has been going the rounds', Censor Stable added ominously, 'that the Commissioner of Police received instructions to stand no nonsense . . . but to take extreme measures . . . if the Commissioner had followed *instructions* there would have been a bayonet charge that night.'[29]

If such instructions had indeed been issued, Commissioner Urquhart paid them no heed, but instead ordered his men to stand firm, as the front rank of marchers pressed upon the bayonet line. 'They came right up against the police bayonets', Constable O'Driscoll later recalled, 'and somebody shouted, "Let us through! We want the Russians!" Another man said, "You would not stick that in me. Get out of the road, or we'll break through!" ' Bottles, stones and bricks now began to whistle through the air from the thick of the crowd, as some of its members were forced forward onto the bayonet points by the crush of hostile demonstrators pushing from behind. Many were highly intoxicated, a condition which only enhanced their capacity for recklessness. 'One could even smell the fumes of liquor in the air', reported Commissioner Urquhart.

As demonstrators were spiked by bayonets and the line, besieged by missiles, began to waver, a squad of ten mounted troopers under the command of Senior Sergeant Bell wheeled into Merivale Street behind the milling crowds. Alerted by the clamour outside the Russian hall, they charged their horses into the crowd without warning from the rear. As women on its outskirts screamed and ran, others were trampled beneath the horses' prancing hooves or buffeted aside and knocked to the ground. The galloping troopers cut a swathe through the huge crowd, which scattered in panic. 'Using their whips freely', the mounted men fought their way to the police lines, which parted momentarily to allow them to dash through.

During this assault, one of the horses was brought down by stones flung by the retreating crowd; three others, plunging in panic directly into the lines of foot police, knocked several officers and men to the ground. As the nine remaining troopers rallied to charge again into Russell Street, the soldiers quickly remobilised. In a pitch of fury, they began tearing hundreds of wooden palings off surrounding fences to defend themselves against the approaching riders. A barrage of palings, bricks and bottles greeted the mounted squad as they emerged once more through the bayonet line. As this point, gun-shots also rang out, marking a serious escalation of the conflict. The use of guns against police by a disorderly crowd was an exceptional departure. Shearers had drilled with rifles during the Nineties' strike wave, but actual gun battles had remained more of a threat than a reality. Dynamite and gelignite charges had exploded along suburban tramlines during the 1912 General Strike, but there had been no resort to firearms. Guns had been carried by opposing forces during the conscription struggles and a military picket had been shot at the Domain in October 1916. Yet during the many conscription riots and the loyalist mobilisations which followed, fists and boots, augmented at times by clubs and broken bottles, had been the principal weapons employed.[30]

William Connellan later recalled seeing Thomas Drane, a returned soldier, draw a revolver and fire several shots at plain clothed Constable O'Driscoll. 'O'Driscoll ducked his head and I thought he was shot', Connellan testified, 'I said, "The poor _____ has got it" . . . I thought I was at the Front for a moment'. (O'Driscoll was afterwards felled by a well-aimed bottle.) But gunmen directed most of the sporadic fire at the mounted troopers. Thomas Cunningham, a returned soldier, mustered a pack of rioters with cries of: 'Right over here, diggers! What are we here for? We want a machine gun to shoot them' — as they and the troopers clashed in a headlong rush in Russell Street. Senior Sergeant Bell's horse was struck across the head and body and reared in the air as it received a bullet wound: "he saw Constable Clark's and Constable Byrne's horses fall. The missiles and revolver shots still continued . . . [Bell] was struck with palings and other missiles thrown by the crowd . . . A soldier in uniform caught him by the front of the tunic and attempted to drag him off his horse . . . The horse plunged forward, slipped and came down . . . "[31]

Bell was knocked unconscious, and later found he had been shot in the left foot, was bruised all over and had broken two ribs in his fall. His mount was bleeding badly from the jaw and nostrils. Turning, he then saw Constable Gooch topple from his horse, 'and later discovered he had punctured wounds in the back'. In all, seven of the ten troopers had been injured: Byrne had been shot twice in the kidney region; Clark was wounded in the arm and back. Three of the horses, one ironically named 'Czar', had also suffered gun shot wounds. One animal had been hit nine times by bullets and was afterwards destroyed.

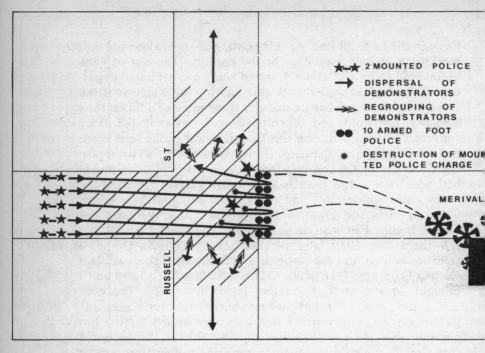

2 MOUNTED POLICE

→ **DISPERSAL OF DEMONSTRATORS**

⇒ **REGROUPING OF DEMONSTRATORS**

●● **10 ARMED FOOT POLICE**

✳ **DESTRUCTION OF MOUNTED POLICE CHARGE**

ST

MERIVAL

RUSSELL

Merivale Street clash, Monday evening, 24 March 1919

With the mounted squad rendered virtually inoperative, the crowd turned its fury once more upon the bayonet-wielding foot police. At the Russell Street intersection, they assaulted the police line in a succession of massed charges, hurling bolts, bricks, fence pickets and bottles, and were subjected, in turn, to indiscriminate bayonet thrusts. A 'thunder of stones and palings' fell against the walls and roof of the Russian hall, shattering windows and reducing the premises to 'a wreck'. Simultaneously, a section of the crowd, numbering seven to eight hundred and brandishing the Australian flag, appeared at the Glenelg Street end of the block. There they rushed the smaller police line hurling rocks at the club house and yelling curses. They lowered the flag on the police bayonets, attempting to push them to the ground with the flagstaff. According to O'Driscoll, 'The Police withdrew the bayonets from the flag and stepped back a pace or two. The crowd pushed the police and cried, "Let us through!" This went on for about half an hour.'[32]

An artist's impression of these combined assaults, published in the *Queensland Police Union Journal* almost three months later,

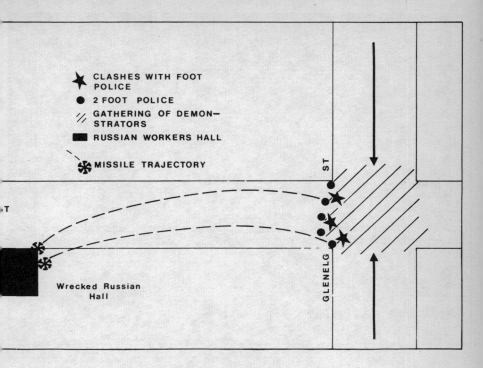

depicts the police line standing resolutely with rifles held at an 'on guard' position, and with square-jawed, imperturbable expressions on their faces (even though one constable is being struck on the head by a brick) in the path of a howling, weapon-wielding mob. The real nature of the official response, however, was far more chaotic. Sub-Inspector McNeill was directing his men when he was hit across the head with an iron bar, the force of the blow chopping through the peak of his cap. The headgear apparently saved his life, but he was then knocked to the ground by a bolting horse. At Glenelg Street, Sergeant Ferguson sustained a fractured skull when an iron railway bolt struck him square in the forehead. At the other end of the block, Inspector Ferguson was using his rifle butt to club demonstrators when he inadvertently stabbed Commissioner Urquhart deeply in the right side of the chest. Brisbane's Police Magistrate, H. Archdall, caught up in one wild crowd surge and driven on to the police bayonets, received a nasty wound in the groin.[33]

For more than two hours, bedlam reigned around the Russian hall. Staccato blasts of guns, crackers and homemade bombs ex-

ploded above the clatter of hooves on asphalt and the thunder of running feet. A cacophony of shattering glass added a sharper register to the slap of palings and the thudding of cudgels and rifle butts. Shrill cries of terrified and wounded horses answered the 'yells, groans and curses' of the desperate men; the cheers of women, calling from the crowd's outskirts and the verandahs of adjacent buildings, encouraged the recklessness of the rioters. Overall, the reek of alcohol blended with the acrid fumes of sweat and gunpowder and the tang of freshly-split blood. 'There must have been over a hundred stabbed with the bayonets', calculated Constable Larkin in a letter to his brother at Cloncurry: 'I know for certain I prodded 6 myself. Zarn who has a brother in the police at Allora made a swing at me with a paling – he missed but I didn't – I stuck him in the side . . . still in the hospital . . . ' As Commissioner Urquhart stood facing this frenzied scene, his shirt-front saturated with blood from his own bayonet wound, the folly of inciting vigilantes 'prepared to go pretty far', may at last have become apparent.[34]

Exhaustion and injury finally harnessed the intensity of the onslaught. A soldiers' deputation was allowed through police ranks to establish that the virtually demolished Russian hall was devoid of Bolsheviks. Surrounding tenement houses had also been heavily damaged by the missiles of the crowd. As the demonstrators began to withdraw from the site, they left a further trail of destruction, smashing the windows of Russian homes, shops and refreshment rooms, breaking in doors and looting stock and belongings. Back in the city, elated loyalists began to gather at several locations. Some attempted to march behind a Union Jack to Government House, while others congregated noisily at North Quay, the General Post Office and in Albert Square. These self-satisfied assemblies roared their approval at the formation of an impromptu Anti-Bolshevik society and vowed to meet again the following evening.[35]

On Tuesday 25 March, it seemed as though conservative and labour press reporters had been witnessing quite different demonstration the previous evening. In the *Brisbane Courier*'s estimation, Bolshevism had 'fairly aroused the blood' and resulted in 'an outburst of loyalty which in some respects was as magnificent as it was altogether spontaneous'. The event was depicted as 'dramatic . . . wild and thrilling', although, it was quickly added, a major confrontation had been 'averted by splendid tact'. 'Nothing of the kind − nothing approaching it in fact − had ever been witnessed before in Brisbane', the *Brisbane Courier* trumpeted: 'The first blow has been struck by the returned men for the honour of the flag for which they fought and suffered.' The events were certainly remarkable and probably unprecedented, for in their hostile intensity they clearly surpassed the mob assaults on Chinese premises in the inner-city and Fortitude Valley in May 1888 and the loyalist demonstrations at the German Turn–Verein club during the war. The London *Times*, usually uninterested in Queensland news, carried small items on the Brisbane riots in seven of its issues between 25 March and 9 April.[36]

Yet the fracas which the *Brisbane Courier* so excitedly lauded (and promised would be supported that evening by 'the largest open air meeting ever seen in Brisbane') was viewed in a radically different light by the *Daily Standard* that afternoon. Brisbane had been converted into 'a Bedlam' by returned soldiers, it editorialised, 'sooled on and encouraged to lawlessness by the capitalist press'. This had culminated in 'one of the maddest and most disgraceful scenes ever witnessed in any part of Australia. It occurred when several thousand returned soldiers and civilians equipped with bricks, bottles, batons, saplings, revolvers, knives and beer attempted to storm the premises of the Russian Association.' But, in the *Brisbane Courier*'s estimation, the soldiers were not really to blame for the mayhem. It was rather the 'truculent but cowardly' Bolshevik band 'that slinks through the city' that had caused 'the whole disturbance'. And, in its wildest flight of fantasy, the paper blamed 'armed supporters of the Bolshevik element', hiding amongst the demonstrators, for the worst of the violence. To the *Daily Mail* as well, the rioters and looters could not have been war veterans; rather they were 'hoodlums' and 'larrikins' who had attached themselves to the margins of the avenging crowd.[37]

The press generally seemed unsure about the precise number of casualties. The Melbourne *Argus* reported sixteen injuries, the *Daily Standard*, eighteen (with 'miraculously no-one killed'), while the *Brisbane Courier* listed nineteen. Fourteen names on this list were mounted or foot police. There was no sign in these press estimations of the 'hundred' rioters Constable Larkin believed had been stabbed, nor even of the six he had 'prodded' himself. Among the five listed, one had been hurt at North Quay and only one had received bayonet 'cuts'. The other three had been, in turn, wounded in the head by a bullet, trampled by a horse (or humans) and struck by a paling. (None of those reported wounded was surnamed 'Zarn'.) In fact, after perusing various police accounts of the riot, nineteen casualties can be enumerated from within their ranks alone — seven mounted troopers had been hurt, as well as a dozen defenders on foot, including Urquhart and Archdall. Civilian casualties can only be guessed at; but, after two hours of savage fighting and charges against the bayonet lines, these were undoubtedly far more numerous than the four conceded by the *Brisbane Courier*. Indeed, Larkin's estimate may have been much closer to the mark, for a need to preserve anonymity would have deterred most of those injured from venturing their names to the press. 'One after another of the soldiers proceeded to the centre of the square to have injuries attended to' by an ambulance van after the riot, admitted the *Daily Mail*, 'And there were eyes that had to be bandaged and bruised heads to be patched, while those who had been wounded on the limbs remained on duty till the end'.[38]

In the conservative papers, the rioters were invariably presented as both the heroes and victims of the clash, and even the labour press maintained a fairly discreet silence about the desolation inflicted upon the Russians themselves. In contrast, the real victims of the affray would describe their ordeal fully as 'a pogrom', directed by soldiers and citizens against their South Brisbane community. At first sight, the designation 'pogrom' — a Russian word implying 'devastation' or 'an organized massacre for the annihilation of any body or class' — appears to be an excessive and inappropriate label. Historically, it resonates with the virulence of localised mob frenzies unleashed upon Jewish communities in nineteenth and early twentieth century Russia: the savage Palm Sunday assaults at Odessa in 1871, the epidemic of anti-Semitic riots following the assassination of Tsar Alexander II in March 1881 at Kiev, Volhynia and Podolia, the Kishinev pogroms of April 1903 and the attacks of the fascistic Union of Russian People upon Jews after the failure of the 1905 Uprising. On the night of 24 March 1919, Russian homes, club rooms and shops in South Brisbane had been destroyed and looted, and yet no Russian name appeared on the press's injuries list. As we have seen, forewarned Russians in the vicinity had all fled into hiding. Some, for instance, had been sheltered by Chinese vegetable gardeners at Earl Street, Thompson Estate, for the Chinese, too, intimately recalled the terror which an Anglo-Australian mob could evoke. Yet the mass assaults of the 23 and 24 March were only the beginnings of the Russians' troubles.[39]

Soldiers returned to the site in the early morning of Tuesday, 25 March, to raise a Union Jack over the gutted Russian hall, apparently inflicting further damage upon nearby homes, now unguarded by police. Throughout that day and others following, Russian venturing onto the streets were chased and beaten. Job dismissals, evictions and boycotts of Russian business premises escalated rapidly in the wake of this physical violence. 'We made things very hot here and I do not know what will take place', wrote a Russian resident, Charlie Galchin, to a compatriot at Pyrmont a week later: 'The Club has been closed. I will not describe to you the details of the pogrom . . . Yes, it was a formal pogrom, exactly like the pogroms of Jews organized during the reign of the Czar . . . All the Russians are in a state of panic. They are being dismissed everywhere from work. The soldiers thrash the Russians in the streets. The Russians have all run away like rats . . . ' Clearly, such beatings had begun at the North Quay riot in the early evening of 23 March, when Bykov had been stabbed. Another Russian witness, apparently not in sympathy with the Bolshevik activists, wrote to a friend in Brisbane General Hospital during the 24th: 'I cannot describe all I have heard. Many Russians were beaten . . . Through the fault of some silly Russians, it falls on all of us, and all is closed down. I met a Russian here and started to speak to him . . . I was nearly beaten for speaking Russian – by Englishmen. We must be as far from Russia as we possibly can. There is danger for the Russians on every step and corner.'[40]

Significantly, no non-Russian source has been uncovered which evokes this same sense of perpetual intimidation and panic. Among Anglo-Australian commentators, only Vere Gordon Childe, then in Brisbane and himself under censorship surveillance for his socialistic and pacifist ideals, remarks upon these events. He fleetingly refers to them as a 'pogrom' in the chronological survey attached to his penetrating study, *How Labour Governs*, written during 1919. Yet when the overall picture of the loyalist attack is etched out – the destruction of property, the lynch-mindedness of the mob, the panic of flight, the desultory beatings, the enforced economic impoverishment and loss of shelter, the intensity of ongoing public hostility and the withholding, in most instances, of a helping hand – the distinct impression of a Brisbane pogrom is forcefully suggested. Additionally, the official onslaught of military raids, the closure of the Russian headquarters and the suspension of *Knowledge and Unity*, as well as the subsequent arrests, trials, imprisonments, internments and deportations, represented a ruthlessly efficient accompaniment to all the rudiments of mob rule; indeed, official sanctions met its demands, both extending and exacerbating its terror, sanctifying it and casting the wretched victim into the role of culprit. 'We are accustomed to any measures of victimization', commented a group of Russians later: 'because of Czardom in Russia, we used to suffer a great deal'. Yet 'the cowardly and uncalled-for revolt by Brisbane reactionaries' had represented an intensification of former tribulations:

> The systematic victimization . . turns out to be worse than the advice of the ex-President of America, Mr. Taft who came to the conclusion that it was the best thing for the safety of the world's democracy to have all the Bolsheviks killed straight away. The Russians are bereft of employment, unrecognized by the State authority as citizens, turned out from their homes and hunted in the streets — that is, outside the prison, of course . . . [41]

Loyalist agitation persisted throughout Tuesday, 25 March. Returned soldiers of the RSSILA, meeting together and, later, in consecutive deputations to Premier Theodore and Colonel W. Mailer at Victoria Barracks, made no apology for their violent excesses of the previous evening. To the contrary, they charged that the state police were the real offenders. 'Ball ammunition was used and two Returned Soldiers at least have been wounded, whilst others received bayonet wounds', complained W.A. Fisher of the RSSILA:

> The Returned Soldiers view with disgust the fact that whilst to meet the Bolshevik party on Sunday the police were not armed, yet to meet the soldiers (who had no quarrel with the police and had *no desire to in any sense create trouble* . . .) they were fully armed . . . This hostile act, the most extreme which can be used by any nation in the support of law and order was carried out without the reading of the Riot Act.
> . . .

The state government was actually cosseting the Bolsheviks, the deputation reasoned, so 'swift and drastic action' by federal authorities in deporting 'these aliens' was needed. If this was not done, the soldiers threatened:

> We feel it is our bounden duty to warn the authorities that grave

breaches of the peace will ensue . . . We have a large number of Returned Soldiers here who are fully determined to use every means necessary to effect our purpose, namely to clear these men out of the Commonwealth . . . unless immediate action is taken . . . there can be no doubt that serious loss of life will be the inevitable result . . . [42]

In retrospect, the effrontery of these RSSILA spokesmen is both startling and chilling. Unequivocally, they were saying that what was not done legally, by the application of state force, would still be accomplished by public violence. Their dark hints at lethal disorder if their demands were not rapidly met was the vocabulary of men convinced that warfare's legitimated brutality could be transferred successfully to the resolution of homefront conflicts. As Colonel Bolton, President of the RSSILA, commented that day, local Bolsheviks must be treated 'as a German spy would be if he were discovered behind the Australian trenches'. Without any qualms, these men calculated that federal anticipation of criminal deeds upon a mass scale would induce an appropriate administrative response.

To press these points home, civilian vigilante leaders and loyalist patrons also began a flurry of correspondence to Acting Prime Minister Watt. Their representations were led by a 240 word telegram from Dr Sandford Jackson of the ULE, claiming to represent 'over seventy thousand' Queensland citizens and demanding 'prompt deportation of all rebels, or in the alternative their internment'. At the same time, Commander William Weatherill, President of the Brisbane Naval Rifle Club, despatched a telegram from a hastily convened meeting of the Brisbane Chamber of Commerce, urging that the 'unchecked growth' of Bolshevik and IWW elements be rapidly stunted by deportation proceedings. Queensland Nationalist federal members, J.G. Bayley, E.B. Corser and G.H. Mackay, added their voices to this ultimatum. To all, Acting Prime Minister Watt replied encouragingly, 'Commonwealth Law authorities already moving in matter . . . You may rely upon Federal Government doing its duty.'

Fortified by this response the following morning, G.H. Pritchard, President of the Cane Growers Association, as well as company director, George Brown, and Dr Guy L'Estrange, a Brisbane medical specialist representing the National Democratic Council (NDC), joined in the hue and cry, encouraging Nationalist Senators from Queensland to do likewise. Senators Crawford, Foll and Givens (the President of the Senate) quickly responded. All advocated the suppression or deportation of this 'dangerous foreign element'. 'If allowed to continue, their agitation will completely undermine the prosperity of the State', warned Senator Crawford: 'There is already a general disinclination to embark upon new or to extend existing enterprise, business people practically without exception regarding it as unsafe to do more than mark time while present unsatisfactory conditions prevail.' In the interests of capitalism, social tranquility and the wounded pride of war veterans, it was concluded, Russian Bolsheviks and other disloyalists would have to go. 'The soldiers have been very patient in the face of continual insults and open disloyalty by a section that has congregated in Queensland, *but who do not belong to that State*', explained Senator Foll: 'They are the scrapings of Sydney and Melbourne and also men whose own country has become too hot for them . . . The returned soldiers are not going to see the Country they have fought for dominated by a pack of hoodlums and anarchists.'[43]

Reports reaching wounded Commissioner Urquhart throughout Tuesday 25 March, were heavy with the threat of renewed violence. The returned men were planning an evening attack on the Roma Street police barracks, he was informed, as well as a demonstration at Bowman House, the newspaper office of the *Daily Standard*. Others spoke of assaulting Russian residences in Deshon Street, Woolloongabba, as well as in Merivale Street once more. Urquhart, who had suffered 'very considerable loss of blood', had been warned that 'any physical exertion might bring on a considerable renewal of Hemorrhage [sic]' and therefore surrendered command to Chief Inspector Short that evening. He remained preoccupied about the numerical weakness of available police, however, even if 'the most extreme measures' were applied by the force. Invoking the spectre of the 1912 General Strike, he called for commonwealth military intervention to augment the strength of his outnumbered troopers. His turn of phrase in this report — 'Returned Soldiers with their attendant rabble' — bears witness to his mounting disenchantment with the vigilantes. Yet he continued to direct his main barrage against the radical aliens. 'Until this plague spot of pestilent Russian revolutionaries is eliminated in Brisbane', he warned, 'there can be no peace or safety for the community'.[44]

That evening, despite driving rain, 'one of the largest open-air meetings ever held in Brisbane' convened in Albert Square to register its defiance and endorse the soldiers' demands. Diatribes delivered here by an array of military officers all followed a remarkably similar rhetorical pattern. Bolsheviks, particularly 'dirty, greasy Russians', were likened to a disease, a microbe – a cancer which needed eradicating. 'Root it out now!' demanded Pearce Douglas, Queensland President of the RSSILA, as Brigadier-General Spencer-Browne, a senior *Brisbane Courier* journalist, called for 'a revolution of loyalty' to begin. 'The imported element before very long, if not deported, was going back to its Maker', shouted Sergeant Buchanan above waves of cheering. 'We are absolutely determined that this crowd has to go', added Major Bolingbroke, the League's publicity officer, 'not only the Russians, but the IWW and Germans (Loud Cheers). They [ie the soldiers] had the fighting strength and they would use it'.

Hotels had been closed early that Tuesday afternoon by proclamation, in the vain hope that absence of liquor would inhibit any proclivities towards violence that night. Yet the incendiary speeches provided sufficient incitement to the volatile crowd for 'the two hours wild mêlée which followed'. It began when a 'disloyalist', who had refrained from removing his hat during a fervent rendering of the national anthem, was attacked. 'Scarcely had the last word of the hymn been finished', reported the *Brisbane Courier* graphically:

> before half a dozen soldiers had grabbed the offender and his hat was torn off his head . . . in a moment there was a wild rush and an angry crowd of probably 2000 persons surged in upon the scene. A dozen police constables or more crushed to the centre of the disturbance and the packed mass of humanity swayed backwards and forwards across the street. The man . . . was forced against the wall of the Albert Hotel and a hundred voices roared, "Make him sing it". "Sing it, man, sing it", roared a police inspector, hoping by that means to pacify the crowd . . . The man steadied himself for a moment and then ducked his head as if to break through, but a fist planked fairly in the face with an "upper-cut" brought him back to the wall. Then he sang or tried to sing . . .

This remarkable description is worth quoting at length for it conveys powerfully the mood of the mob – communal rage stoked once more to a virtually lynch-like intensity. Upon finishing his tortuous performance, the unnamed singer was beaten in any case, and his molestation ended only when his assailants were distracted by the cry, 'On to the *Standard*!'[45]

A large portion of the crowd then broke into a wild, disorderly rush along Adelaide Street in the direction of Bowman House,

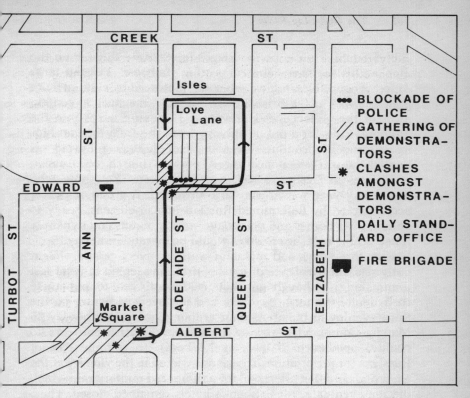

Inner city clashes, Tuesday evening, 25 March 1919

which was already heavily guarded by forty constables and two non-commissioned officers. Nevertheless, stones soon began to fly from the rear of the dense mass of demonstrators, and revolver shots once more rang out. One of the gunmen, a returned soldier and stockman named James Mills, was grabbed by police after firing twice but 'the violence of the crowd' allowed him to escape. 'Somebody fired a shot past my "lug"', Mills later testified, 'and I thought I would have a shot too . . . I was not the only one who had a revolver. All the others had them too.' Mills had bought his gun and fifty cartridges that morning at a second hand shop in the city. As he informed the proprietor, 'We will have some sport tonight. We knocked 'em last night and will knock 'em again tonight.'[46]

Returned soldiers yelling, 'Let us get inside and we'll give them Bolshevism!' rushed the doors of Bowman House, as a shower of rocks smashed its windows. During the riot, several more men received the same rough handling as the hapless individual at

Albert Square, while police fought to extricate them from the mob and place them aboard passing tramcars. Yet the large squad of constables, which was soon reinforced by a dozen more police as well as the Brisbane Fire Brigade, managed to contain most of the violence and prevent a successful surge into the building. Calls for a public apology from the *Daily Standard* for its afternoon headline, 'Riotous Ex-Soldiers', followed as demonstrators were encouraged next to march on Russian residences in Deshon Street, South Brisbane. Yet those who proceeded there were once more thwarted. A group of police, accompanied by determined Russian Jewish citizens, ready to defend their homes and synagogue with shotguns and dynamite if necessary, kept the crowd of would-be marauders at bay.[47]

After three days and nights of warlike invective and violent outbursts, the virulence of loyalist protests seemed to be at last diminishing. Although gunshots had continued to punctuate their demonstrations, bayonets had not been necessary on the third evening to puncture their ardour. During Wednesday 26 March, Commandant Irving persuaded 'returned officers to counsel obedience to law', as he began to compile lists of Russians for deportation. Thousands waited in the vicinity of the *Daily Standard* that afternoon for a rumoured military raid which did not eventuate. All Brisbane's hotels remained closed. Thus, when loyalists met that night, near the *Standard* office in Edward Street, 'in one solid cheering mass from Adelaide Street to Ann Street', there was only a faint hint of the violence which had marked their prior mobilisations. 'The crowd, although quite orderly, showed that they were not to be trifled with', reported Military Inquiry Agent, R. James, to General Irving the following morning. Officers of the RSSILA counselled the immense throng, estimated at anywhere between seven and fifteen thousand, 'not to behave in a riotous manner but to leave it to their League and get satisfaction through the proper channel'. The only rabble-rouser was ex-Sergeant Buchanan, who reiterated that the *Daily Standard*'s insults should still be 'rammed down their neck [sic]'. Furthermore, he falsely asserted, 'about one hundred armed men were to be brought in from the country districts against returned soldiers'. Yet his rumour-mongering was countered by Major Taylor, who spoke at length about 'responsible . . . rightminded and sensible' behaviour: 'he wanted to inform those who had come there in search of "fun" that there was not going to be any fun . . . He appealed to all loyalists to

wait one week for a reply from the Government . . [and] pleaded with the crowd not to do anything rash or riotous as they had
the sympathy of all the decent-minded people of Brisbane
behind them . . .'48

This de-escalation of activism was aided the following night
(Thursday 27 March) by a terrible storm which lashed the city
for more than four hours and prevented any street gatherings occurring. For the first time in five nights, rain-swept Brisbane was
described by the *Telegraph* as being 'normally peaceful'. Yet, on
Friday evening, civilian loyalist leaders, supported by RSSILA
officers, emerged once more to sponsor another monster
assembly in Albert Street. The general mood of this meeting remained aggressive, but was now overlaid by a swaggering sense
of achievement and celebration. In short, the nature of the
gathering was predominantly declamatory and ritualistic, rather
than turbulent. Three large platforms, each with a Union Jack
flying above it and presided over by either the Mayor or an ex-
Mayor of Brisbane, catered to the jingoism of the crowd, as the
Tivoli Theatre orchestra, from the adjacent picture palace, accompanied the throng as it sang of 'Rule Britannia'. Yet despite
this veneer of respectability, the speeches, delivered principally
by civilian spokesmen, remained riddled with threats and
violent innuendoes. 'If constitutional methods failed', warned
John Adamson, the renegade Laborite, 'they would be strong
enough to do what else was necessary.' Bolsheviks, added NDC
organiser, the Hon. T.C. Bierne MLC, should be granted no
toleration and, in fact, should be 'bayonetted on the spot'. E.H.
Macartney, Leader of the Parliamentary Opposition, who was
welcomed onto the podium by prolonged cheering and song, was
in a similarly demagogic mood. 'If the Government did not do its
duty, then, when the time came the people would do it for them',
he predicted. Overall, speakers seemed to be walking a perilous-
ly thin line between keeping another riot at bay, whilst main-
taining persistent pressure upon the authorities by inciting
further disturbances.49

Thus, immediately following this rally, a reporter from the
Daily Standard became the target of a near riot in the vestibule of
the *Courier* building in Queen Street. A group of returned
soldiers spotted 'a red flag badge' on his coat lapel. The victim, H.
Nicoll, was forced to fend off an attack by a dozen or so war
veterans with a loaded revolver, as he backed away from them
and ultimately found refuge on the fire-escape of the Queens-

land Irish Association Club. He huddled there for over an hour, before he could slip quietly away. Commissioner Urquhart's official comment upon this incident was a characteristic one. 'This Nicoll is a troublesome and turbulent person', he concluded, 'and if not restrained will cause serious trouble.'[50]

Such a response — of singlemindedly branding the victim as the culprit — summarised the wider official reaction by state and federal authorities, which was already unfolding as Urquhart wrote. In this regard, governmental and mob responses were to prove interlocking and complementary ones. State force and private violence now combined to belabour both the radical and the alien — 'the scum, the sore on society . . . this hideous thing in our midst', as the conservative newspapers stereotyped them. That Friday, the *Bulletin* appeared upon Brisbane newsstands, with a particularly lurid cartoon by Norman Lindsay on its inside cover. On a throne, from which Czarist autocracy had been deposed, sat a worse tyrant, 'Bolshevism', represented as a demented thug, brandishing a large meat cleaver in his right hand. Blood dripped from it onto the arm of a slaughtered woman who lay at his feet, her right breast exposed. The crowned assassin's right foot pressed down upon the shoulder of a male corpse which had fallen, face-forward beside her, as a vulture squatted expectantly upon the apex of the throne. 'The King is Dead — Long Live the King', read the illustration's mordant title.

In an editorial devoted to 'Bolshevism in Brisbane', the *Bulletin* loosely argued that it was the duty of every 'democrat' to insist upon the suppression of 'cranky ideas'. 'Being a foreigner', the paper reasoned: '[the Bolshevik] does not know what the democratic institutions of this country are. *The majority of us can do absolutely what it pleases*. This shows that these foreigners are in the wrong place. Their outlook does not call for punishment by imprisonment. It calls for deportation.' However, the *Bulletin*'s quirky logic about the essence of Australian democracy was not to be extended so far as to permit any foreign element to 'do absolutely what it pleases' — even when that pleasure was confined to the public display of a suppressed emblem.[51]

The exposure of the red flag had resulted in unprecedented scenes of riot, demagoguery, victimisation and destruction. It had provided an effective signal, not for a leftwing revolt, but for a massive resurgence in Brisbane of xenophobia, imbricated tightly with political intolerance and unleashed vigilantism. Part

The king is dead — long live the king! (*Bulletin*, 27 March 1919)

of this great mobilisation had been visceral and uncoordinated, drawing onto the streets thousands of agitated citizens, often unsure of what their next move would be. Yet behind this undisciplined mob response lay a premeditated scheme of political engineering, which ranked soldiers behind officers for the dirtier tasks of direct confrontation; whilst, in their wake, bourgeois, loyalist spokesmen and the conservative press could parade – at a more respectable distance – baying persuasively for a timely retribution for alien lawbreakers as a counter to further bloodshed. Taken together, they composed a neatly structured and seemingly irresistible alliance, delivering their grim ultimatums, before which both state and federal authorities already appeared inclined to bow.

Exactly one week after Zuzenko and Bykov had exposed their red flag, a procession of 1,750 returned soldiers – almost six times the numerical strength of the three hundred radicals in the previous Sunday's parade – marched behind a large Union Jack and a Caledonian pipe band along virtually the same route to the Domain gates. 'All the famous regiments were represented', claimed the *Brisbane Courier*, and included men from Coolangatta, Ipswich 'and outlying districts'. Near the Moreton Bay fig tree, which Norman Jeffery had climbed a week earlier to congratulate his comrades on their 'solidarity', Pearce Douglas of the RSSILA jubilantly addressed laughing, cheering soldiers about 'rooting out', deporting and shooting 'anarchists'. The veterans' demonstration proved a fitting close to a seven-day cycle during which loyalism had commanded the streets and radicalism had been rapidly driven from them.

Yet these 'days of the pogrom', as Peter Petroff Kreslin was soon to dub them, were merely a foretaste of more sombre days ahead for the Russians and their Anglo-Australian supporters. The arm of the state, they were now to discover, was capable of delivering them a more telling blow than the loyalist who swung a paling or fingered the trigger of a gun.[52]

Chapter 5

No Sympathy for You

It happens in life that for the
sake of one's ideals and ideas,
men go to prison, are exiled
to Siberia and even commit
suicide, but make no compromises.

Konstantin Klushin[1]

The Brisbane Domain on Sunday afternoon, 6 April 1919, was devoid of its usual array of platform speakers. Instead, noted the *Daily Mail*, picnic parties were scattered across a grassy expanse which now looked 'beautifully fresh and green' after so much rain. Groups of happy youngsters romped among the swings, see-saws and merry-go-rounds in the adjacent playground. Indeed, added the *Toowoomba Chronicle*, an 'altogether different class of people' now seemed to be frequenting the place. Gone were the 'Domainiacs', those strange 'long-haired men to whom a shower bath would have been a blessing', observed a *Daily Mail* columnist, '[those] hard faced persons with soft hands, men of enemy origin, IWW propagandists and others [who] beat the air' and shouted their wild harangues. 'Common sense' and 'normalcy' had apparently been restored. The area adjacent to the speakers' rotunda 'where the OBU propagandists, the Internationalists and Pacifists were wont to hold forth was practically deserted', for, as the *Chronicle* explained: 'Several of the principals are now in gaol; a number of Russians who were always to be found there are to be deported and many who were at first disposed to sympathise with the sentiments expressed at these gatherings are, as one of them remarked, "full up" . . . '[2]

'Repressed and terrified', perhaps, would have been a better description, for authoritarian conformity as well as autumnal fragrance was very much in the air. Ever since the riots, a fortnight earlier, the letter columns in the conservative press had been deluged by practical hints about establishing loyalist

Peace, perfect peace! (*Worker,* 24 July 1919)

bureaux throughout Queensland, organising 'simultaneous loyalty meetings' all over Brisbane and designing loyalty badges for all right-minded citizens to wear. 'If a man is not for the Empire, he is against it', reasoned a *Brisbane Courier* correspondent, 'and everyone should make it his business to know of his neighbour whether he be a loyalist or a rebel.' It definitely was not a good time to be in any degree 'radical' in Queensland. 'If any permanent good is to be done, those who preach and print revolution will have to be dealt with, as well as those who have revolutionary flags', the *Courier* editorialised on 4 April: 'The undermining movement carried on by extremists has received a check, and the engineers like hunted rats have scurried to their holes. If like rats also, they are not dug out, they will resume operations as daringly as before, as soon as they imagine the danger has passed.'[3]

Before the first week of anti-Bolshevik demonstrations was over, loyalist citizens had begun posting lists of 'suspect Russians' to Military Command and commonwealth police headquarters. Alice Osborne of South Brisbane, for instance, supplied an index of Russian cab-drivers whom she claimed 'gloried' in their Bolshevik beliefs. Another informant, signing himself 'Under the Union Jack', wrote of mysterious doings by Bolshevik Russians, hiding out with their 'documents . . . and gold' at Thompson's Estate, near Woolloongabba. Their presence might result in another Hounditch scare, commented the writer, harking back to sensational events in London's East End as early as 1911, when police had besieged a group of Latvian anarchists. Commonwealth constables were kept especially busy pursuing these chimeras and discovering that most led them precisely nowhere. A purported Bolshevik sympathiser called 'Solovdohin' at Thompson's Estate simply did not exist, while another named 'Patroochini', allegedly living at Coorparoo, had actually left Brisbane in 1911. Other rumours took these policemen further afield than the outer Brisbane suburbs. On 31 March, Constable Stewart was summoned to Coolangatta on the New South Wales border to investigate information supplied by David Kerr, an inquiry agent of the Brisbane Tramways Company, about Russians disseminating revolutionary propaganda to passing trains. His trip once more was fruitless.[4]

On the same day, Constable Foote arrived at Cleveland, Moreton Bay, in response to reports that strangers had been seen 'wandering about' in the region. Again, the investigation proved abortive. The strangers may indeed have been CIB men, themselves making enquiries about a Russian Pole, working as ₹ blacksmith at Birkdale station, Foote surmised. Or perhaps the alleged Russians had vanished into: 'the dense scrub called locally "The Never Never Lands" at Capalaba or Lota Park. This dense country extends right away from Thorne Siding to Manly and is a very big stretch . . . where men could remain hidden for weeks . . . A mounted search party would be necessary to get these men out.' As Foote sat ruminating upon these possibilities on the return train journey to Brisbane, five young men entered his railway carriage at Manly. Ever alert for suspicious signs, Foote observed:

> two of them [were] wearing their shirt collars over their coat collars *in the manner that is said to show that they are Bolsheviks.* One of these men was also wearing a small red flag badge in his coat, but removed this before reaching South Brisbane station. All five . . . were carrying sugar bags, apparently full of clothing and blankets . . . and it is *quite feasible that they had been on a visit to the Russians* . . . [5]

Such false leads and absurd conjectures were merely reflections of the intense fear and hatred which the Brisbane Red Flag riots had agitated. 'The Russians had accumulated a fairly large stock of rifles, revolvers, swords, sabres and other lethal weapons', reported the *Toowoomba Chronicle* sensationally on 8 April:

> Practically every dealer in arms in Brisbane was visited and many could have sold several times the number they had on hand. The Russians bought these arms *by proxy* in order to cover up their tracks. As a result of the raid on the part of the military, the arms in question were not secured, and there is much speculation in certain quarters as to their present location.

The spectre of armed Russians, anxious to rise in revolt, continued to haunt unsettled imaginations. On 7 April, the Visiting Justice to the Diamantina Hospital for the Incurably Ill in Brisbane discovered that two incapacitated Russian patients had revolvers in their lockers. Apparently, these had been supplied by Ipswich friends as a defensive precaution, in response to the prevailing Russophobia. The matter was immediately turned over to Military Intelligence. Meanwhile, under a headline, 'Armed Russians', the *Brisbane Courier* reported that two foreign desperadoes had attempted to gain admission to the hospital wards for nefarious purposes. Similarly, in early April, the Censor's office was alerted to the fact that a Russian at Kuridala, a copper mining centre south of Cloncurry, had purchased a quantity of blasting powder from Brisbane, and that the man in question was an associate of the Russian anarchist, Nicholai Lagutin. Two military raids had already been conducted upon Lagutin's premises by this time – one prior to the riots, when printed matter and a hunting knife had been seized, and one following them when 'nothing implicating' had been found. Yet the tenuous association drawn between Lagutin and the blasting powder was to prove a stubborn one. Several months later, he was still under close surveillance as a man who would 'stop at nothing'. As Brigadier-General Irving commented fancifully at this time to the Chief of General Staff, 'He was the Russian who had control of *about two hundredweight of ammunition and arms* when the former trouble with the Russians in Brisbane arose'. Even Archie Eastcrabb, the IWW unionist bashed at Hughenden, was under investigation in April 1919, after it was learned that he had once served an apprenticeship at an Essex gunpowder and cordite factory[6]

As reverberations of the riots spread across Queensland, curious and extravagant reactions were recorded statewide. At Gayndah, on 3 April, for instance, three youths armed with rifles bailed up a local farmer at his home to lecture him on the meaning of the Brisbane disturbances. A Russian railway gang at Coomera was raided by local police after its members were overheard talking about the Brisbane Red Flag procession of 23 March in the station's refreshment room. At Haden, a small township on the Darling Downs, every conceivable mischief was immediately laid at the Bolsheviks' door. 'Lawlessness seems to have become more Bolshevistic and acute,' argued 'A Wideawake Visitor' on 5 April:

> The recent assault of the local baker, an incendiary attempt on the new two-storied hotel, stone-throwing on the roofs of the houses of loyalists, the wholesale theft of poultry, to say nothing of the garrulous, howling hoodlums, cursing and swearing about the roads till 2 o'clock in the morning are among some of the recent misdeeds. The latest has been an attempt to wreak vengeance on a returned soldier by pulling his sulky to pieces . . . as well as overturning a closet in the yard of a loyal German . . .

The perpetrators were 'visitors from the outlying districts', the informant alleged, terrorising the quiet township with 'the Bolshevik war cry'. Similarly, on 30 March, a rumour spread through Rockhampton that thirty Russian Bolsheviks, fleeing

Brisbane, had invaded the town. The local RSSILA was alerted and commonwealth police Sergeant, A. Marshall, called for reinforcements. In fact, the men were part of the normal influx of seasonal labour into the Lakes Creek meatworks, which was about to re-open. Nevertheless, as a precautionary measure, Marshall demanded that the Lakes Creek manager supply the names of 'all aliens, more particularly Germans and Russians'; and the following day, a list of forty was received.[7]

The hysteria so widely engendered was therefore both acute and fanciful. If, in retrospect, such responses seem by their undoubted spuriousness farcical, it is salutary to remember the grim earnestness with which loyalists gathered in virtually every urban centre of Queensland to harness the panic towards political ends. On 28 March at Hughenden, for instance, a group of graziers declaring 'We will have to smash up these Bolsheviks!' caused a near riot in the main street; while, four nights later, four hundred loyalists met there to defend the honour of Australian womanhood from the menace of Bolshevik 'marriage laws'. At Townsville, returned soldiers and rejected volunteers called upon 'all loyal workers' to cease labouring 'with any Bolshevik', and arranged for all war veterans 'at a given signal' to go to the immediate assistance of police combatting subversives. Indeed, RSSILA members, congregating in dozens of centres, vowed to strike 'a sure, steady blow' against radicals and aliens in their local districts and to send reinforcements to Brisbane, if necessary, to join the 'Bolshevik hunt'.[8]

Officials in the various intelligence organisations seemed incapable of remaining aloof from this general hue and cry. In fact, by their words and actions, they often appeared to be heading it. Captain Stable, for instance, called for federal action against the 'Bolsheviki' as early as Monday morning, 24 March, before the worst rioting had occurred. Military raids, beginning that same day, continued upon the homes and clubrooms of known Brisbane activists and named Russians over subsequent weeks. At one boarding house in West End, five Russian males resided who had all fought with the AIF. The five were 'quiet, well behaved men', attested their landlady, and were 'always in early at night . . . playing cards amongst themselves'. Nevertheless, by 24 April, their rooms had been raided twice by military agents and they were each compelled to report regularly to local police. The library of the Brisbane branch of the Australian Socialist Party, an organisation so small and ineffectual that it had 'not been functioning for some time', was raided by commonwealth police in April, and books of all kinds, 'from the Holy Bible to the Materialist Conception of History . . . Sociology, Psychology . . . both for and against the present social system', were confiscated. 'There seems to have been a panic in the military departments lately', observed James Riddell, the ASP's former secretary, 'taking the shape of indiscriminate raids on civil persons' property . . . perhaps it is the idea . . . to revert back to the very dark ages and to chain the minds of the people in one groove of thought . . . '⁹

On 27 March, the Russian club rooms in Merivale Street were officially closed, under Para. 17(B) of the *Aliens Restriction Order*. Two days later, the publishing firm of Stott and Hoare, which had printed various pamphlets as well as *Knowledge and Unity* for the Russians, was visited by Military Intelligence and their business relationship with the URW severed. This move effectively silenced the Russian press for several months. In a raid on one Russian tenement, all books and papers, membership lists, accounts and minutes of the 'Souse of Russian Workers' were seized for censorship perusal. Russians feared arrest even if they ventured into the Brisbane GPO — where the Censor's office was located — to collect their mail. 'The organization witnessed violence belonging to medieval times', a petition from six Russian Bolsheviks later charged:

> books, papers, journals, office papers, documents and correspondence all were torn into pieces — even the office broom was broken in two — showing the destructive madness which operated while the building was under military guard . . . They may have crippled the organization, but morally and spiritually it still lives with us, because it is the bone and marrow of every Russian immigrant, who will never submit to any form of Czardom, even if subdued . . . ¹⁰

Similarly, on 27 March, in a raid on the South Brisbane home of Norman Jeffery, secretary of the OBUPL, all that organisation's official papers were seized. Lieutenant Wearne, who led this assault, naively asked Jeffery, 'why, if he belonged to the OBU, he had a Red Flag' in his possession? 'We are all Internationalists', Jeffery patiently explained. On the same day, a Melbourne Street second-hand shop was also raided, after it was discovered that the OBUPL had conducted a private meeting in its large cellar the previous evening. In the meantime, the State Labor Government had prohibited all public meetings in Brisbane, although loyalists seemed to experience no difficulty

Victoria Barracks,
24th November, 1919

To A.P.M.

Sir,

While on duty at Albion Park Race Course on
22nd November, 1919, Captain Wills, Intelligence Officer
drew my attention to a man wearing a red tie with a black
stripe through it. The man was dressed in a Military
Uniform. I immediately found the man and asked him his
name. He gave his name as Pte. McPherson, 49th Battalion,
and said he was receiving treatment at the Rosemount
Hospital. This man's tunic was unbuttoned at top thereby
exposing the wearing of the red tie.

(Signed)   F. N. CROUCH, Cpl.

The O.C.

Intelligence Section.

Forwarded.

(Signed)   J. B. HEMPSTED, Lieut.
25/11/19.   A.P.M., 1st M.D.

The hunt for 'red' subversion continues. (Australian Archives: BP4/1, item
66/4/2165)

in securing the Police Commissioner's exemption from this order. On 3 April, David Burns, an OBU member, wrote to a fellow militant in Melbourne: 'No meetings are allowed now . . . and the Trade Unions have been approached and they turned us down, so you can realize our difficulties . . . Norman Jeffery got six months and all the others who have come before the beak have received the same . . . I don't know if the organization will go out of existence or not'.[11]

The fate of Jeffery and his cohorts 'before the beak' serves, at a basic level, to highlight the rapprochement now occurring between Theodore's Labor Cabinet and W.A. Watt's Nationalists in the arraignment of radicals and Russians. Although the absent Premier Ryan would later indicate that the State was constrained under Section 120 of the Constitution to provide its police, courts and prisons at the Commonwealth's behest, his explanation did not account for the avidity with which his deputy, Theodore, entered into that arrangement. After the political estrangement wrought by two conscription referenda and subsequent disagreements over future war prosecution, it now seemed as though state and federal governments were happily colluding to curb Wobbly and Bolshevik influences in Queensland.

In a gentlemanly exchange of telegrams, beginning on 25 March, Watt agreed that military authorities would restrain the soldiers' propensity for 'tumult', if state police provided the names of those breaching commonwealth regulations. However the names collected identified persons 'who carried red flags', not rioting soldiers; and these names, in turn, had already been forwarded to Military Command by Commissioner Urquhart on Monday morning, 24 March — well before the Acting Prime Minister's request had been made. Thus, on 25 March, General Irving began issuing warrants for War Precautions violations and, the following morning, Theodore promptly informed Watt that 'the cases will come up for hearing early next week'. Commensurate action against riotous loyalists, thereby, had been neatly sidestepped in favour of a two-pronged assault upon Russian and Anglo-Australian leftists. Police and military now cooperated in a broad sweep against this target group, selecting some for trial (and virtually automatic imprisonment) and others for internment and deportation.[12]

By Saturday, 29 March, the Defence Department had been informed that twenty-one red flag prosecutions had been launched, ten of which were to be heard at the Brisbane Magistrate's Court on Monday, 31 March. The manner in which these cases were selected became a matter of considerable leftwing comment. More than one hundred red flags had been paraded on 23 March, and General Irving's secret agent had actually identified some forty-two of the bearers. Yet, of those on the list, only seven were selected for prosecution; while a further seven, who were unlisted, would also be imprisoned. In all, sixteen 'red flag' cases would be heard: one man, E.N. Free, the Labor parliamentarian, was simply fined, but the other fifteen – including Joe 'Nugget' Doyle of Samsonvale fame – were all incarcerated. The prosecution list, however, did possess one sort of internal logic: five of the accused were allegedly members of the Union of Russian Workers, while another seven belonged to the OBUPL. The remaining two (excluding Doyle), Bob Carroll and George Taylour, were strong sympathisers of either the Wobblies or the Bolsheviks.[13]

Although ten members of the Queensland Socialist League were named as flag carriers, none were officially touched. One of their number, Jennie Scott Griffiths later commented on how strange it seemed that so many men from one organisation 'who prepared no flags, nor brought any with them to the Trades Hall . . . would be picked out as victims for punishment . . . ' At his trial on 2 April, Norman Jeffery made this accusation more bluntly. Examining defence witness, William Barty, Jeffery asked:

> Is it not a fact that persons prominent in public life carried the red flag in the procession?
> [Barty:] Yes. Many well known persons flew the red flag . . . but none of them have been served with a summons.
> [Jeffery:] Gross discrimination has been shown . . . One organization has been singled out for prosecution . . .

And so one of the surviving centres of IWW activism – the OBUPL – was about to receive its humiliation from the state apparatus. Both Commissioner Urquhart and Captain Stable, several months before, had been urging 'a hard knock such as stiff sentences of imprisonment of ten or twenty of them'; and now the opportunity to deliver this short, sharp shock had apparently arrived.[14]

A large crowd, restrained by police, assembled outside the City Police Court on Monday, 31 March. The courtroom was packed. Nine defendants faced the Bench, with Police

Magistrate H.L. Archdall presiding, still recovering from a week-old groin injury incurred during the riots. The tenth man summoned, Alexander Zuzenko, was unavailable, explained Sub-Inspector Brosnan, as he was 'at present in the custody of the military authorities'. Brosnan, who had been thwarted by Zuzenko and Bykov at the start of the Red Flag procession, *was* present, however, to conduct the case for the prosecution. He was supported by Inspector Ferguson, another participant at the disturbances, and both men were assisted by J.C. Roberts of the commonwealth legal firm of Chambers, McNab and McNab. Thus, even before the opening words of the first trial were uttered, it appeared that the cards of justice had been more than a little stacked. 'None of the defendants were defended', the *Telegraph* succinctly observed.[15]

Herman Bykov, the badly injured victim of the OBUPL riot of 23 March, was the first defendant to appear. He seemed relatively unconcerned about his own fate but, in a state of intense agitation, demanded to know why Zuzenko was not present. After several fruitless interchanges with Archdall, he then addressed the court at length, an oration reported next morning in the conservative press as 'A Russian Outburst'. 'From a capitalist point of view I undoubtedly am guilty', Bykov stated: 'because I dared to wave the red flag of the workers . . . I did so because as a Russian Maximalist, I recognize only one State, Soviet state of toil . . . and as an Internationalist, . . . only one flag, the red flag of the workers of the world, which is now the national flag of our fatherland . . . ' He had acted thus, he explained, to protest against Allied intervention into Soviet affairs and to support the repatriation, via the port of Odessa, of all Russian Bolsheviks in Australia. Yet, although clearly guilty in the eyes of the State, he continued:

I am not a criminal, but merely a political prisoner of Australian capitalists. I was stabbed and beaten with sticks by some ignorant and probably drunken soldiers who do not understand what Bolshevism really is. Bolshevism is the section of Socialism which stands for revolutionary socialization of all means of production, for the benefit of the producers. I spent seven years in the Czar's dungeons and in exile in Siberia. I was glad to come in prison again for the final victory of the Red Flag. I believe that time will come, and the Socialists and workers of Australia will understand why I and my comrades are fighting for the realization of our Socialistic ideals . . .

Despite Bykov's optimism and loquacity, his ideals and his delivery in 'broken English' were greeted with gales of laughter.

The conservative press depicted him as a buffoon. Had this 'raving Russian' been imprisoned in Siberia for theft or bigamy, asked the *Bulletin* scornfully: 'As he insists on wrecking things here to get level with the late Czar's ghost, he has . . . to be got rid of. But perhaps he was never in a dungeon. He may be a grocer's assistant unhinged by reading penny dreadfuls.' 'You are making quite a number of demands,' Archdall admonished him, as he passed sentence of six months imprisonment. The Russian was led from the court, threatening a hunger strike as 'my last protest against the starvation of Russian citizens in Hughes's land' as peals of derisive laughter rang in his ears.[16]

The next case was heard in a much lower key, although it was potentially more problematical. Whereas Bykov had proudly admitted to displaying the flag, Paul Leischmann, a Russian boiler-maker from Ipswich, denied the charge of assaulting Acting-Sergeant Patrick Davis 'five or six times with a stick' during the procession. It was a case of mistaken identity, Leischmann pleaded, for he had carried his young son throughout most of the march. The boy had been handed a small red flag, but Leischmann took it from him and rolled it up. He was not even a member of the Russian Association. Yet Archdall duly sentenced him to seven months imprisonment with hard labour. With Leischmann's sentence, it appeared as though a guilty verdict would be the mandatory outcome of each trial, whatever the defence presented. The characterisation of Archdall by the left as a man whose 'spirit of class bias' had been reinforced by a painful bayonet prod, and who could pass 'brutally savage sentences . . . without a blush', seems, by such evidence, to be somewhat vindicated.[17]

When Norman Jeffery (in his 'melodious voice') next requested an adjournment, because of a biased press and an inflamed public mind, Archdall curtly admonished him for his impudence'. But it was now rather late in the day, and Archdall held the hearing over until Wednesday, 2 April. When Jeffery reappeared, he argued that he had held only a furled flag, but was nevertheless proud to have carried it as a symbol of his ideals and his friendship with the Russians. 'Was it the size of a blanket?' Archdall scornfully asked. 'No', came the reply. 'It was between the size of a blanket and a postage stamp.' When the laughter subsided, Jeffery continued: 'The carrying of the red flag is to me a right which no Act can abrogate . . . Laws . . . which are an affront to our intelligence should be repealed. I trust the time will soon come that Bolshevism . . . will come into Australia . . . [until that time] I will carry the OBUPL flag.' As Jeffery spoke on about convincing returned soldiers of their 'real' anti-capitalist interests, there was an outburst from a man sitting in the press gallery, wearing an RSSILA badge. Archdall glanced sharply in his direction, but said nothing. The man was Johannas Tilanus, a clerk sent by Military Intelligence to cover the trials. Jeffery was then sentenced to Boggo Road Gaol for six months. George 'Gunner' Taylour, following Jeffery to the stand, received the same leaven of justice. Russians should be 'treated as human beings', he argued, and their repatriation pleas acknowledged. 'I would like to ask the authorities', he ventured, 'why the red flag was permitted to fly during the first three years of the war from all working class halls and homes without interference . . . [and] why the red flag is banned in Australia and allowed to fly in Great Britain?' His queries went unanswered as he was duly convicted.[18]

A close examination of this series of trials, continually strikes home the inflexibility of the bench, the atmosphere of witch-hunt which pervaded the court and the comparative resilience and sincerity of the defendants as they struggled with their statements. At the trial of Jerry Cahill, a cooper from Tipperary who had formerly participated in the Dublin Transport Strike with James Connolly, both Brosnan and Archdall attempted repeatedly to inveigle him into incriminating his brother, Ned, who was also to be tried. Even his most direct responses were greeted with disdain. For instance, when he answered that he lived at Toowong, Archdall could not resist playing to the gallery by enquiring whether or not he resided in the cemetery there. Thus provoked, Cahill finally stated:

> I'd like to say that I did carry a flag, but didn't carry it in defiance. I carried it as a symbol of an ideal . . . the uplifting of the human race and the betterment of their condition . . . You cannot shatter my body unless you also shatter my heart . . . therefore, though you put my body in prison, my thoughts will live . . . I will now say that I am proud of each one and the way they have met this crisis, and I will do it again for the same ideals involved. I'll be there just the same.[19]

And so these political trials were to continue, as the Russians, Steve Tolstobroff, Mark Ostapenko and Ludwik Roslan, were each sentenced and imprisoned. Roslan, a Russian Pole with a wife and six children, was the last to be tried, after he was flushed by police from six weeks' hiding. Ostapenko, a railway worker with a family of three, spoke the most eloquently of the three when he remarked:

> I was cautioned as a child against displaying a red flag to a bull and I never thought that the antipathy of that animal would also be shared by human beings . . . We [Russians] left our native land to escape persecution and firmly believed that in coming to Australia we would find freedom and peace . . . we now find ourselves regarded as people without rights, and have been forced to flee from infuriated mobs who have been prejudiced against us . . .

He denied either carrying a flag or assaulting two policemen, but was sentenced to seven months gaol, nevertheless.[20]

Among the remaining Anglo-Australians, Percival James led the court on the merriest dance when he claimed to have been mopping his forehead with a red handkerchief rather than waving a flag. In exasperation, Archdall finally ruled that even 'the carrying of a red handkercief in such circumstances would probably — and almost undoubtedly — be an exhibition of a red flag'. James received his conviction with a bow and a sardonic 'Thank you!' to the Magistrate, and was taken away to the cells. The other three OBUPL members to be tried — James Huggot, William Elder and Gus Orance — were described as 'mere youths'; and both the court and the press gallery were somewhat startled by their oratory. 'The time will come', Elder predicted hopefully, 'when instead of having misery, starvation and unemployment with all its attendant privations, the working class will, through their own might . . . own collectively and control the industries . . . ' Orance, described in the *Brisbane Courier* as being 'of foreign appearance', spoke of the imminent 'psychological moment' for capitalism's overthrow. As he recited several foolscap pages of this 'pompous stuff', observed the *Daily Mail* columnist, 'The lad became so excited at times that he had to stop, and in one place his voice failed him altogether. He had arrived at the passage dealing with "the glorious Red Flag" . . . ' Such propaganda, the press concluded, must have been concocted by 'the brain of another person'. Yet it is just as likely that all three were avid pupils of the radical speakers' classes, held weekly at Trades Hall, and had now discovered a political forum far superior to any Domain soapbox.[21]

It was not until 7 July 1919 that the entire spate of Red Flag trials ended. Joseph Doyle, still suffering from the effects of pneumonia, chose one month's gaol rather than be fined for 'the first offence of this nature'. In the meantime, Edgar Free had quietly paid his fine and Bob Carroll, who had gone into hiding rather than pay his, was discovered at Bundaberg in mid-June and sentenced to two months imprisonment. In all, fifteen men had been sentenced to a total period of seven years incarceration for breaching a War Precautions regulation, more than four months after the war had ended.[22] The prisoners and their sentences are shown in the table.

Red Flag Prisoners			
Name	Sentence (in months)	Date sentenced	Date discharge due
Herman Bykov	6	31.3.19	13.8.19
Paul Leischmann	7	31.3.19	13.8.19
George Taylour	6	2.4.19	15.8.19
Norman Jeffery	6	2.4.19	15.8.19
Steve Tolstobroff	6	3.4.19	16.8.19
Jerry Cahill	6	4.4.19	17.8.19
Ned Cahill	6	4.4.19	17.8.19
William Elder	6	4.4.19	17.8.19
James Huggot	6	4.4.19	17.8.19
Percival James	6	7.4.19	23.8.19
Gus Orance	6	7.4.19	23.8.19
Mark Ostapenko	7	13.4.19	29.8.19
Louis Roslan	7	22.4.19	7.9.19
Robert Carroll	2	16.6.19	15.8.19
Joseph Doyle	1	7.7.19	6.8.19

In stark contrast to these rigorous penalties, rioting ex-soldiers were handled with conspicuous leniency. Although thousands had participated in the disturbances, the police had somehow managed to collar only three of them. As Trevor Botham notes, the size of this catch seems ludicrous when 'evidence clearly indicates (by a comparison of misdemeanours) that the returned soldiers and their supporters had outdone their opposition'. Approximately 150 State police had been on duty during three nights of disturbances, as well as commonwealth policemen and Military Intelligence agents. Yet amidst all the picket-wielding, stone-throwing and gunfire, the arrest sheet for each evening read, consecutively, zero, two and one. Commonwealth agents, in turn, had taken the names of precisely no-one. At Merivale Street, the two men secured were returned soldiers, Thomas Luke Cunningham, a professional actor, accused of leading a charge of more than 150 paling-swinging veterans against the mounted police, and Thomas Drane, described as a 'North American colored man', charged with attempting to shoot

Constable O'Driscoll. The third, stockman James Mills, was summonsed after indiscriminately firing his pistol outside the *Daily Standard* offices the next evening. The essentially token nature of such gestures was highlighted when each man was repeatedly placed upon remand, until interest in the riots had waned, and then despatched with only a light fine. Clearly, the attempted murder of a policeman was regarded more benevolently than the public display of a handkerchief-sized flag.[24]

The imprisonment of this Brisbane Fifteen, however, was merely the milder of the coercive responses upon which state and federal authorities collaborated. At 12.42 a.m. on Thursday, 27 March, Acting Prime Minister Watt, in response to concerted public pressure to 'uproot Bolshevism', ordered Commandant Irving to collect the names of 'Russian aliens in your opinion undesirable and prominent in recent disturbances'. The next morning, CIB detectives, Hegarty and O'Roarke, arrested Alexander Zuzenko near Coorparoo (then an outer Brisbane suburb), after he had allegedly 'eluded capture for four days'. Zuzenko, depicted as the head of 'the Bolsheviki in Queensland', was delivered to military authorities and placed in a cell at Victoria Barracks to await 'immediate deportation'. In the meantime, Irving had compiled a list of seven other Russians – Michael Wishnevsky, Herman Bykov, Konstantin Klushin, Peter Kreslin, Frank Madorsky, Walter Markin and Michael Rosenberg – for arrest and deportation. All had been 'very prominent' in the 23 March demonstration, he claimed. Contrary to this assertion, however, the Russians themselves would later argue that neither Klushin, Markin, Rosenberg nor Madorsky had even been present at the Red Flag march. The seven were chosen, it was alleged, because Intelligence linked them closely with the URW executive. Their arrests were calculated to put that organisation out of operation. Of the seven, the most contentious and revealing case was that of 'Frank Madorsky'.[25]

'Madorsky' was the last to be arrested as he left work at the Australian Meat Export Company in South Brisbane on Saturday, 5 April. Yet the man peremptorily seized at the factory gates was not 'Madorsky' at all. The winding trail which had led detectives to him had begun with a fruitless search for a fictitious 'William Jim'. 'Jim' in turn had been identified as 'Madorsky' and when he too could not be found, it was decided by 4 April that he was operating under the alias of 'Frank Melville'. The next morning, 'Frank Melville' inexplicably became 'Wolf Weinberg', purportedly a 'Russian Jew' working at the meat processing plant. Thus, Weinberg, alias 'Melville' alias 'Madorsky' alias 'Jim', was duly arrested. In actuality, commonwealth records show that Frank Madorsky had already left Australia aboard the S.S. *Nikko Maru* on 3 June 1917. At Thursday Island, his belongings had been searched. Syndicalist publications and several letters from Wobbly activist, Tom Barker, were found in his cabin. Anxious to be rid of him, however, federal authorities had finally decided 'to let the man proceed with leaving the country'.[26]

The 'undesirable' Frank Madorsky could hardly have been 'very prominent' in a Brisbane march almost two years later, as Irving confidently claimed. But who, then, was Wolf Weinberg? To begin with, he was not Jewish, but a Pole of Russian extraction; and 'Wolf Weinberg' was his only name. He was the son of Louzeroff and Hanorofa Weinberg, born at Lotz; and, since his arrival in Australia, he had had no connection with radical or revolutionary politics whatever. He was, by profession, an entertainer – a dancer and contortionist – who had left Poland in 1912 to appear at the Grand Opera House in Calcutta. From there, he had travelled with various circuses throughout India and Java. Arriving in Sydney aboard the *Tasman* in 1914, he had performed at several theatres and cinemas in Surry Hills, before becoming a clothing factory worker at Redfern. In 1918, he had travelled to North Queensland, working itinerantly at various hotels, meat processing plants and mines. By Christmas 1918, he was in Brisbane, working as a wool-washer at Cannon Hill, before commencing employment at the South Brisbane meatworks. He later wrote:

> leaving work on Saturday [5 April], I was accosted by two detectives who asked me, "Are you a Russian?" I stated, "No." Asked my name, I said, "Weinberg". Then they said: "The Victoria Barracks wants you" and I was arrested. I was asked if I knew any people. I said no as I had not been in Brisbane very long. Then they said I was a Bolshevik and detained me, sending me to Sydney. I have been five years in Australia and have never belonged to any association whatever and do not agree to Bolshevik principles of any kind and intended to become Naturalized and settle in Australia . . .

Yet Military Intelligence was to stick stubbornly to its original interpretation; and, without the mechanism of hearings to accompany internments, who was successfully to gainsay it? On 22

April, Sydney headquarters asked the Defence Department, ' . . . for what reason is he [i.e. Weinberg] detained?' The reply came that his real name was 'Madorsky' and that he was now a 'Prisoner of War [sic]'.[27]

This arbitrary and wrongful detention is a startling example of the hasty manner in which CIB detectives and military authorities cooperated to secure the eight Russian deportees. On 1 April, Lieutenant-General Legge, the Chief of General Staff, wired Irving, urging him to arrest all seven listed Bolsheviks *before soldiers' meeting tomorrow*. Federal forces, by now, were clearly dancing nimbly to the returned soldiers' tune. At this meeting, called by the RSSILA at the Brisbane Stadium, loyalist demands intensified. Official action against 'the Russian procession' was insufficient, stated Brigadier-General Spencer-Browne of the *Brisbane Courier*. What they wanted was total censorship of all Bolshevik propaganda, the dismissal of all Russian workers and the deportation of *any* disloyalists. These must include all undesirable aliens, added Major Bolingbroke, as well as the IWW, the Sinn Feiners and any other 'rebels' in Australia. 'They wanted to accomplish their ends by constitutional means', he concluded, 'but if they failed, then there were others. They had all "hopped over" before, and he supposed they could do it again (Cheers).' Yet it was Colonel A. Sutton, a Brisbane medical specialist and 'a leading figure in society circles', who honed the threatening innuendo to its sharpest edge. 'If they could not get their way by peaceful means', he suggested, 'there were other resources. Some of them early on the Peninsula knew the history of their bombs. There were plenty of jam tins in Brisbane . . . '[28]

Such blatant mob advocacy apparently bound the Defence Department more enthusiastically to its task. Yet the Russians were not to be as rapidly taken as Legge had hoped. By the time of the RSSILA meeting, only Klushin, Kreslin and Markin were in custody, with Rosenberg, Wishnevsky and Weinberg to join them that evening and over the next three days. (Bykov, of course, was already in Boggo Road Gaol). In the interim, however, Irving began compiling further lists, with the expressed intention of deporting 'all undesirable aliens (other than alien enemies)'. On 2 April, a register was compiled of twenty-three Russian spokesmen from centres as diverse as Cairns, Townsville, Ingham, Ayr and Innisfail in the north, Selwyn and Cloncurry in the west, and Brisbane, Samsonvale and Ipswich in the south. When it was learned, the following day, that the depleted Bolshevik ranks had rallied by appointing a new 'Soviet executive' of nine, including the radical Dutchman from Townsville, Barend Meyer, this entire 'Vigilance Committee' was added to the list. Eight other Brisbane Russians were presently under investigation. Two days later, Irving also recommended that the eight Red Flag offenders already gaoled with Bykov 'be deported immediately on the expiration of their term of imprisonment' as either Wobblies, Sinn Feiners or 'prominent leaders' of Bolshevism.[29]

As early as 27 March, this mounting anti-radical crusade had also reached Sydney, where it was rumoured that Russians and others intended holding a supportive Red Flag demonstration at the Domain the following Sunday. Although no such protest occurred, military raids nevertheless were ordered upon the Sydney Russian 'Soviet', the Social Democratic League and the Industrial Labour Party. Additionally, Major-General George Lee recommended, on 7 April, that five other 'dangerous' Russians be deported. Of these, only Peter Timms, allegedly 'the leading member of the Sydney Soviet', was actually apprehended. Timms was a Lettish Social Democrat, formerly arrested at Riga for insurgent activities during the abortive 1905 Russian uprising. He had served seven years in a series of Russian prisons before escaping from Siberia to Australia. His outspoken advocacy of physical force and his close association with Brisbane Bolsheviks led to his downfall. He was imprisoned with Zuzenko at Darlinghurst to await the arrival of the other interned Russians. Writing in support of such comprehensive official action, Irving observed that all men listed were 'undesirables of the worst type and very clever propagandists'. 'They are distributed all over Queensland for the sole purpose of spreading Bolshevism', he avowed, and had 'conjointly done everything possible to bring about a revolution here'. Yet, paradoxically, he had to admit, 'it is with great difficulty that we get *any information at all* concerning their activities because . . . they secretly move about with revolutionary matter on their person [sic] . . . hand in hand with the IWW of Queensland'.[30]

A combination of factors, however, would conspire to thwart Irving's expansive designs. First, a report from Captain Ainsworth of the SIB to his superior, Lieutenant-Colonel Jones, on 26 March had somewhat strained the veracity of Irving's communications. For, in utter contradiction of the Military Commandant's appraisal, Ainsworth reasoned:

> The Russians as an entity *do not threaten the disruption of Australia from any point of view*. Suppress their paper and where are they. They have no money, no influence in the community, whilst in supposing them to be sufficiently extreme to resort to armed force, their numbers and cohesion are so ridiculous that they could do nothing. Again, the majority of them are just like sheep and as stated to you here in December, if you dealt with a dozen whose names I supplied to you at that time, the Russian menace would cease to exist.

More pragmatic considerations soon lent considerable force to Ainsworth's assessment. On 1 April 1919, Governor-General Munro-Ferguson contacted the Secretary of State for the Colonies in London to determine the accuracy of a recent press report that 100 'Russian Jew Bolshevist propagandists' were to be deported from England that month. If this was so, he queried, could similar action be taken by the commonwealth? The response was not encouraging. All Russian ports were closed, he was informed, due to military reverses suffered by the invading Allies and White Armies in both northern and southern Russia. There was no certainty as to where the deportees could be landed. Furthermore, he was strictly admonished, 'In no circumstances should Russian deportees be sent from Australia to the United Kingdom for trans-shipment to Russia.'[31]

Consequently, on 10 April, Watt's Cabinet decided that Irving had presented insufficient evidence to warrant immediate action and called for more information. Irving seemed perplexed. What additional intelligence could he provide, he pleaded, beyond his own assurances that these 'undesirables' were intent upon 'more drastic measures of revolt'? Undaunted, he persisted with his single-minded endeavour to widen the pool of deportees. On 17 April, for instance, he asked Defence whether British IWW members, 'the original promoters . . . of Bolshevism', who were scattered across Queensland could not be deported. In mid-May and early June, he reiterated his complaint that incriminating evidence against the radicals seemed impossible to obtain as they were 'protected by their supporters and sympathizers'. Finally, on 28 June, he hopefully presented yet another list of five Russian Bolsheviks for deportation.[32]

Meanwhile, the prompt removal of Queensland's Bolshevik 'ring-leader, A.M. Zuzenko, had been officially approved. After languishing more than a fortnight in Darlinghurst, Zuzenko was taken in mid-April aboard the S.S. *Bakara*, bound for Odessa. During this voyage, however, after it was learned that the port was closed to Allied shipping, he was conveniently off-loaded at

Colombo, Ceylon, and abandoned there. His pregnant wife, Civa Rosenberg, unaware of his fate, had followed him to Sydney, accompanied by her mother, Doris, whose own husband, Michael, was now also in detention. Here they lived in destitute circumstances, along with Mrs Timms, Mrs Mary Wishnevsky and Jean Reid, who claimed to have married Klushin in Brisbane 'according to Russian Soviet rules'. The Defence Department refused to grant these dependants and their children any living allowance on 23 April. Ultimately, they were forced to subsist upon a pitiful handout of ten shillings per week from the New South Wales government. In response to Civa's constant badgering of the military concerning her husband's whereabouts, she was eventually informed 'she was going to meet him'. In late May, she was forcibly placed aboard the S.S. *Ulimaroa* 'in a state of distraction'. As Percy Brookfield later protested, 'She did not know whether she was to get off at Colombo or what was to happen to her.' As it eventuated, Civa did not join Zuzenko in Colombo. Finally, 'with a young child at her breast', she was disembarked at Alexandria in Egypt. In late July 1919, Peter Simonoff, unconsciously reflecting upon Civa's plight, remarked in a letter to Brisbane compatriots, 'I have a great anxiety about our comrade . . . Zuzenko. If [he] . . . is *sent to Egypt*, he will find himself under the most hellish conditions . . .'[33]

The other six Russian deportees had also been forwarded to Darlinghurst in early April; Bykov remained behind to finish his sentence at Boggo Road Gaol. Before leaving Enoggera Army Barracks for Sydney, Peter Kreslin attempted to smuggle out a letter to 'all Comrades left behind', but it was intercepted. 'I am, together with the rest, a prisoner', he wrote:

> What will happen I have absolutely no idea. It is a dirty mean trick to seize us from the ranks of society, just like thieves, behind a corner. They are trying to isolate us here . . . We are watched like treasures . . . Visitors are absolutely forbidden . . . A curious fact is, and why all this happened? "Arrested prominent Bolsheviks": It is just a huge joke . . .

Yet, despite his understandable cynicism and insecurity, Kreslin struggled hard to maintain an optimistic outlook. Even the fury of reactionaries during 'the days of the pogrom', he speculated, 'proves that they are beginning to feel the coming danger and that revolutionary measures are infecting the masses'. The disturbances, the imprisonments and deportations, he anticipated: 'will strengthen the ranks that are left. No matter how

few had suffered materially through the procession; no matter
that temporarily the Souse is crippled, our cause will get a
tremendous forward push. This storm washed some of the
mildew from the brains of many, and the slaves are beginning to
take notice if they are not idiots . . . '

Kreslin's isolation had apparently saved him from grasping
how vast the wave of repression had been. Furthermore the promise of ultimate repatriation to 'our free motherland' still served
to inflate his spirits. 'One thing — we expect to land in Russia
some time', he concluded: 'where we will be better understood
and do more useful work. It is a positive fact that permission to
leave will be granted very soon. It is already given by Watt, the
PM, but only to Odessa. . . . I wish you all happiness and a
speedy meeting *at home* . . . '[34] In contrast to Kreslin's buoyancy,
however, the hapless Wolf Weinberg remained in a condition of
utter despair. On 7 April, as the camp authorities prepared the
interned men for transportation to Sydney, Weinberg apparently
made an unsuccessful suicide attempt 'by eating a box of
matches'. In the light of what now lay before them, perhaps
Weinberg's response was a somewhat more appropriate one than
Kreslin's.[35]

On Monday, 7 April, the six interned Russians were herded into a filthy railway waggon at Enoggera with a guard of twelve
soldiers and taken in handcuffs to Brisbane Central Station to
board the Sydney mail train. At Wallangarra on the New South
Wales border, where the differing railway gauges of the two
states met, the small party was forced to halt, for influenza
quarantine restrictions necessitated waiting for another military
guard to be sent from Sydney. These men arrived four days later.
Back at the station, on 11 April, an additional complication arose
due to fear of contagion, for the Sydney guard were legally
prevented from making any physical contact with their Brisbane
counterparts. In solemn pantomime, the Queensland guard
therefore marched their prisoners across the platform and halted
precisely one yard away from the Sydney train. The New South
Welshmen had been warned that 'if they leave the carriage, it
becomes a breach of quarantine'. Thus, as the Queensland
soldiers released the prisoners, their Sydney escorts reached out
and hauled them aboard, ostensibly to prevent the spread of
pneumonic influenza across the border. Upon arrival in Sydney,
the prisoners discovered that their meagre possessions had been
rifled in transit and practically everything of value was missing.

Walter Markin, for instance, had lost his money-belt, books, blankets and items of clothing. Kreslin found that his watch and chain, camera, dress studs, dancing pumps and diploma had disappeared. Klushin's Russian passport and Rosenberg's watches and jewellery had been souvenired, as had Wishnevsky's money, badges, books and even a photograph of his wife. 'I will consider it a pure robbery', he complained, to no avail.[36]

Within Darlinghurst detention centre, the prisoners were soon stripped of more than precious material possessions. They were locked in groups of four (with Timms and Zuzenko) in single-cell 'stone cages . . . compelled to lay [sic] on a musty cement floor, only a few, dirty undisinfected blankets being allowed . . . ' The cramped cells were poorly ventilated and one was unlighted. 'Is this supposed to be British fair play and justice?' they protested on 24 April: 'Feeding us with rotten food . . . not allowing us to buy food with our own money, debarring delivery from outside . . . not allowed to smoke . . . absolutely ignored by the ad-ministration . . . letters kept for weeks without being sent . . . our wives and children left absolutely to starve . . . ' 'Cease to treat us like dogs', they pleaded — but the prison staff turned a deaf ear to their demands. 'You can knock at the stone walls with your head as much as you like,' they were told. 'You, being Bolshevik must expect as much from us returned soldiers.' Thus, on 24 April, with Zuzenko now deported, the remaining seven declared a hunger strike as 'the extreme measure of protest against unbearable oppression'.[37]

There is no record of the duration or outcome of this action; but on 12 May the five Russian Red Flag prisoners at Brisbane's Boggo Road similarly decided to refuse food until the state recognised them, not as criminals, but as political prisoners. Led by Bykov, they protested against the quality of the prison diet, the condition of their cells, their forced labour detail and the cen-sorship of their correspondence. This latter prohibition had hit the Russians severely, for as the majority of them could not write in English and prison officials could not decipher their letters, none of their mail was being forwarded. When the Home Secretary, John Huxham, visited the prisoners on 25 April: 'There was a pathetic scene when three of the Russians, who are married men with families . . . asked . . . [him] about their wives and children. One of the Russians, scarcely able to speak

English, with tears streaming down his cheeks had to get Bykov's assistance as interpreter . . . '

'The victim decides upon such a strike only when he is ready to die rather than be subjected to impossible treatment,' it was forcefully argued. The resistance continued for four days before the state government capitulated. Gradually, the treatment of the Red Flag prisoners improved, until, by June, they were no longer compelled to work forty-eight hours at mat and broom-making for sixpence per week. Instead, they passed their time 'reading, writing, studying and debating the issues of the day'. They wore their own clothing rather than prison garb and their food was provided by a Red Flag Prisoners Defence Committee, formed by sympathetic radicals outside the gaol. An interpreter was hired to censor their mail and weekly family visits were granted.[38]

The irrepressible revolutionaries were jubilant at their victory. Although 'four of our lads' were down with influenza, George Taylour wrote from 'His Majesty's State Hotel' to Pierce Carney of the Townsville AMIEU, ' . . . the spirit of the Reds is still as of old . . . the fight is on and we are up to our necks in it. Tell the lads not to forget that we are in here and let that knowledge spur them on . . . ' Addressing Harry Holland, in a similar vein in early June, Taylour continued:

> although it is a long time since the Albury Trials when Tom Mann and yourself were principals, the usual system of our enemies is still perpetuated, even in a Labour [sic] State. It is quite apparent that we here in Queensland have no Webbs, Hollands or Brookfields in the Labour Party . . . [Yet] there is a movement on foot for Prison Reform in Brisbane and as you have been a victim of the system (which operates against working agitators) . . . I would be very pleased if you could give me any information regarding the Prison system in Maroiland [sic], it is I believe a lot [more] advanced than ours . . .

Even in gaol, it seemed the agenda of agitation was never abandoned. The British-Australian prisoners mounted a campaign for prison reform, and, following their hunger strike, the Russians too became active spreading revolutionary propaganda. Bykov's writings on freedom of thought and political struggle 'simply smothered the gaol . . . and it was three months later that the authorities caught him red-handed'.[39]

Yet outside the prison walls, an enforced torpor had descended upon Brisbane's radical sects. Initially, the BIC had shown some fight by reviving, on Friday evening, 28 March, the leftwing vigilante organisation of the 1916 conscription campaign – the Labour Volunteer Army (LVA). This body had formerly been 'very efficient in proving that the quarrelsome soldier element could not bully townspeople', reported the *Daily Standard*. Men attending this meeting were urged 'to purchase firearms' and fight for 'the freedom of all militant organizations'. By the next morning, 320 had been enrolled. Anticipating a clash between the LVA and returned soldiers, Commandant Irving ordered the formation of a 'guard for military arms and ammunition' and the call-up of additional personnel for a 'limited period of home service'. Yet such moves proved unnecessary. At Commissioner Urquhart's urgings, Acting Premier Theodore met with BIC officials and ordered them 'to desist from such action'. Consequently, little more was heard of the LVA. Urquhart's recalcitrance was also to prevail when Theodore attempted to enrol 2,000 special constables on 26 March, to combat any resurgence of loyalist violence. The Commissioner argued that, as the BIC was supporting this move, he was too 'suspicious of [the] source they [ie the 'specials'] would be drawn from.' Urquhart flatly refused the Acting Premier's request, at the same time grumbling about 'the lack of cooperation' between Cabinet and his Police Department – and Theodore capitulated to his demands.[40]

A fortnight later, the battered Brisbane 'Soviet' elected a new executive, which promised further demonstrations of protest. Such bravado, however, was to little avail. As Peter Simonoff remarked, upon his release from Darlinghurst in mid-July, 'I was thunderstruck with the complete chaos in our organization and the arrest of our comrades.' The Russians now found themselves far too preoccupied with the immediate problem concerning their livelihood to agitate for political ideals. Concerted campaigns of job dismissal, boycott and eviction had severely affected their already precarious economic security, introducing prolonged hardship. Russians employed at Darra, Rocklea, Cannon Hill, Pinkenba and Ipswich were summarily dismissed. In the meatworks and railway yards, and on the wharves, canefields, farms and mining fields of Queensland, the situation was precisely the same. 'Bitter feeling existed in the North against these aliens', noted Captain Wills in May. Although the Hampden Mining Company, near Cloncurry, had advertised for five hundred workers, no aliens were wanted, 'which means the biggest field for employment in the North is closed to these individuals'. Another two hundred Russians were unemployed at Townsville and 'getting very desperate'. 'Since the Brisbane upheaval, they find it impossible to get work of any kind,' Wills reported. 'Their sole subsistence is the Government ration of 10/- per week . . . The stress of poverty is very acute.' Similarly, from Bingera Plains, near Bundaberg, the spokesman of the Russian community of forty-one pleaded with the Acting Prime Minister: 'hasten our departure without driving us to despair. Soon there will be no course left for us but to go to Local Authorities and ask them to gaol us . . . let us go from this Babylon prison. We will spend our last money and very soon face family starvation . . . Let us go from Australia to the old contry [sic] . . .'⁴¹

On 9 April, the BIC petitioned the Queensland government to halt the 'dismissal of foreigners merely because of their nationality', but discovered, several days later, that this very policy was being implemented by the state-run Labour Bureau in Brisbane. Acting Premier Theodore bluntly told a Russian delegation on 25 April 'he could not alter the recent regulation prohibiting the employment of unnaturalized aliens'. Furthermore, he would not intervene to halt the eviction of Russians from their homes, beyond providing them with 'tents and flys' for temporary accommodation. The Russian responded, 'We are not going to live in tents in cold and damp weather like this, especially with families of six or eight children . . . we demand houses like any other citizens . . . ' Their consequent determination 'not to leave the houses until forced into the street by the landlords' met with little outside support. In early May, the Brisbane Censor remarked upon the prevailing 'antipathy of the general public against the Russians and the sympathy with the soldiers in the action taken . . . ' A Russian relief committee formed to help compatriots in material need found that any money orders, issued in the name of the Russian Workers Association, were automatically rendered void. In Brisbane, 'everyone remained deaf and dumb' to its pleas, the committee noted. 'The only people who responded were those living in the country.'⁴²

In desperation, on 18 June 1919, four members of the Brisbane Soviet, P. Shohnovsky, T. Kislica, G. Tocaroff and A. Melcharek, addressed a long appeal to 'the People's Commissary of the Russian Socialist Federative Republic of Soviets', V. Ulianoff — that is, to Lenin himself. Since before the war, they wrote, the casual employment of Russians in Australia had always meant only 'a bare living and no chances of any savings'. During the war period, Russian Consul D'Abaza's policy of 'enlist or starve' had brought much renewed suffering. And, since November 1917, the émigrés' unanimous adoption of 'the revolutionary programme of Bolshevism' had doubled their hardships:

> On several occasions we attempted to defend the principles of the social revolution, that were being misrepresented by the reactionary press, by making the public demonstrations where we tried to show to the people of Australia the good will of the Russian social revolution towards the toiling masses of the world, with the assistance of our Australian comrades. But since the procession of March 23, 1919, which brought about the disturbances and pogroms on the Russian Workers Association and Russians in general, our hardships became quite unbearable. Fourteen Russians are arrested and put into different State prisons where, in each case, the prisoners had to declare a hunger strike in order to obtain just comparatively human treatment.

Additionally, both Zuzenko and his wife, Civa had been 'forcibly taken' and separately deported, they knew not where. Furthermore, they informed Lenin:

> The State Government of Queensland refused to recognize us as citizens and given [sic] special instructions to the Labour Bureau not to employ the Russians at the Government Works. Position is unbearable. We have put into the labour press several protests . . . demanding free deportation to Russia and also we sent several telegramms [sic] of protest to the Federal Government asking for a permission to leave Australia, but up to the present time we did not receive any answer. The local press continues to agitate against us as undesirable.

They appealed to Lenin to mediate with the British government for their release and repatriation. 'We understand that for the class-consciencious [sic] workers it is better to remain where they are and help the Revolution in Russia be explained', they concluded, 'but our presence here brings now rather negative results, because unpreparedness of the workers of Australia and its reactionary press at our expense prolongs the excessive expression of patriotism and emperialism [sic] keeping the masses in ignorance of social movements in Europe.' If the Soviet government would only grant free passages to those unable to pay, they promised, the repatriates, who were 'all working people, accustomed to any work', would pledge themselves 'to pay the expense . . . by personal exertion in any way the Soviet

Government will find it necessary'. Vladimir Ilyich Lenin was never destined to read their entreaties, however. The petition had been handed to the Dutch Consul in Brisbane for transmission to Russia, via the government of Holland. The Consul, considering it to be 'a breach of etiquette . . . to forward the letter in question', conveyed it, instead, to Brigadier-General Irving, for action by the Commonwealth Department of Defence.[43]

As the Russians' plight became critical and the other radical movements languished, the loyalist mobilisation passed from strength to strength. The full panoply of loyalism was displayed, for instance, on Tuesday evening, 8 April, when leading Brisbane citizens mounted a stage at the Exhibition Hall, decorated with the pennants and shields of Bullecourt, Messines, Zeebrugge and Jutland. The audience was packed with returned soldiers and other patriotic citizens, flanked by 'grey clad war nurses'. The meeting had been endorsed by the Queensland Justices Association, the Mayor informed them, and he was there himself to assert that there was only one remedy to their present difficulties: 'Eradication or deportation'. 'If this vermin was not got rid of', added John Ambrose Walsh, a prominent Brisbane solicitor, 'there would be a revolution − a revolution that would be to the honour of the British Constitution − a revolution at the ballot box.' 'Purge out the rebels now distracting our land', chorused the Queensland Congregational Union, two days later. Even the previously impartial Queensland Governor, Hamilton Goold-Adams, entered the lists as an anti-Bolshevik crusader at a demonstration arranged by the Royal Society of St George in late April. 'It had now been shown to be necessary for those of English blood to be up and doing', Goold-Adams declared, unequivocally, to loud applause, ' . . . and no-one could find fault with any of them that were determined that the constitution should not be thrown aside and torn to shreds and patches.'[44]

In the meantime, the RSSILA's mobilisation of returned soldiers was also proceeding apace. On Sunday afternoon, 6 April, in response to news that the Labour Volunteer Army might be reforming, war veterans gathered at the Exhibition Grounds to organise a private army of their own. Two thousand men gained admission upon displaying their RSSILA badges and discharge certificates to hear their President, Pearce Douglas, assure them that 'as soldiers they had gained the right of issuing

Loyalist Concert and Demonstration

(His Worship the MAYOR OF BRISBANE presiding)

At the Organ: Mr. VICTOR GALWAY, Mus. Bac.

The Artistes include: Mrs. S. B. HARRIS, Miss NORRIS, Miss LENA HAMMOND; Messrs. LONGBOTTOM, W. T. DOWN and WISHART.

TO-NIGHT - - APRIL 8th.
CONCERT 7 to 8 p.m.

At 8 p.m. various speakers (including Returned Soldiers) will propose the following motions :—

1. "That this Meeting of the Citizens of Queensland fully endorses the actions of the Returned Soldiers and Sailors' Imperial League and pledges itself to loyally support the soldiers in all lawful efforts to suppress disloyalty and ensure just treatment to Returned Soldiers, and, whilst congratulating the Federal Government on the action which it is now taking, is further of the opinion that such action must be complete and continuous in order to rid the community of the present evil."

2. "That, in the opinion of this Meeting of the Citizens of Queensland, it is the imperative duty of the Federal and State Governments within the ambit of their respective powers, to take immediate proceedings against all persons who have acted in any manner disloyal to King and Empire or who have committed any breach of the War Precautions Act or Regulations, either by the display of prohibited flags or otherwise."

3. "That these resolutions be forwarded to the proper authorities urging prompt action."

GOD SAVE THE KING.

Papers relating to demonstrations in Brisbane in March 1919, subsequent prosecutions and related matter, known as "Red Flag Incident" (Jan)1919-1920(Feb), 8 April 1919 (*Australian Archives*: BP4/1, 66/4/3660) manifestoes to the Government'. The men were then divided into eight district divisions by Major Bolingbroke, the League's 'chief advisor'. Each division of this 'Army to Fight Bolshevism' (AFB), covering the entire Brisbane area, then selected a commander and four non-commissioned officers to lead them. The names, addresses and occupations of all participants were recorded 'so as if they were wanted in a hurry, they could be called upon'. Instructions, objectives and meeting places were next discussed. Similar country divisions were also forming, they were told. The South Brisbane division, under Major Hart, was ordered to report to Musgrave Park the following weekend for drill practice; the North Brisbane group was to assemble near the Boys' Grammar School 'in cases of emergency'.[45]

Thus, with 'alacrity and military precision', the first of Australia's secret armies – those shadowy and prolific vigilante organisations of the inter-war years – was launched as a direct outcome of the Red Flag riots. Four days later, a fighting fund to 'exterminate' Bolshevism was opened and, in several weeks, £15,000 had been subscribed by anonymous donors. 'The "Diggers" are marching!' enthused the journal of the Returned Soldiers and Citizens Political Federation (RSCPF) now simply called *The Leader*. And the 'marching orders' of this anti-Bolshevik throng would surely save Queensland from 'the market of free love' and 'the rule of the wild beast'.

> Bolshevism shall not rule us!
> IWW shall not rule us!
> . . . We are going over the top!
> Diggers, fall in!

Commissioner Urquhart's painful wound, however, had left him less comfortable about the wisdom of vigilante armies of any nature. On 7 April, he demanded to know 'whether the enrolment . . . of men along military lines is an infringement of Sect. 118 of *The Commonwealth Defence Act of 1903?*' Yet a query to the Crown Solicitor disclosed, five days later, that no such breach had occurred; and the Defence Department, apparently, was never approached upon the matter.[46]

There the issue rested; for, by late April, Urquhart's attention was diverted once more towards the left, when he discovered that the IWW-inspired Builders' Union (the ABIEU) and the remaining Russian Bolsheviks once more intended carrying red flags, in the Eight Hour Day procession on 5 May. Any such display, he warned, will 'undoubtedly result in riot and turmoil,

Another skeleton escapes (*Worker*, 10 April 1919)

besides which anything which has hitherto occurred in Brisbane will be a mere bagatelle'. Over subsequent days, both Commandant Irving and Sub-Inspector Short echoed his alarm; while, from Captain Wills, came the disturbing news that northern revolutionaries (principally from Cloncurry) intended 'getting armed' and carrying the red flag through Townsville streets on May Day. If interfered with, Wills warned, they planned using force: 'they thought by this means that it would act as a signal for a general revolt throughout Queensland'. The qualms of Urquhart, Irving, Short and Wills were soon conveyed to the officers of the anti-Bolshevik Army, and, in a series of 'secret' meetings, called by 'unsigned advertisements in the Tory press', the private divisions were rapidly mobilised to discuss tactics for 5 May.[47]

They were working 'in conjuction with the Commonwealth Intelligence Department', recruits were told, and if the red flag or any 'substitute' was carried in the May Day march, 'it is our duty to attack it'. At one such meeting of the Fortitude Valley division at Earl's Court Picture Palace, New Farm, on Wednesday evening, 30 April, Captain Gray advised the two hundred present to be 'thoroughly organized' for 5 May. They were to gather at 8 o'clock that morning at the Soldiers' Residential Club in Wharf Street, wearing white arm bands. Some four thousand war veterans were expected to participate, and those who were trade unionists would actually join the procession. The rest 'would be allotted to their various positions under officers'. They would mingle with the crowd and 'when any Bolshevism or any they deemed "disloyal" appeared, they could soon be together'. Furthermore, all along the march route, naval 'squabbles' (i.e. signallers) with flags would be 'posted on the high buildings'. These would remain 'all in touch with one another' and 'would signal from any point where soldiers were required'. 'I am not going to tell you to carry revolvers', Gray remarked: 'If you do that, you do it yourselves, but there are some handy things about as long as that (he illustrated the length by showing the measurement across the four fingers of his clenched hand). These weapons . . . [had] been used elsewhere with tremendous results . . . [and were] found to be extremely dangerous . . . ' If drastic action were necessary, another officer intimated, 'a little more than sand-bags and sticks would come into play'. 'What about ammunition?' a returned soldier asked Gray, but he made no response. 'What about supplies?' the question was then rephrased. 'There are plenty of supplies,' Gray assured him. He would like to say more, he explained, but there might be 'spies' in the audience.

'We shall be there waiting and go right into it again if the Military wants us', an enthusiastic soldier informed Military Censorship on 1 May. Yet, just how fanciful was this assertion by the 'secret committee' of the AFB that Military Intelligence had actively solicited their aid? Such a question is perhaps best answered by the Military Commandant himself — for the towering figure of Brigadier-General Irving was present 'in mufti' on the morning of 5 May to address the vigilantes, assembled in their divisional ranks under the command of Major Bolingbroke. 'It is an excellent idea of the League to have the men divided into districts,' Irving told them:

> In case a necessity arose, you would be of great assistance to me. In fact I had, after the recent trouble in Merivale St., certain information given to me through Army Reserve Officers and *I would have been able, had the emergency arisen, to send out to the districts . . . and ask for assistance.* I know the men are loyal to me and I thoroughly appreciate the district scheme . . .

Following this frank endorsement, a voice from the ranks asked him, 'Say three hundred men at least carry rebel flags, Sir, can the Authorities gaol such a number?' 'We do not want to see any extremist take the law into his own hands,' Irving replied. '*Any piece of red bunting waved is objectionable.*'[48]

The naval scouts and military vigilantes assumed their positions on the taller rooftops, in the waiting crowd and among the processionists; but there was little that was 'objectionable' to challenge them. With so many Brisbane revolutionaries imprisoned or interned, the threatened renewal of soldier violence was enough to cow what remained of the local left into submission. The Brisbane labour movement effectively censored itself. Even the huge red banner, with three large golden '8's emblasoned upon it, which traditionally led the procession, made no appearance that year. Instead, more than one thousand returned soldiers were allowed to swamp the march, which seemed more like another Anzac Day procession than any symbolic expression of working class solidarity. A 'uniformed warrior', carrying the commonwealth flag, led the parade and was followed by row upon row of 'war-scarred men in quartet formation, swinging to the step of march music, their brass medals and batallion colours standing out conspicuously'. Behind them came loyalist 'ladies' waving Union Jacks; all were 'heartily cheered' by the street spectators. In contrast, any labour display (such as the giant torch featuring the motto 'Keep the Union Spirit Burning') was received 'in cold silence'. Almost hidden among all the loyalist pageantry, one forlorn calico banner petitioned the unsympathetic crowd to 'Remember the Red Flag Prisoners: Help their Wives and Children'. The banner was white — only the appeal upon it was lettered in red. There were also a few conspicuous red streamers about, the *Daily Mail* complained, which would have been better 'cut out'.[49]

And so a 'cleansed' May Day march passed on its way, leaving an emasculated Queensland labour movement in its wake. On the rooftops, the naval sentinels laid down their signalling flags while, in the streets below, 'secret army' recruits left their revolvers and other weaponry concealed to applaud their fellow marchers. This 'orderly and striking pageant', extolled by the *Brisbane Courier* next morning, certainly bore no resemblance to the bloody and abandoned rout which Merivale Street had hosted some six weeks previously. But a rout it had been nevertheless, and not a fist, broken bottle, 'jam tin' bomb or paling had been brandished in anger.

Conclusion

Militants are Hard to Kill

They will never fly the red flag in Brisbane again, or any other rebel flag.

Major Bolingbroke

We know that in the near future, the red flag of freedom . . . will once again float from the flagstaffs and the homes of the proletariat . . . Get wise. Unite.

Red Flag Prisoners' letter[1]

If one were seeking to attach a tidy finale to the Red Flag crisis period, the opening weeks of May 1919 would seem an appropriate time to locate it. For, even as loyalist returned soldiers overwhelmed the Labour Day procession of 5 May, another drama was unfolding itself which would soon clear the streets entirely. Despite every quarantine precaution, the tell-tale signs of 'Spanish' influenza — shivering, racking debility and, often, a 'plum-coloured' tinge upon the skin — were beginning to display themselves among the local population. On 1 May, the first influenza death was reported from Lytton, near Moreton Bay, and during the next fortnight, another seven hundred cases of infection were notified. Soon, the heart of Brisbane seemed 'absolutely dead' as the epidemic wreaked its havoc. Stores were deserted and schooling abandoned. Any place 'where persons regularly or occasionally congregate or assemble for worship, education, meeting, amusement, entertainment, dancing, physical culture or athletics' was closed down. All open-air gatherings were assiduously shunned. The fear of Bolshevism, so skilfully sustained, now yielded to a more intimate and tangible terror and the anti-radical crusade retired behind gauze masks and locked doors.[2]

Yet such a neatly structured ending contradicts the more disorderly processes of historical change. At its worst, this gloomy hiatus, stretching from May to July, hospitalising thousands and killing hundreds, merely inhibited the spread of conflict. Loyalist forces continued to enrol recruits. The RSCPF

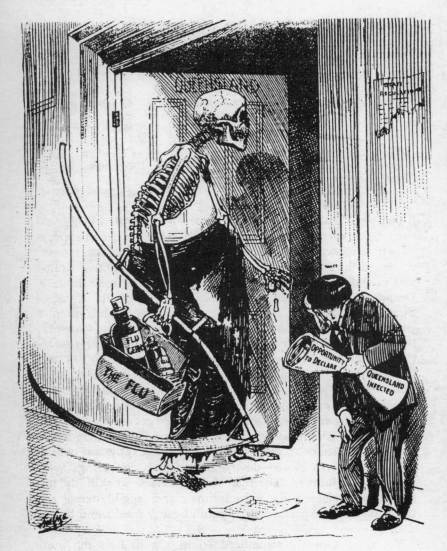

At last (*Worker*, 8 May 1919)

To Our Readers.

MANIFESTO

The Returned Soldiers & Citizens' Political Federation.

(QUEENSLAND DIVISION.)

Head Office, Darragh's Buildings,
Queensland Street, Brisbane.

Fellow Citizens, —

With the passing of the World War, those who have fought and worked for the overthrow of autocracy and for the triumph of Right and Justice are now asked to rally round the banner of true Citizenship with view of obtaining for our Country a Government of the People, for the People by the People.

For this purpose the Interstate Conference of Soldiers' Political Parties resolved upon the formation of the Returned Soldiers' and Citizens' Political Federation, which now links up the Commonwealth with Federal and State Platforms, based upon common objectives.

The Returned Soldiers' and Citizens' Political Federation is building on sound foundations, the first principle of which is service in the interest of the whole community.

This Organisation is out for a square deal to the returned man.

It is pledged to a distinctly non-party platform, which aims at the overthrow of the present pernicious party system.

It is neither Liberal nor Labour.

It has no associations with any other political organisation.

It is playing a lone hand for clean, impartial politics.

It stands for the same principle for which our men have fought and died — Right, Justice and Progress.

To our Readers (*The Leader*, 1 June 1919)

journal, *The Leader*, already with 9000 subscribers, claimed a 150 per cent readership increase and expanded its size to thirty pages. Yet this organisation was soon eclipsed by the RSSILA, which had played such a key role in the riots, rallies and loyalist ceremonies. Sixty-eight sub-branches 'fearlessly' endorsed the League's campaign against the radicals. More ex-soldiers enroll-ed over the next three months than during the previous year. As its ranks swelled by almost 3,700, its President, Pearce Douglas, jovially complained that expansion was so rapid, 'badges cannot be supplied in sufficient numbers'. The clashes had 'done more to unite the soldiers than years of organizing would have ac-complished', the RSSILA admitted, as it consolidated its rightward political direction.[3]

Dr Sandford Jackson's ULE also continued to gather adherents prepared to fight Bolshevism to the bitter end. By May, it had reconstituted itself under the grander title of the King and Empire Alliance (KEA), and now represented one hundred patriotic organisations. In July, it received the fillip of endorse-ment from Lord Jellicoe, First Sea Lord of the Admiralty, visiting Australia to promote closer Imperial bonds. Its inflexibly 'loyal and righteous' pose did not, of course, seduce everyone. In late 1919, for instance, Military Intelligence paid a call upon a For-titude Valley herbalist who had ridiculed the KEA as a 'tinpot . . . Tory show', full of 'clap-trap' ideas. Yet, with more than 70,000 members at its mid-year peak, the KEA must have extended its influence through virtually every level of Queensland society, securing its base among the 'respectable' lower middle class, the small proprietor, the self-employed and the white collar worker. In size, it was by far the largest and most rapidly constituted voluntary mobilisation of citizens in Queensland's history. A fair impression of the KEA's immensity is gained when it is com-pared with the entire trade union movement of Queensland at that time (some 87,000 members in 102 unions) – a membership accumulated over forty years of exhaustive activism.[4]

In March 1920, precisely one year after the riots had begun, the KEA was still protesting against the 'very large number' of Russians disseminating disloyalty across the state. 'We are press-ing for all we are worth with the authorities . . . for their removal,' the Alliance noted. 'We know that the contamination of these Russians with British workers is carried on largely and in most insidious ways.' Within several months, with the elec-tion of the Storey Labor Government in New South Wales in

April, the KEA, under the command of Major-General Sir Charles Rosenthal, was established in this state also. Like its Queensland prototype, it sought to have a 'formidable striking force' at the ready if required; its secret army appurtenances, which soon captured the imagination of D.H. Lawrence, were organised by Major Jack Scott.[5]

The fascist ingredients of loyalist vigilantism, patriotic outrage combined with quasi-military discipline, were to provide an alluring formula. In early July 1919, General Sir Cyril Brudenell White, eulogised by C.E.W. Bean and described by Sir John Monash as 'far and away the ablest soldier Australia has ever produced', returned to his home state of Queensland. At a welcoming dinner, organised by the KEA on 11 July, White spoke of tightening 'the bonds of loyalty' and never allowing them to 'degenerate'. Several years later, in 1923, the general organised the White Guard in Melbourne, a paramilitary auxiliary to the state's strike control forces. This secret loyalist guard may well have been modelled on Brisbane's Army to Fight Bolshevism (AFB) of 1919.[6]

An element which linked Queensland's RSSILA and KEA, as well as Brisbane's AFB, with the Scott–Rosenthal secret force in New South Wales and the White Guard in Victoria was the evident appeal of proto-fascism. One of its sturdier roots can be traced to the warfront trenches. As Barrington Moore Jr comments upon the 'Nazi conception of people's community' in interwar Germany: 'The main content of the notion has its roots in an idealized recollection of life in the trenches, contrasted with the disappointments of civilian existence. Life in the trenches purportedly was one of comradeship and mutual support, not one of anonymity and cutthroat individualistic competition.'[7]

This nostalgia for a system of manly association and military discipline stirred the spirit of the Australian returned soldier at least as much as the German. 'In his heart there is a yearning for the old military system, which made life so hard and yet so easy', admitted one Queensland war veteran in April 1919. Confronted by a society bewilderingly different from the one they had left – a society which itself had been harshly transformed by the rigours of warfare – ex-soldiers fumbled for both explanations and solutions to their sudden disillusionment. With peace had come poverty for many a returned warrior, wrote another Queensland veteran, threatening to reduce those comrades 'to flotsam and jetsam on the dark shores of life's dreary river'. So,

The new offensive (*Aussie*, 15 April 1920)

he plaintively asked, 'Why not peace with organization?' 'King's Army regulations' were altogether 'more wonderful even than the Bible,' he recalled. 'They allow for everything and provide organization for everything. What a pity the better part of war organization is not used in times of peace . . . [where] effort and service counted most . . . Why cannot the bands play, the people march in ceremonial orders and have carnivals to enliven peace, *so that it works.*'[8]

Such militaristic idealism chafed against high unemployment, rampant inflation, industrial turmoil, uncomprehending families and all the social and psychological readjustments to civilian life the returning soldier now had to negotiate. In the freezing trenches of 1917, writes Paul Fussell, 'cold, tired and terrified' men had dreamed very different dreams about the nature of that homecoming. In their fantasies they had embraced the simple securities of home life or basked in the heat of a 'broiling' tropical sun. For Australian, and particularly Queensland troops, these yearnings meshed into a sanctification of the good life, on a homefront of 'shining Southern beaches/ where the warm Pacific breaks'. Such inflated expectations had crumpled dramatically against the harsh realities of that homefront. Anticipating some perpetual Eden, the men had returned instead to post-war Brisbane, where unemployed men trudged the streets in hundreds, vainly seeking work; where an inflation rate approaching 15 per cent gave them 'shell-out shock'; and where conspicuous aliens and revolutionaries preached the downfall of the world order they had battled to defend. Instead of the easy security they had craved, they discovered there were now fresh campaigns of survival to be fought. Faced with this impasse, they gathered strength by resurrecting the virtues of military order and 'digger' camaraderie from the very trenches they had hungered to leave.[9]

'Imagine that the Aussie Nation is the Aussie Army', a popular soldiers' magazine suggested earlier in 1920:

> Your State is the Divvie, your suburb or district is the Battalion. Your Member of Parliament is the Orderly Officer . . . Don't allow that loyalty and comradeship and national pride that you learnt on the Battlefield to be lost. Sixty thousand of your cobbers died for it, thousands more have suffered terribly for it and many are still suffering . . . Make your splendid old ESPRIT DE CORPS into a still more splendid ESPRIT DE NATION.

This well-regulated Arcadia evokes 'an imaginary return to the security of the family, of childhood, if not even the womb'. For here, it is fondly believed, 'all the quarrels, pains and uncertainty that are part of life in every society . . . will . . . vanish to be replaced by the comradeship of affectionate, trusting relationships'. The route to this El Dorado was signposted simply and beguilingly – rightwing formulae for change were virtually bereft of complex socio-economic analyses of inequality or injustice. Instead, their impulsive plan was to solve problems simply by rooting out all apparent 'evil and pollution'. Just as the injustices of capitalism were attributed to the evil 'profiteer', so too, the ills of social instability were blamed upon the contaminating alien and revolutionary. If these polluters were tracked down 'in a manly, "old fashioned" way', it was argued, 'the unpolluted could live happily ever afterwards in a "people's community" '.[10]

The radical dissemblers were merely 'squibs' who could be easily dealt with by 'a good crack under the chin', stated Major Russell of the RSSILA. Their ideals were 'mad, fanatical . . . piffle . . . absolute tripe'. If a social atmosphere 'polluted with such pro-Hun utterances' was rigorously purified, other soldiers reasoned, then people could breathe easily one more. Once the Bolshevik 'disease' was eradicated, predicted the KEA, Queensland would become 'the happy and contented country which it should be'. Addressing the problem of a 14.2 per cent unemployment rate, Corporal Thorpe promised cheering soldiers, 'If all aliens were cleared out of Queensland there would not be one unemployed man walking about'; and, if all their radical cohorts joined them, added 'Digger Dick' expansively, the outcome must inevitably be 'happy homes for the people'.[11]

Idealised warfront formulations thus blended with grimmer trench-life solutions – the solutions of the violent sortie, the frontal attack, the bloody enemy clearance. Future hopes masked intenser hatreds, which could be rapidly converted into destructive action. This hatred, as the events of 1919 demonstrated, was easily aroused and precisely targeted. Its wellsprings lay in 'the dissonances and humiliations' of war for, to quote Eric Leed, the veterans' 'grievances were universal because their sufferings had been unimaginable'. Psychologically, stated one returning digger, 'We are not the same men who went away . . . We are entirely different men.' 'Something had altered in them,' observed war correspondent Philip Gibbs. 'They were subject to queer moods and queer tempers . . . Many were easily moved to passion when they lost control of themselves; many were bitter in their speech, violent in opinion, frightening . . . ' He did not know how to deal with such men, admitted Mackay's police magistrate, after a soldiers' riot there in mid-April. Their minds seemed so over-excited that they quickly 'lost their heads'. Some of his comrades had 'returned mentally deficient as a result of the trials they had suffered', warned an RSSILA member a week later. 'It only requires the least trouble for these men to cause bloodshed.'[12]

Once unleashed, the inclination of such violence was protofascist rather than insurrectionary; its target the weak and powerless, the scapegoated outsider and the isolated, socially unpopular agitator. In short, it took the form of 'oppressor's violence directed against the victim'. As Barrington Moore Jr points out, rightist popular movements 'do display a strong tendency to select weak targets – or, in plainer language, to destroy the weak and helpless'. When, conversely, leftist force was released, its method, usually was 'not the pogrom'. Instead, its conventional targets were 'the symbols and embodiments of oppressive power: kings, aristocrats, government officials, men of power and substance generally'. The glorified, or at least, socially sanctioned aggression of the Australian ex-soldier almost invariably took a rightwing political deviation.[13]

Unlike conscript troops, who had a clearer mandate to blame the system which had consigned them forcibly to the firing line, members of that uniquely volunteer force, the AIF, tended to vent their post-war spleen against unpopular 'outgroups' – the foreign migrant, the pacifist 'shirker', and the anti-war radical. The Brisbane Red Flag riots were a classic example of this propensity. Incidents in Townsville in May, Brisbane again in October, Proserpine in November and Charleville in December 1919 provided further confirmation. Red Flag violence carried 'no flavor of novelty', asserted *Labor Call* in early April. 'In almost as many words . . . the soldiers were urged forcibly to prevent the holding of anti-conscription meetings and of peace demonstrations . . . [F]rom amongst the returned soldiers, the reactionaries wish to raise the Australian Black Hundreds [ie: counter-revolutionary vigilantes in Csarist Russia].'[14]

The forging of rightwing vigilante alliances between ex-soldiers and 'reactionary' civilians, however, cannot be attributed solely to military indoctrination and warfront experiences. Even though that exposure had allowed soldiers to experience 'living *outside* class, but in ranks', war's impact upon the homefront had, if anything, sharpened class awareness and magnified class antagonisms. As Armageddon lumbered on, loyalism had become increasingly a matter of ruling-class directive and middle-class duty. From these social ranks, either as leaders or followers, the loyalist vigilantes had sprung. Their willingness to resort to extra-legal activism – carried potentially to the same point as the German *Einwohnerwehr* (the arming of civilian volunteers as a local security force) – dovetailed neatly with the soldiers' rancour and miltancy.[15]

As ruling groups feel the reins of hegemonic power slipping from their grasp, they quickly resort to coercive measures to defend their interests. In Gramscian terms, 'ruling groups resort to force when their hegemony breaks down or when it has not yet been established'. The conscription fights, the disillusioning latter stages of the war and the insecurities of post-war reconstruction had all placed the ruling class under incredible stress. Furthermore, the survival of a vigorously reformist Labor government in Queensland had increasingly denied these men the corridors of power. Their obstructionist controls in the Upper House were gradually being pruned away, just as their economic privileges were being whittled down by more equitable Arbitration awards, state-run enterprises and threateningly uniform land-tax reforms. Even the powerful conservative press was gamely challenged in Queensland by a pugnacious leftwing alternative.[16]

Especially after mid-1918, the warfront enemy lost its potency as a serious external menace. A commensurate internal threat seemed necessary to maintain loyal allegiances. Thus loyalist leaders sought to build a popular base upon a groundswell of outrage against the 'Bolshevik monster', even if this meant recruitment in the streets, the discharge depots and returned soldier club rooms. To some, this Bolshevik conspiracy embraced the Labor Government itself, and the ultimate goal of agitation was not simply the intimidation of a few thousand Russians, but a recapturing of the state apparatus. It is no mere coincidence that the three men, who, in March 1920, began organising the 'economic blockade' of Queensland among London loan merchants, had been embroiled just one year previously in the Red Flag agitations – Robert Philp and Alfred Cowley as patrons of the anti-Bolshevik ADU, and solicitor John Ambrose Walsh who had displayed himself even more prominently upon the

COMMONWEALTH OF AUSTRALIA.

PRIME MINISTER.

Fellow-Citizens

By your votes to-day you will decide
the future of Australia. Prussian militarism has
been defeated but those disloyal & Bolshevik
sections within our gates who did everything
to hamstring recruiting & to disrupt and destroy
the Empire during the war now seek to
befool the people in order to effect their
disloyal and destructive purposes.

Australia stands at the cross-roads.
Which path will you tread? That is the
great question which by your votes you
will this day decide.

I ask you to follow the party that
led you during the war: that party that
stands for a free Australia within the Empire
for sound finance: for just and capable
government for all irrespective of class or creed.
& for a bold progressive policy which will
give employment to the workers deal
effectively with the profiteers & ensure prosperity
to this great Commonwealth.

Yours truly

W. M. Hughes

Letter from W.M. Hughes (*Brisbane Courier*, 13 December 1919) loyalist hustings. Others tended to blame Trades Hall 'for this and all kindred happenings' and to hope that loyalist agitation would strike at 'the root of the Industrial or Bolshevik plant here' by curbing the power of 'the Industrial Council Bosses'.[17]

Yet many more directly feared the counter-hegemonic threat posed by the revolutionaries themselves. It was not for nothing that the Nationalist Government had placed Military Intelligence, Censorship, the SIB and the commonwealth police all on their tail. As Verity Burgmann notes, 'Ruling classes, unlike historians, have not generally been in doubt about the importance of agitators.' Though the militants' numbers may have been comparatively few, their strategical influence was potentially great. For they not only articulated workers' grievances with daring and flamboyance, they also channelled those grievances towards creative social alternatives. 'It is always an activist minority that promotes . . . new standards of condemnation', observes Barrington Moore Jr:

> They are an indispensable if insufficient cause of major social transformations . . . Their task is to find and articulate latent grievances, to challenge the dominant mythology, to organize for a contest with the dominant forces around them. The outside agitators do the hard work of undermining the old sense of inevitability. They are also the travelling salesmen for the new inevitability . . . [18]

Thus, to the loyalists generally, Bolshevism in Queensland seemed powerful, deeply entrenched and hydra-headed. In fighting it down and out, no tactic seemed too extreme or illegitimate. Did it really matter if they behaved 'unconstitutionally', Major Bolingbroke had asked his cheering followers. The Constitution needed 'a bit of ginger' injected into it in any case. The self-confidence and ease with which American vigilante solutions were adopted by civilian as well as ex-soldier suggest a long tradition of similar activism, stretching well beyond the Hughenden purge of October 1918. Stretching back, perhaps, to the armed frontier 'posses' which had progressively decimated Queensland's Aboriginal population, or the larrikin mobs of urban rioters who had intermittently harassed non-European migrants – the Chinese, Melanesian, Cingalese and Malays. The tradition also encompassed that constellation of forces which had provided strike-breakers, special constables or militia to counter worker demands in times of industrial crisis: the 1860s , the 1890s and the 1910s.[19]

In mid-May 1919, this older vigilante wave had broken

momentarily against the new, when a group of pastoralists, substantial farmers, businessmen and returned soldiers met secretly at Toogoolawah in the upper Brisbane Valley to answer the anti-Bolshevik call. In response to a warning from Major Bolingbroke that a Bolshevik 'rising' was imminent in Brisbane, 'Tory squatter' E.F. Lord of Eskdale station revived his Legion of Frontiersmen whom he had led previously into the capital to help crush the 1912 general strike. 'We are behind you to a man', Lord assured Bolingbroke. When the SOS was received from Brisbane, the mounted men would assemble at a predetermined place and he would command them. The fact that Lord and his new 'Frontiersmen' ultimately did not ride — for no 'rising' was contemplated by the beleaguered radicals — seems less significant than the certainty that the vigilantes were again ready and willing to do so whenever required.[20]

The cast of mind which bound loyalist civilian and ex-soldier inflexibly to the one cause was not simply motivated by perceptions of economic self-interest, although economic fears arising from tense job competition or presentiments of social revolution no doubt played their significant part. But such anxieties were subsumed by that simplistic sense of 'community' which achieves cohesiveness by rigorously targeting its putative enemies. Loyalism nourished a form of national identification which was Anglophile, monarchical and conservative, reinforced by powerful injections of chauvinism and xenophobia. It was, in short, as racist as it was reactionary, condemning Russian residents as much for their ethnicity as for their ideologies. Russians in the Red Flag procession of 23 March 1919 were 'showing their teeth like wild animals and dripping saliva', Malcolm Ellis later asserted confidently in the Melbourne High Court. Racism was a well-ingrained reflex, almost certain to invoke an uncritical, ratifying response, and in 1919 its resonances were abundant. The severity of the trauma inflicted upon the Russian émigré ghetto can best be understood by reflecting upon the explosive hatreds which triggered the loyalist backlash — hatreds which fused anti-revolutionary spectres with anti-foreigner ones. Such antipathies erupted when 'the outsiders, the foreign enemy' were freighted with the burden of all society's ills, and then attacked for their perfidy. Only their obliteration, it was confidently predicted, could eliminate social suffering.[21]

One further influence upon the self-assurance which infused loyalist activism needs to be mentioned. By 1919, the federal Na-

The affection nauseous (*Worker*, 2 October 1919)

tionalist government and private organisations shared a practically identical view of loyalism. Indeed, the commonwealth's executive actions represented loyalist intolerance writ large. During the war, its official processes had become more authoritarian, as it expanded the means of proscription and coercion, using agents, police, card files, censorship and propaganda 'to stamp out dissent and reduce social and cultural space to an absolute minimum'. Its prognosis of social danger was virtually synonymous with that of the vigilantes, and it recruited functionaries from their ranks. In condemning leftists and aliens, both shared a vocabulary of suspicion and misconception, adopting the same tones of hysteria and disgust. The government's official reaction to the Merivale Street rioting was clearly exonerative of the vigilantes. Revolutionaries must be countered, 'horse, foot and artillery', Prime Minister Hughes maintained; and, from London, he expressed himself as being unequivocally 'delighted to see' the way Australian soldiers had dealt with the Brisbane Bolsheviks. Simultaneously, his deputy, Acting Prime Minister Watt, had endorsed the agitation by explicit acts of internment and deportation, inflicted upon the soldiers' prey. It is not surprising then that loyalist mayhem seemed fully clothed in the robes of integrity.[22]

In the intense polarisation induced by the red scare, the middle ground proved to be the most unstable and treacherous of all. Though the Queensland Labor government gave every appearance of holding firm to it, as the local political world turned topsy-turvy, they too were pitched inexorably to the right. Their vocal condemnation of rioting reactionaries stopped short of the arrest and imprisonment of leading rightwing rabblerousers; they introduced no emergency measures to deal with quite extraordinary circumstances of social disturbance and victimisation. Parliament, in recess since late 1918, was not recalled and the riots were never debated within its walls. No special constables were enrolled; no leftwing defence committees were mobilised; no mass meetings were called; no political strikes encouraged. To the contrary, any worker initiatives were rapidly stifled, as trade union leaders prevaricated and acting Premier Theodore moved expeditiously to cooperate with Acting Prime Minister Watt.

To the radicals, Labor's reaction was 'a living disgrace', the sellout of an alliance forged through the bitter anti-conscription struggle. Yet to the government, that betrayal was pragmatic, a change of dancing partners to suit a new political tempo – a neat pirouette to the right, as post-war 'necessity' tapped it roughly on the shoulder. Its major concern lay in keeping matters orderly and holding on to power; and, in doing so, qualms about a loyalist backlash were at least equalled by qualms about a radical *putsch*. Indeed, evidence strongly suggests that, overreacting to indications of a worldwide spread of revolution, Laborites feared more the potential danger of their radical cohorts. In early October 1919, Theodore called for CIB lists of 'particularly virulent and dangerous men' in Queensland for increased police surveillance. Significantly, no loyalist identities were included in this broad coverage of 'Agitators and Propagandists'. Without exception, the hundreds indexed were from the radical left – socialists and pacifists, Wobblies and OBU advocates, Anglo-Australian and Russian Bolsheviks, Finns, Poles and German radicals. The Labor Government was unerringly reflecting rather than confronting the preoccupations of a society 'ripe for radical and racialist witchhunts'.[23]

In winking at the extreme right, in gaoling radicals for publicly displaying Labor's own official colour, in fudging the defence of vulnerable Russian residents, Theodore's Cabinet sanctioned the pogrom and validated the reactionary and antidemocratic forces in Queensland society. If, by so curbing revolutionary militancy, their intention was to defend moderate reform, their victory would prove to be a limited and ultimately Pyrrhic one. Just one year later, ruling-class loyalists, deftly wielding capitalism's 'proper weapons', would begin their successful campaign of bringing that reformist government (and, incidentally, the society that it governed) to its knees. To what extent their brazen triumphs in the Red Flag crisis had steeled them to their task is difficult to assess. Yet, as the historian, Tom Cochrane shows, the ruthless economic strategy of financial blockade would wrest a gradual and painful capitulation from Theodore. In the October 1920 state election, Labor's support fell by an alarming 5.91 per cent and ten seats were surrendered. The party would rally only slightly in 1923 and slip back again in 1926 as, one by one, its progressive initiatives were abandoned. If the Red Flag phase of 1917–20 reveals the shedding of a radical guise by Labor, then the years 1920–24, even more crucially, expose the loss of its reformist heart. To what kind of political husk was Premier Theodore referring when he unblushingly asked satisfied conservative parliamentarians in late 1923, ' "Do you admire us as we are, or as we were?" (Laughter).'[24]

By early 1919, the Queensland labour movement was clearly the most ideologically amorphous in Australia. On the one hand, the Parliamentary Labor Party (PLP) had retained its conservative wing, which elsewhere had hived off into Nationalist ranks during the conscription crisis. On the other, it had largely tolerated and sometimes aligned itself with its far left sectors, which elsewhere had suffered wartime repression. One end of the labour spectrum held state power while the other promoted its overthrow. Such unwieldy diversity no doubt carried the seed of imminent fratricide. Yet Labor's actions should not be seen as predetermined or unavoidable. Indeed, it seems fairly certain that, had T.J. Ryan been present as Premier, he would have handled the issue very differently. Ironically, the absent Premier was actually attending an International Socialist Conference in Amsterdam – along with Russian and German delegates – at the same time as the last Red Flag defendants were being sentenced in the Brisbane Magistrates Court. His return to Queensland in June coincided with the improvement of gaol conditions for the Red Flag prisoners and, for the first time, radical deputations canvassing the question of early release received a sympathetic hearing. Furthermore, the Premier explicitly stated that the War Precautions regulation, banning the flag, was not only unwise but 'as an infringement of Magna Charter [sic] . . . there were very grave doubts as to whether . . . [it] was valid'. Significantly, during the entire crisis, this was the first time that the regulation itself had been officially addressed as an oppressive rule which required testing. On 15 July Ryan's Full Court challenge against the regulation as 'ultra vires and unlawful' failed. However, the pressure he brought to bear upon Acting Prime Minister Watt for their early release allowed clemency to be extended to ten of the Red Flag prisoners four days later, as part of the Peace Celebrations. Ryan's functionalist attitude – that undue 'interference with the safety valves of freedom' was simply 'bad tactics' – was a classically liberal one. As such, it stood in marked contrast to Theodore's roughshod battering of the radical left. Under Theodore, Labor in Queensland would adopt an increasingly conservative and authoritarian tone, ever suspicious of 'extremists' within its ranks, and apprehensive of the very idea of revolutionary change.[25]

It is probably not prudent to suggest that a post-war workers'

Premier Theodore (*Smith's Weekly*, 12 February 1921)

revolution was never feasible in Queensland. Certainly both revolutionary and counter-revolutionary preconditions were present to some extent, although the latter predominated. A small minority of revolutionary activists, euphoric over Bolshevik successes in Russia, no doubt badly misread the overall mood. Yet indications of widespread discontent and agitation were not altogether absent from the scene.

Wartime experience had rapidly worsened existing inequalities and working-class distress. There is no denying that workers suffered from long hours of labour, arbitrary discipline, minimal social welfare and unemployment provisions, as well as general material hardship. Yet, more significantly, the war had brought a sudden escalation to this level of suffering, provoking an incensed response. As Barrington Moore Jr observes, 'For standards of condemnation to take hold, the suffering has to increase rapidly enough so that people do not have time to become accustomed to it.' And this it undoubtedly did. Large-scale unemployment had created great uncertainty in the labour market, while unprecedented price inflation and the rapid fall in real wages had piled excessive material hardship upon the average consumer. The War Census on wealth and poverty had exposed glaring plutocracy in Australia; and, as Moore again comments: 'Plutocracy may be the form of social order whose legitimacy is most liable to challenge.' Total war, furthermore, had dramatically disrupted normal routines, attenuating family bonds, inducing many to fight, fall wounded or die, while curbing the civil freedoms of others, threatening them with conscription and exposing them to intense anxiety and bereavement. '[T]he familiar social networks and sanctions that had tied individuals to the status quo underwent severe strains and had to be recreated — or else broken down altogether.'[26]

Thus, insofar as revolutionary agitators detected a desperate animus among certain sections of the working class, particularly manual, unskilled, itinerant or migrant labourers and the unemployed (as well as an entire social order in an uncertain state of flux), their perceptions were fairly accurate ones. It was the means of converting this anger into revolutionary condemnation, in order to capitalise upon prevailing instabilities, which eluded them. It would be safe to say that the overwhelming mass of Queensland workers were not in a revolutionary 'frame of mind'; but then, even in actual revolutionary situations, the labouring mass seldom, if ever, are. 'I would hazard the suggestion that in any of the great revolutions that have succeeded, the mass of the followers have not consciously willed an overturning of the social order', Moore writes. 'To the extent that angry little people want something new, it generally amounts to their perception of the old order minus the disagreeable and oppressive features that affect them.' It is the activists themselves — the workers' own 'organic intellectuals' — who propose startlingly novel solutions and push worker expectations and rage towards their attainment.[27]

In Queensland, this anger broke in two waves. The first wave, in its condemnation of the wastefulness and immorality of warfare, remained essentially an anti-militaristic rather than a full anti-capitalist onslaught. But with the Armistice and Allied victory, its momentum was largely spent, with only the myriad shallows of private grief remaining. Secondly anger against parlous working and living conditions burst forth in the massive strike wave of 1918-19, involving 26,000 men in 153 disputes, and resulting in 770,544 work days lost. Once more these battles were fought for changes, long postponed by the agenda of total war. Yet they represented only limited bread and butter gains (economism) rather than any profound social alternative.

The radicals' failure to mobilise apparent discontents towards a revolutionary goal no doubt has many explanations. In hindsight, one can suggest that this enthusiastic minority did not possess sufficiently persuasive strategies to counter the ruling class and challenge that benumbing sense of social inevitability which is implanted by the dominant culture. Despite their verbosity, they were tactically inchoate. Additionally, they had no answer to the robust coercive mechanisms the state could also employ. Propaganda, censorship, surveillance, the police, the military and the courts kept them continually on the run. Furthermore, many militants were 'outside' agitators in a very real, geographical sense — Wobblies from interstate, socialists and Bolsheviks from overseas. Parochialism and racism once more detached them from the working-class mainstream. It was the Russians, with their Leninist strategies, who were clearly the most ideologically advanced of the revolutionary sects. Yet, because of language difficulties and cultural suspicions, they seemed, to many Australian workers, to be the most inchoate of all. Furthermore, their energies were dissipated by the harsher task of economic survival and their commitment to make revolution locally while at the same time securing their group's

The germs of revolution (*Worker*, 13 February 1919)

repatriation. Their exile status, in short, compounded their inef-
fectuality. Among workers generally, apathy, deference, fatigue,
incomprehension and complacency also played their part – as
did a more immobilising sense of trepidation about the unknown
ordeals a revolution might unleash. Most, understandably, dragged their feet or headed the other way at the prospect of becoming revolutionary cannon-fodder. The memory of recent
crushing defeats in the general strikes of 1912 and 1917 hardly
inspired their confidence.[28]

The status quo may have seemed tainted to these men and
women, but not absolutely unsound. The sense of moral outrage
– of the 'injustice' about which Barrington Moore Jr writes –
was not sufficient to forge that 'iron in the soul' necessary to take
a revolutionary chance. Militants had attempted to mount a campaign around the injustice of suppressing the Red Flag, but that
was essentially a limited, liberal-democratic issue. When their
civil rights protest was answered by pogrom, that development,
too, failed to engender the sense of outrage necessary to escalate
any counter-struggle towards insurrectionary ends. The outrage
perpetrated may have been gross enough, but because it was
directed largely against the despised Russians, its impact was
greatly reduced by xenophobic prejudices. Had a working-class,
Anglo-Australian suburb, rather than an ethnic ghetto in West
End, been similarly attacked the outcome would have been
vastly different.

Furthermore, despite war-induced desperation, workers *en
masse* were more prepared to stake out their rallying grounds
around a reformist Labor government than to engage in a heady
revolutionary outbreak. Although the militants had rejected
liberal, parliamentary reform as the path towards a just society,
what most working-class voters seemed to prefer was a gradual
improvement of their circumstances within a 'tolerable' social
order. Labor, in offering them a small sample of socialisation,
the alleviation of immediate grievances and a promise of decent
living standards in the future, appeared to answer this need. The
government, in short, dealt with workers as they generally
seemed to be, not as radical intellectuals hoped they might yet
become – fired with a passionate commitment to establishing a
new and more humane social order.

Thus the radical thrust of 1918–19 was easily contained. In
fact, it was left virtually undefended by potential supporters; it
was swamped by hostile adversaries, and then it was brutally

put to rout. By the time of the Peace Celebrations in July, the humbled radicals were gingerly re-emerging. Fewer than one hundred 'reds' gathered at a Dutton Park picnic in South Brisbane to welcome the ten pardoned men, watched over in their revelry by Federal Intelligence agents. Perhaps when the War Precautions Act was repealed, one of the picnickers ventured hopefully, 'we can fly all the red flags possible'. Such acquiescence was a far cry from the bold revolutionary calls of six months earlier. Domain gatherings had recommenced the previous month, with an 'average crowd' of sympathisers turning out to hear the speakers. 'So the ball is started once more', wrote Jennie Scott Griffiths, with a hint of weary sarcasm. 'On with the dance, let joy be unconfined'.[29]

By September, Agent 77 was reporting that radical organisations and activity had been re-established. The Wobblies were meeting at their new Albert Street rooms; the Socialist League had been revived; the Workers School of Social Science was attracting pupils, and radical females, formerly of the Women's Peace Army, had formed a Labour Girls Club. Jim Quinton and Norman Jeffery were preaching the OBU message to wharfies and meatworkers, while Nicholai Lagutin addressed the Russian 'Souse' on anarchism and sabotage. Simultaneously, 'Curly' Johnston and Charles Lee, an IWW activist from the United States, were agitating among the local unemployed. At outlying Queensland centres — Longreach in the west in May, Goombungee on the Darling Downs in July, Dululu and Eton in the central districts in August, and Babinda in the north in October — the fitful struggle to fly the red flag continued; and, in Brisbane, 'Curly' Johnston became the last rebel to be imprisoned (in January 1920) for waving the flag at the Domain the previous July. Yet, despite this flurry of renewed activity, the sense of an assured direction and momentum seems to have deserted the radical cause. Confident predictions about the imminence of social deliverance were undermined by an encroaching pessimism. 'The hope of obtaining palliatives from the Government large enough to tide over the reconstruction period decreases daily', wrote a Brisbane correspondent to the *Socialist* in August, 'and failing THAT, the workers have nothing but a period of successive strikes, lockouts and riots to look forward to.'[30]

As the last Red Flag prisoner, Ludwick Roslan, was being released from Boggo Road Gaol in September, the eight interned

Russians in Sydney were being prepared for deportation. On Thursday, 18 September, Bykov (who had joined the others in mid-August), Rosenberg, Kreslin, Markin, Klushin, Timms, Wishnevsky and Weinberg were taken in a military police van to Pyrmont Wharf, escorted by five soldiers, and placed on board the S.S. *Frankfurt*, bound the following day for Odessa. In mid-April, Lieutenant-General Legge of military command had promised that wives and children of the deportees might accompany them and, if of inadequate means, have their fares paid by the commonwealth government. Yet this promise was not honoured. The soldiers prevented families, relatives and friends, waiting by the wharf, even from contacting the eight men or handing over money collected in Brisbane to finance them. 'For what reason, nobody seems able to say', commented the *Daily Standard*, 'nor were the deportees seen again after they boarded the transport.' Although an angry protest at Sydney Town Hall against this 'cruel scandal' erupted into a riot, both the *Brisbane Courier* and the *Daily Mail*, whose editorials had clamoured for deportations throughout April, somehow missed reporting the entire tawdry episode.[31]

The ultimate fate of the deportees is presently unknown. Of the four about whom something is sketchily understood, only one, Peter Kreslin seemingly reneged upon his original Bolshevik enthusiasm, and found employment as an interpreter at the American consulate in Vladivostok in late 1923. Alexander Zuzenko became the captain of a Soviet cargo vessel, plying between Leningrad and London, but was also embroiled in Comintern activities overseas, returning as a courier to Australia on at least one occasion during 1922. In this capacity, he doubtlessly continued to liaise with Peter Simonoff who, upon re-entering the USSR, became controller of Comintern activities throughout the British Empire. Michael Rosenberg also joined the Soviet Foreign Service. Finally, and tragically, it appears that Rosenberg, Simonoff and Zuzenko were all liquidated in the Stalinist purges of the Old Bolshevik party between 1936 and 1939. Yet Civa Rosenberg – the only female activist to be deported – is still alive and well in the Soviet Union at the time of writing.[32]

Russians in Queensland had clearly borne the brunt of the loyalist excesses of 1919. In effect, they had been caught in a crossfire, as Australia's first fullblown anti-communist scare converged with one of its latter-day race riots. Anti-Bolshevism, laced with Russophobia, had inflamed popular prejudices against any minority tendencies favouring internationalism, working-class solidarity and revolutionary zeal. Nor were the Russians merely a passive sacrifice in this loyalist conflagration, although clearly they had been victimised and punished in dramatic ways. For certain Russians were also self-conscious activists in promoting social unrest and encouraging the deportations they hoped would follow. Russians seeking repatriation after the riots had a longer wait and a more tenuous journey homeward than the deportees. In March 1920, it was agreed that Russians might leave if in possession of a 'military permit' and a guaranteed return passage via a 'neutral' country. This plan, however, came unstuck as various groups of migrants were stranded, in severe destitution, at Singapore, Shanghai and Hong Kong, while British and Chinese authorities complained of their presence, and the Japanese refused to land them. This policy, furthermore, had included only Russians with sufficient funds to leave. As Lagutin complained in February 1920, 'workless and poor Russians, unable to pay their own fares' were virtually marooned in Australia.[33]

The riots, imprisonments and deportations failed to suppress local Russian militancy and resolve. By late 1919, details of the Third International (Comintern) had begun to spread through Australia, and Simonoff had helped initiate the formation of an Australian Communist Party (ACP). In August 1920, the first issue of a monthly magazine, *The Communist*, appeared in Brisbane, edited by Russian sympathiser, George 'Gunner' Taylour. *Knowledge and Unity*, revived in late July 1919, soon became the Queensland party's official organ. Branches of the ACP rapidly grew in Brisbane, Townsville, Cairns, Childers and Innisfail, as a propagandist cadre organised by Simonoff became particularly active. Regular intelligence summaries, compiled by Major H.E. Jones of the SIB and conveyed monthly to MI5 at Scotland Yard, invariably depicted communism as 'spreading rapidly', particularly in North Queensland, where it was feared that even 'whole districts have "gone communist" '.[34]

As severe as the conservative backlash had been against an openly proclaimed Russian 'Soviet' and a thinly disguised IWW local, the lively militants, though temporarily overawed, were never entirely silenced. The subsequent contest between radical and anti-radical forces remains to be adequately explored, but it is clearly an ongoing struggle which continues to be waged energetically. Queensland's political history has been described elsewhere as a largely conservative process, in which radicalism has remained a 'real but exceptional' force. An 'embattled but significant minority' has continually tried to keep a torch of militancy alight, in the face of reactionary gales. The Queensland Russians' attempts to publicise their revolution and assist with the struggle against local political and industrial 'bosses' and a 'lying Tory press', is just one incandescent historical moment in this unfolding saga.[35]

In confusing a small civil liberties march with an incipient revolutionary uprising, conservative forces in 1919 demonstrated their own disquietude in an uneasy reconstruction period, as well as a penchant for violent extremism, clearly surpassing those other brands of ideological 'extremism' which so alarmed them. As the present ideological inclination in Queensland continues to the right, it is both instructive and sobering to recall how such reactionary consolidations were initially mobilised. Resilient and at times resurgent, radicalism's critical refrain has more consistently been a lamentation than a battle cry since 1919. Yet, either plaintively or boldly, that song continues to be sung in Queensland, chiming discordantly against today's tranquillising coda, celebrating happier lives in a stronger state:

> . . . and I will do it again for the same ideals involved. I'll be there just the same . . .
>
> Jerry Cahill[36]

Abbreviations

AA	Australian Archives
ABIEU	Australian Building Industrial Employees' Union
ACCC	Anti-Conscription Campaign Committee
ACP	Australian Communist Party
ADL	Australian Defensive League
ADU	Australian Democratic Union
AFB	Army to Fight Bolshevism
AIF	Australian Imperial Forces
AMIEU	Australian Meat Industry Employees' Union
APA	Australian Peace Alliance
APL	American Protective League
ASP	Australasian Socialist Party
BIC	Brisbane Industrial Council
CIB	Criminal Investigation Bureau
CPD	Commonwealth Parliamentary Debates
CPE	Central Political Executive
IIW	International Industrial Workers
ILP	Industrial Labor Party
IWW	Industrial Workers of the World
JWA	Jewish Workers Association
LVA	Labour Volunteer Army
LVC	Loyal Vigilance Committee (of Toowoomba)
MLA	Member of the Legislative Assembly
MLC	Member of the Legislative Council
NDC	National Democratic Council
NPC	National Political Council

OBU	One Big Union
OBUPL	One Big Union Propaganda League
PLP	Parliamentary Labor Party
QCE	Queensland Central Executive
QPD	Queensland Parliamentary Debates
QRU	Queensland Railways Union
QSA	Queensland State Archives
QSL	Queensland Socialist League
RSCPF	Returned Soldiers and Citizens Political Federation
RSPNL	Returned Soldiers and Patriots National League
RSSCLL	Returned Sailors, Soldiers and Citizens Loyalty League
RSSILA	Returned Sailors and Soldiers Imperial League of Australia
SIB	Special Intelligence Bureau
UFL	Universal Freedom League
ULE	United Loyalist Executive
URW	Union of Russian Workers
WPA	Women's Peace Army
WPO	Workers' Political Organisation
WWF	Waterside Workers' Federation
YMCA	Young Men's Christian Association

Notes

Introduction

1. *CPD* 15 (1917-19), 13719; H.J. Rosenbaum and P.C. Sederberg, *Vigilante Politics* (University of Pennsylvania Press, 1976), 1-29; some recent exceptions include A. Moore, "Guns across the Yarra, Secret Armies and the 1923 Melbourne Police Strike", in *What Rough Beast? The State and Social Order in Australian History*, ed. Sydney Labour History Group (Sydney: Allen and Unwin, 1982), 220-33; M. Sturma, "Myall Creek and the Psychology of Mass Murder", *Journal of Australian Studies*, 16 (1985): 62-70; A. Metcalfe, "Fraternity and Terror: The Organization of Violence in Everyday Life", *Mankind* 14, 5: 373-82; G. Reid, *A Nest of Hornets: The Massacre of the Fraser Family at Hornet Bank* (Melbourne: Oxford University Press, 1982); R.B. Walker, "Violence in Industrial Conflicts in New South Wales in the late Nineteenth Century", *Historical Studies* 22, 86 (1986): 54-70.

2. R.M. Crawford, "The Australian Pilgrimage of Arnold Wood", *Journal for the Royal Australian Historical Association* 48 (1963): 412; R. Gerritson, "The 1934 Kalgoorlie Riots: A Western Australian Crowd", *University Studies in History* 5 (1967-70): 42-75.

3. R. Lawson, *Brisbane in the 1890s: A Study of an Australian Urban Society* (St Lucia: University of Queensland Press, 1973); G. Lewis, "Queensland Nationalism and Australian Capitalism", in *Essays in the Political Economy of Australian Capitalism*, ed. E.L. Wheelwright and K. Buckley (Sydney: ANZ Book Co., 1978), 116; G. Davison," Unemployment, race and public opinion: reflections on the Asian immigration contraversy of 1888", in *Surrender Australia? Essays in the Study and Uses of History*, ed. A. Markus and M.C. Ricklefs (Sydney: George Allen & Unwin, 1985), 104-5; W.L. Thorpe, "A Social History of Colonial Queensland. Towards a Marxist Analysis", 217-93; R. Evans, "The Battles of Brisbane: The Conscription Struggle 1916-17", *Brisbane at War*, ed. Helen Taylor, Brisbane History Group Papers 4 (1986): 5-15; R. Evans, *Loyalty and Disloyalty: Social Conflict on the Queensland Homefront, 1914-18* (Sydney: Allen and Unwin, 1987); H. Gregory and J. Thearle, "Casualties of Brisbane's Growth: Infant and Child Mortality in the 1860s", and L. Cazalar, "When the Plague Came to Queensland", *Brisbane: Housing, Health, the River and the Arts*, Brisbane

History Group Papers, 3 (1985), 57-70, 79-89; *Brisbane, Aboriginal, Alien, Ethnic* ed. R. Fisher, Brisbane History Group Papers 5, (1987).

4. A.G.L. Shaw, "Violent Protest in Australian History", *Historical Studies* 14, 60, 559-60; M. McKernan, *The Australian People and the Great War* (Melbourne: Nelson, 1980), 224 (my emphasis); G. Souter, *Lion and Kangaroo: The Initiation of Australia* (Sydney: Collins, 1976), 286; H. Mc-Queen, "Shoot the Bolshevik! Hang the Profiteer! Reconstructing Australian Capitalism 1918-21", in *Essays in the Political Economy of Australian Capitalism* II, ed. E.L. Wheelwright and K. Buckley (Sydney: ANZ Book Co. 1978), 186; R. Morris, "Mr. Justice Higgins Scuppered; The 1919 Seamen's Strike", *Labour History* 37, (1979): 52; M. Waters, *Strikes in Australia. A Sociological Analysis of Industrial Conflict* (Sydney: Allen and Unwin 1982), 125.

5. *Direct Action*, 1 June 1915.

6. D.J. Murphy, *T.J. Ryan. A Political Biography* (St Lucia: University of Queensland Press, 1975), 420-21; J. Harris, *The Bitter Fight. A Pictorial History of the Australian Labour Movement* (St Lucia: University of Queensland Press, 1970), 263-67; R. Fitzgerald, *From 1915 to the Early 1980s. A History of Queensland* (St Lucia: University of Queensland Press, 1984), 15-16; T.J. Botham, "The Red Flag Riots: Conservative Reactions" B.A. (Hons) thesis, Australian National University, 1975); Raymond Evans, *Loyalty and Disloyalty. Social Conflict on the Queensland Homefront* (Sydney: Allen and Unwin, 1987) 151-70.

7. Governor-General to Secretary of State for the Colonies, 3 September 1920, CP 78/22, 1921/67, AA, Governor-General, Official Report to Secretary of State for the Colonies, 29 October 1917, Co 148/159, 63864, 226-7, PRO.

1   This Damn Slaughter

1. D. Abse, *Ash on a Young Man's Sleeve* (Harmondsworth: Penguin, 1982), 14.

2. *Sun*, 19 May 1918; M. Ferro, *The Great War 1914-1918* (London: Routledge and Kegan Paul, 1973).

3. H. Foote, Commonwealth Police report, 15 February 1918, BP230/4, AA(Qld).

4. J. Keets to B. Keets, 25 December 1917, Q.2631, AA(Vic); *Brisbane Courier*, 1 January 1918.

5. H. Foote, report, 18 March 1919, BP230/4, AA(Qld); R. Evans, "Loyalty and Disloyalty: Social and Ideological Conflict in Queensland during the Great War", 180-228.

6. C. Peiniger to Military Intelligence, 3 October 1918, BP4/1, 66/4/3053, AA(Qld); *Daily Mail*, 6 November 1918; Governor-General, Affairs report to Colonial Office, 24 September 1918, CO418/169, PRO; F. Watson, *A Brief Analysis of Public Opinion in Australia during the Past Six Years* (Sydney: Tyrrell's, 1918), 16-18; "Secret Service", *Queer Queensland: The Breeding Ground of the Bolshevik* (Brisbane: Privately Published, 1918), 44-45.

7. T. Walker, Military Intelligence report, March 1918, BP4/1, 66/4/2360, AA(Qld); Manifesto of Anti-Conscription Coordinating Committee, Queensland, September 1916, BP4/1, 66/5/142, AA(Qld).

8. Governor-General, Affairs reports, 10 December 1917 and 18 February 1918, CO418/159 and 169, PRO.

9. N.G. Butlin et al., *Government and Capitalism* (Sydney: Allen and Unwin, 1982), 75-77; D.P. Copland, "Australia in the World War: Economic", in *Cambridge History of the British Empire*, vol. 7 (Cambridge: Cambridge University Press, 1933), 593-94; Governor-General, Affairs report, 19 April 1918, CO418/169, PRO; W. Aderman to T.J. Ryan, 19 March 1918,

PRE/A584, 2905 of 1918, QSA; Queensland Society for the Prevention of Cruelty, *35th Annual Report 1917-18*.

10. G.H. Knibbs, *The Private Wealth of Australia and Its Growth* (Melbourne: McCarron, 1918); L. Soltow, "The Censuses of Wealth of Men in Australia in 1915..." *Australian Economic History Review* XII, 2: 125-41; *Soldiers and the Labor Movement* (Brisbane: Worker, 1919): 5-8.

11. S. Dobbs to T.J. Ryan, 22 July 1918, PRE/A 596 in letter 8512 of 1918, QSA; *Socialist*, 23 October 1914; Governor-General, Affairs reports, 21 January and 19 April 1918, CO418/169, PRO (my own emphasis); *Capitalist Patriotism* (Anti-conscription leaflet, 1916); *Brisbane Courier*, 1 October 1918.

12. *Worker*, 1 August 1918; *We Apologise: The Tory Papers of Australia* (Queensland Labor election pamphlet, 1918); *Brutality of the Vote* (Anti-Conscription pamphlet, 1916).

13. Brisbane Industrial Council to Captain R. Cottam, 7 February 1918, BP4/1, 66/4/2360, AA(Qld).

14. *Daily Standard*, 29 January 1918.

15. Summary of Ryan's Disloyal Associations, 1918, B197, 2021/1/270, AA; *National Leader*, 23 November, 1917; Evans, "Loyalty and Disloyalty", 396-97.

16. Censor's reports, Brisbane, 13 and 18 February 1918, BP4/1, 66/4/2360, AA(Qld); Captain G. Ainsworth, Card Index on Radicals, BP230/2, AA(Qld); Ryan's Disloyal Associations, B.197, 202111/1/270, AA; D.J. Murphy, *T.J. Ryan: A Political Biography* (St Lucia: University of Queensland Press 1975), 350.

17. T. Walker, Intelligence report, 17 March 1918, Censor's reports, 13 February 1918, BP4/1, 66/4/2360, AA(Qld).

18. *Sydney Morning Herald*, 28 December 1917; Evans, "Loyalty and Disloyalty", 294-308.

19. C. Cunneen, *King's Men* (Sydney: Allen & Unwin, 1983), 133; SIB List of IWW members, Brisbane, 29 August 1917, BP4/1, 66/5/115, AA(Qld); G. Ainsworth, Diary, 1 September 1917-30 April 1920, BP 230/3, AA(Qld).

20. W.M. Hughes to T.J. Ryan, 8 March 1917, PRE/A559 in-letter 7514 of 1917, QSA; Ainsworth, Diary, BP230/3, AA(Qld); F. Cain, *The Origins of Political Surveillance in Australia* (Sydney: Angus and Robertson, 1983), 36-38.

21. Intelligence report on Brisbane Domain meeting, 21 April 1918, BP4/1, 66/4/2459, AA(Qld); Governor-General, Affairs reports, 10 December 1917 and 22 January 1918, CO418/159 and 169, PRO.

22. W. Anderson, reports, December 1917-January 1918, BP4/1, 66/4/1817, AA(Qld); W.A. Fisher to W. Anderson, 13-28 December 1917, BF230/4, AA(Qld); Constable W. MacGregor-Davies, report, 8 January 1918, "Political Meeting at Domain" report, 10 February 1918, BP230/4, AA(Qld).

23. Censor's report, 21 September 1918, CP447/3, S.C.5(1), AA; M.H. Ellis, *A Handbook for Nationalists* (Brisbane: NPD, 1918).

24. Commonwealth Police reports, 2-7 May 1918, Intelligence and Censor's reports, 2-5 May 1918, BP4/1, 66/4/2360, AA(Qld); Ainsworth, Diary, 1-4 May 1918, BP230/3, AA(Qld).

25. Intelligence report, 8 May 1918, BP4/1, 66/4/2360, AA(Qld); *Brisbane Courier* 4 May 1918; Brisbane Industrial Council, memos to Cabinet 9 June, 12 July and 13 September 1918, PRE/A 618 in-letter 2889 of 1919, QSA; Sergeant L. McCallum, report, 2 May 1918, BP4/1, 66/4/2360, AA(Qld).

26. General G. Irving, report, 3 May 1918, BP4/1, 66/4/2360, AA(Qld); Evans, "Loyalty and Disloyalty", 311-13; E. Fried, "Russians in Queensland 1886-1925", 44.

27. H. Ruzki, Breaking the Chains of Bondage, BP4/1, 66/4/3557, AA(Qld); Irving, report, 3 May 1918, BP4/1, 66/4/2360, AA(Qld).

28. *Brisbane Courier* 2 and 3 May 1918; Intelligence report, 29 June 1918, BP4/1, 66/4/2360, AA(Qld); D. Griffiths to E. Griffiths, 21 June 1918, BP4/1, 66/4/3360, AA(Qld).

29. *Workers' Life*, 22 November 1917; "Russians and *Workers' Life*" file, 1917-18, BP4/1, 66/4/2072, AA(Qld); Evans, "Loyalty and Disloyalty", 27-32.

30. Russian Workers' Association to Dutch Consul, 18 June 1919, BP4/1, 66/4/3660, AA(Qld).

31. Fried, "Russians in Queensland", 21-34; H. Bykov, "Russia in Australia – Diary of a Tramp", BF4/1, 66/4/2165, AA(Qld).

32. *Daily Standard*, 14 June 1919; Evans, "Loyalty and Disloyalty", 183; Fried, "Russians in Queensland", 59; A. Rabinowitch, *The Bolsheviks Come to Power* (New York: W. Norton, 1978), 325-26; T. Poole and E. Fried, "Artem: 'A Bolshevik in Brisbane'", *Australian Journal of Politics and History* XXXXI, 2 (1985): 243-46.

33. Constable A.M. Short, "IWW in Queensland", 21 October 1918, BP4/1, 66/4/1817, AA(Qld); Censor's notes, 5 November 1918, QF2400, AA(Vic).

34. P. Perfileff to A. Zuzenko, 5 November 1918, BF4/1, 66/4/1817 AA(Qld).

35. "Russians and *Worker's Life*", BP4/1, 66/4/2072, AA(Qld); K. Klushin, "Parliament and Soviet", BP4/1, 66/4/3660, AA(Qld).

36. K. Klushin, "No Sympathy for You", BP4/1, 66/4/3660, AA(Qld).

37. "Citizens of the World" conference, 28 December 1915, BF4/1, 66/4/2165, AA(Qld); *Daily Standard*, 13 August 1919; Russian Workers' Association to Dutch Consul, 18 June 1919, BP4/1, 66/4/3660, AA(Qld).

38. *Brisbane Courier*, 8 March 1919; Queensland Governor's Affairs report to Colonial Office, 17 December 1917, CO418/161, PRO.

39. F. Bullcock to AWU President (Qld), 28 October 1917, COL/A1109, in-letter 1886 of 1918, QSA; F. Williams and W. Read to Home Secretary, 19 November 1917, COL/A1102, in-letter 10592 of 1917 QSA; Toowoomba Industrial Committee to Brisbane Industrial Council, 8 November 1917, COL/A1102, in-letter 10270 of 1917, QSA; T.J. Ryan to W.M. Hughes, 21, 24 and 29 September 1917, PRE/A571, in-letter 13536 of 1917, QSA.

40. M. Perks, "A New Source on the Seventh ALP Federal Conference, 1918", *Labour History* 32 (1977): 75-79. Early voting figures revealed an undeniable trend in favour of ending Labor's involvment with recruiting. Plumbers at Bundaberg voted twelve to one in support of this, while Ipswich colliers recorded a favourable majority of 804 to 528. Western shearers solidly endorsed the proposal by 770 votes to 156. See intercepted correspondence, QF2113, 2117, 2292, AA(Vic).

41. Ellis, *Handbook for Nationalists*, 53 and 57; *Daily Standard*, 20 May 1918; Brisbane Industrial Council memo, 26 May 1918, PRE/A590 in-letter 5878 of 1918; W. Dunstan, AWU to T.J. Ryan, 3 July 1918, PRE/A594 in-letter 7553 of 1918; "Volunteer Hunting", *Aussie*, 15 May 1920; W. Richardson to Military Intelligence, 16 September 1918, BP4/1, 66/4/1817, AA(Qld).

42. *Brisbane Courier*, 4 October 1918; *Daily Mail* 29 October 1918; Evans, "Loyalty and Disloyalty", 401-2.

43. "T.J. Ryan's Libel Action against Hobart *Mercury*", in Jennie Scott Griffiths' cutting books (privately owned); Evans, "Loyalty and Disloyalty", 322-28, 390-95; *Daily Mail*, 7 August 1918; *Brisbane Courier*, 11 October 1918.

44. *Daily Standard*, 1 May and 25 July 1918; *Daily Mail*, 10 August 1918; *Truth*, 4 August 1918; Intelligence report, 25 February 1919, BP4/1, 66/5/115, AA(Qld).

45. *Brisbane Courier*, 6 September 1918; R. Evans, "'Some Furious Outbursts of Riot'. Returned Soldiers and Queensland's 'Red Flag' Disturbances", *War and Society* III, 2 (1985): 75.

46. *Truth*, 4 August 1918; *Daily Standard*, 2 August 1918; A.F. Gorman, correspondence, 10 June-2 July 1918; BP4/1, 66/5/115, AA(Qld); H. Scott Ben-

nett and R.S. Ross, *The Story of the Red Flag* (Melbourne, 1918); Captain Wills Intelligence report, 25 November 1918, BP4/1, 66/5/115, AA(Qld).

47. *Daily Mail*, 29 July 1918; "Domain Disturbance" file, BP4/1, 66/4/2944, AA(Qld).
48. *Daily Standard*, 21 August 1918; *Telegraph*, 7 August 1918.
49. *Brisbane Courier*, 9 August 1918; *Daily Mail*, 9 August 1918; *Daily Standard*, 9 and 10 August 1918; Evans "Furious Outbursts", 81.
50. For information on "the Zabern incident", see B. Tuchman, *The Proud Tower* (London: Hamish Hamilton, 1966), 345; *CPD* 76, 10 October 1918, pp. 6835-37.
51. *Daily Standard*, 2 October 1918; General Irving to Defence Dept, 1 October 1918, BP4/1, 66/4/2165, AA(Qld).

2   The Tory Mob

1. *National Leader*, 21 June 1918.
2. J. Toland, *No Man's Land. The Story of 1918* (London: Eyre Methuen, 1980), 297-462; M. Ferro, *The Great War 1914-1918* (London: Routledge and Kegan Paul, 1969), 218-21; L.F. Fitzhardinge, *The Little Digger 1914-1952* (London: Angus and Robertson, 1979), 342.
3. T.J. Ryan to Secretary of State for the Colonies, 1 October 1918, Pre/A602, 11171 of 1918, QSA; *Brisbane Courier*, 3 October 1918.
4. P. Argus, Ipswich to T. Moroney, 9 October 1918, AA, QF2075; D.J. Murphy, *T.J. Ryan. A Political Biography* (St Lucia: University of Queensland Press, 1973), 400.
5. *Brisbane Courier*, 2 and 4 October 1918; *Daily Mail*, 27 August 1918.
6. R.K. Murray, *Red Scare. A Study of National Hysteria* (New York: McGraw Hill, 1955); M. Dubovsky, *We Shall Be All. A History of the Industrial Workers of the World* (New York: Quadrangle, 1969), D. Kennedy, *Over Here. The First World War and American Society* (New York: Oxford University Press, 1980).
7. *Croydon Mining News*, 11 April 1918; Kennedy, *Over Here*, 81-82; *Brisbane Courier*, 24 October 1918.
8. G. Ainsworth, Official Diary, 20 and 23 October 1917, BP23013, AA (Qld); H. McQueen, "Shoot the Bolshevik! Hang the Profiteer! Reconstructing Australian Capitalism, 1918-21", in *Essays in the Political Economy of Australian Capitalism* II, ed. E.L. Wheelwright and K. Buckley (Sydney: ANZ Book Co, 1978), 203; T. Botham, "The Red Flag Riots: Conservative Reactions", 34; R. Rivett, *Australian Citizen. Herbert Brookes 1807-1963* (Melbourne: Melbourne University Press, 1965).
9. "The Works of Sir Thomas Urquhart, reviewed with David Urquhart's 'The Pillars of Hercules'", *Quarterly Review* 86 (1849-50): 415-23; R. Boston, *The Admirable Urquhart: Selected Writings* (London: Gordon Fraser, 1975); E. Riddell, ed, *Lives of the Stuart Age, 1603-1714* (London: Osprey Publishing Co., 1976), 418-19; I. Wilks, *South Wales and the Rising of 1839* (London: Croom Helm, 1984), 162-63.
10. J.H. Hornibrook, *Bibliography of Queensland Verse, with Biographical Notes* (Brisbane: A.H. Tucker, 1953), 76; H.A. Kellow, *Queensland Poets* (London: George Harrap, 1930), 73-74; F.R. Urquhart, *Camp Canzonettes, being Rhymes of the Bush and other things* (Brisbane: Gordon and Gotch, 1891), 20-21; *Telegraph*, 15 December 1920; R. Armstrong, *The Kalkadoons. A Study of an Aboriginal Tribe on the Queensland Frontier* (Brisbane: W. Brooks and Co., n.d.), 134.
11. W.M. Hughes to T.J. Ryan, 8 March 1917, Pre/A559, 7514 of 1917, QSA; Commissioner Urquhart to Home Secretary, 22 August 1917, Col/A1097,

8658 of 1917, QSA; G. Ainsworth, Official Diary, 1 September 1917 and subsequently, BP230/3, AA (Qld); Botham, "Red Flag Riots", 34-39.

12. *Daily Mail*, 26 August, 2 and 9 September 1918.
13. Hornibrook, *Bibliography of Verse*, 22; *National Leader*, 9 and 30 November 1917, 6 September 1918; Ainsworth, Diary, June-July 1918, BP230/3, AA (Qld).
14. *National Leader*, 23 February 1917; J.J. Stable, "Review of Industrial and Political Situation in Queensland", 9 February 1919, CP447/3, SC5[1], AA.
15. R. Munro-Ferguson, 24 August 1918, quoted in F. Cain, *The Origins of Political Surveillance in Australia* (Sydney: Angus and Robertson, 1983), 65; J.J. Stable, Memorandum, 21 September 1918, CP447/3, SC5[1], AA.
16. W. Preston Jr, *Aliens and Dissenters. Federal Suppression of Radicals, 1903-1933* (New York: Harper and Row, 1963), 93, 156; H. O'Connor, *Revolution in Seattle. A Memoir* (Seattle: Left Bank Books, 1981), 95; Dubovsky, *We Shall Be All*, 385-87; Kennedy, *Over Here*, 263-64.
17. *The Leader*, March 1919; "Disloyalists at Brisbane", 11 October 1918, BP4/1, 66/4/3035, AA (Qld).
18. D. Hunt, "A History of the Labour Movement in North Queensland", 348; R. Evans, "Loyalty and Disloyalty: Social and Ideological Conflict in Queensland during the Great War", 437-43; *Brisbane Courier*, 25 October 1918.
19. Censor's notes, 23 October 1918, QF2186, AA.
20. *Brisbane Courier*, 25 October 1918; W.J. Byrne, Intelligence report, 23 October 1918, BP4/1, 66/5/115, AA (Qld).
21. E. Martin, Hughenden to J. Tilanus, Intelligence, 27 October 1918, BP4/1, 66/5/115, AA (Qld); E. Campbell, Hughenden to B. Matthias, Sydney, 1 November 1918, QF2317, AA; *Brisbane Courier*, 23 October 1918.
22. Captain Wills, report, 15 December 1918, BP4/1, 66/5/115, AA (Qld); Inspector Harlan, report, 18 October 1918, Col/A1165, 8892 of 1918, QSA.
23. *Daily Standard*, 25 October 1918; *Brisbane Courier*, 21 October 1918.
24. Adjutant General to Military Command, 6 November 1918, BP4/1, 66/5/115, AA (Qld); Censor's notes, 30 October 1918, AF2222, AA; Acting Prime Minister to Premier Ryan, 12 December 1918, Col/A1165, 8892 of 1919, QSA.
25. *Darling Downs Gazette*, 26 October 1916; Warrant Officer Kimber to Captain Wood, Intelligence, 26 October 1918, BP4/1, 66/4/3084, AA (Qld).
26. *Brisbane Courier*, 8 November 1918; Censor's Notes, 30 October 1918, QF2224, AA.
27. T.J. Mills, Queensland Loyalty League to State Commandant, 24 October 1918, BP4/1, 66/4/3035, AA (Qld); *Daily Standard*, 4 November 1918; *Brisbane Courier*, 8 November 1918.
28. List of IWW members, Brisbane, 1918, BP4/1, 66/5/115, AA (Qld); Commonwealth police report, 10 November 1918, BP4/1, 66/4/1817, AA (Qld); *Brisbane Courier*, 9 November 1918.
29. Constable Norton, report, 8 November 1918; Sub-Inspector Brosnan, report, 9 November 1918, Pol/J36, 42429 of 1918, QSA.
30. S. O'Neill, Brisbane to M. O'Neill, Innisfail, 14 November 1918, QF2362, AA; Evans, *Loyalty and Disloyalty*, 412-14.
31. *Daily Mail*, 14 November 1918; Charles White, sworn statement, 14 November 1918, BP4/1, 66/5/115, AA (Qld); *Townsville Daily Bulletin*, 19 November 1918; Captain Wills, report, 18 November 1918, BP4/1, 66/5/115, AA (Qld).
32. Captain Wills, report, 27 October 1918, BP4/1, 66/5/115, AA (Qld); T. Thorpe to T.J. Ryan, 31 October and 1 November 1918, Col/A1165, 9989 of 1919, QSA; Hunt, "Labour Movement in North Queensland", 351; "Secret Service", *Queer Queensland: The Breeding Ground of the Bolshevik* (n.p.d.) 22, 42.

33. *Townsville Daily Bulletin*, 15 October 1918; Captain Wills, report, 16 November 1918, BP4/1, 66/5/115, AA (Qld); *Daily Mail*, 15 November 1918.
34. Captain Wills, report, 16 November 1918, BP4/1, 66/5/115, AA (Qld); *Townsville Daily Bulletin*, 19 November 1918.
35. *Brisbane Courier*, 25 November 1918 and 16 March 1919; Commissioner Urquhart, notes, 30 November 1918; F. Urquhart to H. Brookes, 23 February 1919, in Botham, "Red Flag Riots", 36, 38.
36. A. Moore, "Guns across the Yarra. Secret armies and the 1923 Melbourne police strike", in *What Rough Beast? The State and Social Order in Australian History*, ed. Sydney Labour History Group (Sydney: Allen and Unwin, 1982), 230-31; Cain, *Political Surveillance*, 170-72; Secret Meeting and Cabinet memo, 18 and 21 January 1919, CP447/2, SC294, AA; R. Darroch, "The Man Behind Australia's Secret Armies", *Bulletin*, 2 May 1978, 60-62.
37. G. Stewart to W.A. Watt, 20 November 1918, CP447/3, SC5[1], AA; G. Ainsworth, Official Diary, 29 November-6 December 1918, BP230/3, AA (Qld).
38. G. Ainsworth, Official Diary, October-December 1918, BP230/3, AA (Qld); J.A. Philp, *Songs of the Australian Fascisti* (Brisbane: Edwards Dunlop, n.d.).
39. A.M. Short, reports, 16 September, 14 November, 27 December 1918, 11 January 1919, BP4/1, 66/4/1817, AA (Qld); *CPD* 88, 17 December 1918, 9512-17; Captain Woods, report, 21 June 1918, BP4/1, 66/5/115, AA (Qld).
40. M.H. Ellis, *A Handbook for Nationalists* (Brisbane: NPC Publicity Dept, 1918); Ainsworth, diary, October 1917; Murphy, *T.J. Ryan*, 351, 354.
41. "Summary of Ryan's Disloyal Associations", November 1918, B197, 2021/1/270, AA. The Summary is unsigned, but Ellis's authorship is clearly revealed, when, in his entry on Tom Barker, he refers to "My 'Handbook for Nationalists'", which he had prepared the previous year. See also M.H. Ellis, *The Red Road* (Sydney: Sydney and Melbourne Publishing Co., 1932), which refers to the "stupid...visionary", "the anarchist...always outside normal reason", louse-ridden Russians as a "monkey's joy", and Lenin as "the poison spider of Communism".
42. Lieutenant-Colonel J. Walker, "Report on Conditions in Queensland", 13 December 1918; J. Legge, memos, 14 February 1919, CP447/3, SC5[1], AA.
43. J.J. Stable, "Industrial Situation in Queensland", 9 February 1919, CP447/3, SC5[1], AA.
44. R. Patrick, "Jackson, Ernest Sandford (1860-1938)", *Australian Dictionary of Biography* 9-457; R.I. Myers, "Ernest Sandford Jackson", *Trephine* 4,2 (1955): 89-90; *Brisbane Courier*, 13 and 29 March 1919; N. Parker, "Dr E. Sandford Jackson", in *People, Places and Pestilence). Vignettes of Queensland's Medical Past*, ed. M.J. Thearle (Brisbane): University Dept. of Child Health, 1986), 13-24.
45. Commissioner Urquhart to William Brookes, 23 February 1919 in Botham, "Red Flag Riots", 37-38.
46. H.L. Foote, reports, 22 February and 3 March 1919, BP230/4, AA (Qld).

3 A Bit of Revoluse

1. H. Foote, report, 4 November 1918, BP230/4, AA (Qld).
2. Return of Brisbane motor vehicles, 1918-19, PRE/A641, 11203 of 1919, QSA; H. Jenson to J. Huxham, August 1918, COL/A1122, 7197 of 1918, QSA.
3. J. Reed, *Ten Days That Shook the World* (New York: Random House, 1935), 74, 112; R. Evans, "Loyalty and Disloyalty: Social and Ideological Conflict in Queensland during the Great War"; W. Thorpe, "A Social History of Colonial Queensland. Towards a Marxist Analysis", 217-93.

4. Brisbane Chamber of Commerce, deputation to E.G. Theodore, 15 May 1919, PRE/A622, 4593 of 1919, QSA.
5. D. Griffiths to E. Griffiths, 21 June 1918, BP4/1, 66/4/3660, AA(Qld); C. Bingham, *The Beckoning Horizon* (Ringwood: Penguin, 1983), 115; J. Lindsay, *The Blood Vote* (St Lucia: University of Queensland Press, 1985), 57; *Daily Mail*, 9 September 1918.
6. G. Ainsworth, Card Index, 1918, BP230/2, AA(Qld); E. Fried, "Russians in Queensland: 1886-1925", 60,64. Simonoff, appointed by Trotsky, failed to have his Consular status recognised by the commonwealth government.
7. Commonwealth Police report, 9 October 1918; A.M. Short, "The IWW in Queensland", 21 October 1918, BP4/1, 66/4/1817, AA(Qld); J.J. Stable, Censor's notes, 3 October 1918, QF2152, AA.
8. J.J. Stable, Censor's notes, 19 October 1918, QF2177, AA; Aliens Prohibition Orders, August-September 1918, BP4/1, 66/4/3036, AA(Qld); M. Rosenberg to Russian Association (undated), BP4/1, 66/4/3036, AA (Qld); Russian Workers Association, resolution, 10 November 1918, PRE/A607, 12862 of 1918, QSA.
9. *Knowledge and Unity*, galley proofs, November 1918, QF2380, AA; A.M. Short, reports, 19 and 27 December, 1918, BP4/1, 66/4/1817, AA(Qld); *Knowledge and Unity*, 31 December 1918; N. Blinoff, Selwyn to *Knowledge and Unity*, 27 February 1919, BP4/1, 66/5/115, AA(Qld).
10. P. Simonoff to A. Zuzenko, undated, QF2166; P. Grant, Newcastle to J. Gibson, undated, QF2228; P. Simonoff to N. Freeburg, 29 October 1918, QF2254; P. Simonoff to A. Zuzenko, 22 October 1918, QF2283, AA.
11. Censor's notes, 6 November 1918, QF2254 and 2283, AA; P. Simonoff to Souse of Russian Workers, 26 July 1919, BP4/1, 66/4/2165, AA(Qld).
12. N. Blinoff, Selwyn to *Knowledge and Unity*, 27 February 1919, BP4/1, 66/5/115; significantly, Military Intelligence interpreted Blinoff's symbolic statement as meaning, literally, "a fire in the Selwyn meatworks is probable in the near future".
13. P. Dukes, *October and the World: Perspectives on the Russian Revolution* (London: Macmillan, 1979), 103-70.
14. Censor's notes, 6 November 1918, QF2214, AA; *Daily Mail*, 11 January 1919; P. Ireland to J. McCarthy, 11 November 1918, QF2393; W. Dobbyn to J. Gritchting, 15 November 1918, QF 2367; *Daily Mail*, galley proofs, 8 November 1918, QF 2341, AA.
15. H. Langridge to *Daily Standard*, 5 September 1918, BP4/1, 66/5/115; P. Brookfield to C. Barrett, 26 March 1919, BP4/1, 66/5/115, AA(Qld).
16. Lindsay, *Blood Vote*, 98; "New Order", December 1918, BP 230/4; A. Norton, report, 20 January 1919, PRE/A614, 670 of 1919, QSA.
17. K. Klushin, "Parliament and Soviet", undated, BP4/1, 66/4/3360, AA(Qld).
18. A. Norton, report, 20 January 1919, PRE/A614, 670 of 1919, QSA; H. Foote, report, 4 November 1918, BP230/4, AA(Qld).
19. J.J. Stable to Deputy Chief Censor, 21 September 1918; J.J. Stable, "Industrial Situation in Queensland", 9 February 1919, CP447/3, SC5[1], AA; W.A. Shepherd to J. Vincent, 24 June 1918, BP4/1, 66/5/115, AA(Qld).
20. Police report on IWW activity, Townsville, 21 August 1917, COL/A1097, 8658 of 1917, QSA; Evans, "Loyalty and Disloyalty", 358-84; Captain Wills, report, 7 November 1918, BP4/1, 66/5/115, AA(Qld).
21. Captain Wills, Report on Townsville street meetings, 6 December 1918; Wills, reports, 7 and 11 December 1918, BP4/1, 66/5/115 AA(Qld); Censor's notes, 26 October 1918, QF 2201, AA.; Captain Hayes, report, 27 September 1918, CP447/3, SC5[1], AA.
22. Wills, Report on Cloncurry and District, 25 November 1918; Wills, Closing of Cloncurry Copper Fields Report, 26 May 1919, BP4/1, 66/5/115, AA(Qld).
23. Case of Paul Freeman, 1918-23, CP447/2, SC292[I], AA.

24. Censor's notes, 13 November 1918, QF2312, AA; W.A. Shepherd to Jack Vincent, 24 June 1918; D. Foley to P. Carney, 26 February 1919; Captain Fisher, report, 11 March 1919; Captain Woods, report, 13 December 1918, BP4/1, 66/5/115, AA(Qld).

25. OBUPL minutes, 23 September 1918; H. Foote, report, 21 October 1918; Commonwealth Police report, 4 November 1918, BP4/1, 66/4/3660, AA(Qld); J. Quinton to "Curly" Johnston, 8 October 1918, QF2088, AA.

26. Intelligence reports on Domain meetings, November/December 1918; Commonwealth Police reports of Domain meetings, November/December 1918; Captain Woods to Commissioner of Police, 17 August 1918; Military raid on J.J. Burke's residence, 21 March 1919, BP4/1, 66/5/115, AA(Qld).

27. H. Foote, report, 8 December 1918, BP230/4, AA(Qld); M. Miller to A. Gorman, 7 October 1918, QF 2156; Censor's notes, 6 November 1918, BP230/4, AA(Qld); Commonwealth Police report, 10 January 1919, BP4/1, 66/4/1817, AA(Qld); *Proletariat*, 8 March 1919.

28. H. Foote, report, 10 November 1918, BP230/4, AA(Qld); Unemployed deputations to Qld Premier, 8 November 1918, PRE/A651, 1529 of 1920; Captain Wills, "Unemployment Agitation in North Queensland", 20 January 1919, BP4/1, 66/5/115, AA(Qld); G. Henry to W. Casey, 3 November 1919, QF 2324, AA; Unemployed demonstration, Brisbane, 23 January 1919, BP230/4, AA(Qld); Evans, *Loyalty and Disloyalty*, 421-25.

29. Theodore to Ryan, 14 February 1919, PRE/A616, 1570 of 1919, QSA; Captain Ainsworth, report (secret), 17 January 1919, CP 78/22, 1921/67, AA; *Queenslander*, 18 January 1919; *Brisbane Courier*, 27 January and 1 February 1919.

30. *Worker*, 30 January 1919; *Brisbane Courier*, 8 and 29 March 1919; *Daily Mail*, 20 November 1918 and 11 February 1919; R. Frederick, Methodist Conference resolution, 5 March 1919, PRE/A617, 1932 of 1919, QSA; Censor's notes, 26 November 1918, QF2398.

31. J.J. Stable, "Industrial Situation in Queensland", CP447/4, SC5(1), AA; H. Foote, report, 30 November 1918, BP230/4, AA(Qld).

32. Stable, "Industrial Situation"; *Brisbane Courier*, 3 and 18 February 1919.

33. *Brisbane Courier*, 11, 14 and 22 January, 14 and 22 February, 8 and 14 March; L. Brophy to P. Carney, 19 February 1919, BP4/1, 66/5/115. AA(Qld).

34. *Brisbane Courier*, 14 February 1919; *Daily Standard*, 9 August 1918. The writer, Mrs M. Tierney of Cleveland, had seven relatives at the Front and a brother-in-law killed at Gallipoli.

35. "Solidarity – or Disruption?", Manifesto of the QCE, 11 March 1919.

36. *Proletarian*, 8 March 1919.

37. *Knowledge and Unity*, 14 February 1919; A.M. Short, report, 30 December 1918, BP4/1, 66/4/1817, AA (Qld); SIB report, 17 January 1919, CP78/22, 1921/67, AA.; J. Grey, "A 'pathetic sideshow': Australians and the Russian intervention, 1918-19", *Journal of the Australian War Memorial* 7 (October 1985): 12-17; C. ("Fanny") Rosenberg, Russian Workers' resolution, 10 November 1918, PRE/A607, 12862 of 1918, QSA.

38. Commissioner Urquhart to Under Secretary, Home Department, 16 January 1919, Gall papers, 621 of 1919, QSA.

39. Constable S. Shersby, report, 22 January 1919, Gall papers, 14404 of 1919, QSA.

40. A.M. Short, report, 17 February 1919, BP230/4, AA(Qld); *Brisbane Courier*, 27 January 1919; *Daily Standard*, 31 January 1919; Captain Blundell to Captain Woods, 27 January 1919, BP4/1, 66/4/3660, AA(Qld).

41. Corporal Crouch, report, 4 February 1919, BP4/1, 66/4/3557, AA(Qld); Governor-General, secret memo to Secretary of State for the Colonies, 23 January 1919, CP78/22, 1921/67, AA.; Intelligence report, 22 February

1919, BP4/1, 66/5/115, AA(Qld); Membership of Brisbane Soviet (undated), BP4/1, 66/4/3660, AA(Qld); *Daily Standard*, 2 April 1919.

42. H. Foote, reports 7 and 18 March 1919, BP230/4, AA(Qld); Intelligence report, 22 February 1919, BP4/1, 66/5/115, AA(Qld).

4   Days of the Pogrom

1. Intelligence report, 8 April 1919, BP4/1, 66/4/3360, AA(Qld).
2. Constable W. Clement, report, 1 March 1919, BP4/1. 66/4/2165, AA(Qld); *Daily Mail*, 7 April 1919; *Brisbane Courier*, 3 March 1919.
3. Brigadier-General Irving, Memo, 4 April 1919, BP4/1. 66/4/2165, AA(Qld).
4. H. Hall to Commonwealth Police, 17 March 1919, BP4/1. 66/4/336. AA(Qld); A.M. Short, Commonwealth Police report, 18 March 1919, BP230/4. AA(Qld); *Brisbane Courier*, 19, 20 March 1919; "Sinn Fein Flag" file, BP4/1, 66/4/3698, AA(Qld).
5. R. Mills, Royal Orange Institute of Queensland to Acting Prime Minister, W.A. Watt, 27 March 1919, BP4/1. 66/4/3698, AA(Qld).
6. *Brisbane Courier*, 19 March 1919; R. Carroll to R.S. Ross, 20 March 1919, MP367, 512/1/898, AA; *Knowledge and Unity*, 26 July 1919.
7. *Knowledge and Unity*, 1, 22 and 29 March 1919.
8. P. Kreslin to M. Polteff, Townsville, B. Rosenberg, Sydney, J. Tooloopoff, Cairns, Schoeinert, Broken Hill, MP367, 512/1/898 AA.
9. School Certificate of P.P. Kreslin, 31 December 1903, BA/1. 66/4/3660, AA(Qld); "We protest" leaflet, 23 March 1919, MP367, 512/1/898AA.
10. *Knowledge and Unity*, 26 July 1919; *Telegraph*, 31 March 1919; Secret Service report, 23 March 1919, CP447/3, SC5[1], AA.
11. R. James, report, 23 March 1919, MP367, 512/1/898 AA; *Knowledge and Unity*, 26 July 1919; *Brisbane Courier*, 24 March 1919.
12. Intelligence reports, 23 March 1919, CP447/3, SC5[1], AA.; *The Age*, 24 March 1919.
13. T. Botham, "The Red Flag Riots: Conservative Reactions", p.3; Police report, 23 March 1919, QSA/A7173/14404; *Knowledge and Unity*, 26 July 1919; R.D. Fisher, report 23 March 1919, CP447/3, SC5[1]; A.M. Short, report, 24 March 1919, BP4/1; 66/4/3660, AA(Qld).
14. H.L. Foote, report, 24 March 1919, BP4/1, 66/4/3660, AA(Qld).
15. Ibid; *Daily Mail*, 9 May 1919.
16. *Daily Mail*, 24 March 1919; Intelligence report; CRS/A3934, SC5[1], AA.
17. *Knowledge and Unity*, 26July 1919; Captain Ainsworth, diary, January-March 1919, BP230/3, AA(Qld).
18. Unsigned to Kalashnikoff, Brisbane, 24 March 1919, QF3515 AA: *The Age*, 24 March 1919; Constable O'Driscoll, report, 23 March 1919, QSA/A71137/14404.
19. Captain Ainsworth, report, 26 March 1919, CRS/AA1969/224; O'Driscoll, report, 23 March 1919, QSA/A7137/14404.
20. *Brisbane Courier*, 24 March 1919; *Daily Mail*, 24 March 1919;
21. *Brisbane Courier*, 19-20 March 1919; *Queenslander*, 18 January 1919; Ainsworth, diary, March 1919, BP230/3, AA(Qld).
22. *Brisbane Courier*, 8 November 1918, 18 and 28 March 1919; *Bulletin*, 18 May 1919; A. Rothstein, *The Soldiers Strikes of 1919* (London: Macmillan, 1980), 78.
23. E. Leed, *No Man's Land: Combat and Identity in World War I* (Cambridge: Cambridge University Press, 1979), 1613-213; R. Evans, "Some Furious Outbursts of Riot: Returned Soldiers and Queensland's 'Red Flag' Disturbances", *War and Society* 111, 2(1985): 92; *Brisbane Courier*, 27 February and 19 May 1919.

24. A.M. Short, report, 24 March 1919, BP4/1, 66/4/3660 AA(Qld); Inspector Ferguson to Commissioner Urquhart, 24 March 1919, Gall Collection, QSA; F.C. Urquhart to E.G. Theodore, 25 March 1919, QSA/A7137/14404.
25. *Daily Standard*, 24 and 27 March 1919; Botham, "Red Flag Riots", 6.
26. J. Wearne, Intelligence report, 25 March 1919, BP4/1. 66/4/3660 AA(Qld); *Brisbane Courier*, 25 March 1919; *Argus*, 25 March 1919.
27. *Brisbane Courier*, 25 March 1919; *Daily Mail*, 25 March 1919; Returned soldiers deputation, 25 March 1919, CRS 479/116 AA; R. James, Intelligence report, 24 March 1919, CRS 479/3/124 AA; E. Canetti, *Crowds and Power* (Harmondsworth: Penguin, 1973), 55.
28. *Daily Mail*, 25 March and 10 April 1919; *Daily Standard*, 25 March 1919; *Truth*, 20 April 1919.
29. J. Larkin, South Brisbane, to L.P. Larkin, Cloncurry, 27 March 1919; Censor's notes, 2 April 1919, MP367, 512/1/898 AA.
30. *Daily Mail*, 10 April 1919; F.C. Urquhart, report, 25 March 1919, Gall Collection, QSA; *Brisbane Courier*, 25 March 1919.
31. *Daily Mail*, 11 April 1919; *Truth*, 20 April 1919; *Argus*, 25 March 1919.
32. Inspector Carroll, report, 25 March 1919, Gall Collection QSA; *Argus*, 26 March 1919.
33. *Queensland Police Union Journal*, 11 June 1919; *Argus*, 26 March 1919; *Brisbane Courier*, 25 March 1919.
34. J. Larkin, letter, 27 March 1919, MP367, 512/1/898 AA.; *Daily Mail*, 25 1919.
35. Inspector Ferguson, report, 26 March 1919, Gall Collection, QSA; *Brisbane Courier*, 25 March 1919.
36. G. Davison, "Asian Immigration Controversy of 1888" in *Surrender Australia*, 104-5. R. Evans, "Loyalty and Disloyalty: Social and Ideological Conflict in Queensland during the Great War", 162-64; *The Times*, 25 March-9 April 1919.
37. *Daily Standard*, 25 March 1919; *Daily Mail*, 25 March 1919; *Brisbane Courier*, 25 March 1919.
38. J. Larkin, letter, 27 March 1919, MP367, 512/1/898; Inspector Ferguson, report, 26 March 1919; Inspector Carroll, report, 25 March 1919, Gall Collection, QSA; *Daily Mail*, 10 April 1919.
39. W.J. Fishman, *East End Jewish Radicals 1875-1914* (London: Duckworth, 1975), 28-29, 280; G. Vernadsky, *A History of Russia* (New Haven: Yale, 1961), 267; F.G. Clarke, *Will-'o-the-wisp: Peter the Painter and the anti-tsarist terrorists in Britain and Australia* (Melbourne: OUP, 1984), 11, 17; M.T. Florinsky, *Encyclopedia of Russia and the Soviet Union* (New York: McGraw Hill, 1961), 257-58; "Under the Union Jack" to Military Command, 30 March 1919, BP4/1, 66/4/3660, AA(Qld).
40. M. Stepanoff to Military Command, 28 March 1919; P. Kreslin to Military Command, 26 March 1919, BP4/1, 66/4/3660 AA(Qld); C. Galchin to B. Rosenberg, 5 April 1919; Unsigned to Kalashinikoff, 24 March 1919, MP367, 512/1/898, AA.
41. C.G. Childe, *How Labour Governs. A Study of Workers' Representation in Australia* (Melbourne: Melbourne University Press, 1923). Information that the draft of *How Labour Governs* was written during 1919 in Brisbane was received, with thanks, from Terry Irving; *Daily Standard*, 14 June 1919.
42. Returned soldiers' deputation, 25 March 1919, CRS 479/3/116 AA; *Brisbane Courier*, 25 March 1919.
43. E.S. Jackson to Acting Prime Minister Watt, 25 March 1919; G. Brown to Watt, W. Weatherill to Watt, 26 March 1919; J.G. Bayley, E.B. Corser, H.S. Foll, T. Givens to Watt, 27 March 1919; Senator Crawford to Watt, 2 April 1919, MP367, 512/1/898, AA.
44. F. Urquhart to E.G. Theodore, 25 March 1919, Gall Collection, QSA.
45. *Brisbane Courier*, 26 March 1919; *Argus*, 26 March 1919.

46. Constable A. Norton, report, 25 March 1919, Gall Collection, QSA; Statement on James Mills, 26 March 1919; BP4/1, 66/4/3660 AA(Qld).
47. R. James, report, 26 March 1919, BP4/1, 66/4/3660 AA(Qld).
48. Commandant Irving to Defence Dept, 27 March 1919, BP4/1, 66/4/3660, AA(Qld); *Brisbane Courier*, 27 March 1919; R. James, report, 26 March 1919, BP4/1, 66/4/3660 AA(Qld).
49. *Telegraph*, 28 March 1919; *Brisbane Courier*, 29 March 1919.
50. Acting Sergeant Warner, report, 28 March 1919, COL/A1148, 3961 of 1919, QSA.
51. *Bulletin*, 27 March 1919.
52. Constable Hogan, report, 30 March 1919, COL/A1147, 3898 of 1919; QSA; *Brisbane Courier*, 31 March 1919.

5   No Sympathy For You

1. K. Klushin, "No Sympathy for You", BP4/1. 66/4/3660. AA (Qld).
2. *Daily Mail*, 7 April 1919; *Toowoomba Chronicle*, 8 April 1919; SIB memo, March 1919, CRS AA1969/224, AA.
3. *Daily Mail*, 15 April 1919; *Brisbane Courier*, 29 March and 1,3,4,7,8,9 April 1919.
4. "List of Suspect Russians", April 1919; "Under the Union Jack" to Military Command, 30 March 1919; Captain Woods, memo, 15 May 1919; A. Osborne to Military Intelligence, 31 March 1919; Constable Maher, report, 15 May 1919 BP4/1. 66/4/3660 AA(Qld).
5. Constable Stewart, report, 31 March 1919; Constable Foote, report, 31 March 1919 (my own emphases), BP4/1, 66/4/3660 AA(Qld).
6. *Toowoomba Chronicle*, 8 April 1919; Visiting Justice, C. Morris, report, 7 April 1919, COL/A1150, 4345 of 1919; *Brisbane Courier*, 9 April 1919; Censor's notes, 14 April 1919, Q4153, AA(Vic); Raids on N. Lagutin, 4 February and 27 March 1919, BP4/1, 66/4/3557 and 66/4/3660, AA(Qld); Commandant Irving, report, 8 September 1919 (my own emphases), BP4/1, 66/4/3557 AA(Qld); Constable Short, report, 30 April 1919, BP230/4, AA(Qld).
7. *Brisbane Courier*, 4 April 1919; Constable O'Roarke, report, 4 April 1919, BP4/1, 66/4/2165, AA(Qld); *Toowoomba Chronicle*, 8 April 1919; Commonwealth Police reports (Rockhampton), 30 March-4 April 1919, BP4/1, 66/4/1817 AA(Qld).
8. *Brisbane Courier*, 1, 19, 28 April and 1 May 1919; *Townsville Daily Bulletin*, 29 March 1919.
9. Censor Stable, confidential cable, 24 March 1919, MP367, 512/1/618, AA; Constable Foote, report, 24 April 1919, BP4/1, 66/4/3660, AA(Qld); Intelligence raid on J. Burke, March 1919, BP4/1, 66/5/115, AA(Qld); Lieutenant J. Wearne, report, 27 March 1919, BP4/1, 66/4/3660, AA(Qld); Censorship, Raid on Russian tenements, 7 April 1919, BP4/1, 66/4/3660, AA(Qld); Constable Short, report, 30 April 1919, BP230/4 AA(Qld).
10. Watt to Irving, 27 March 1919; Raid on Russian tenements, 7 April 1919 BP4/1, 66/4/3660 AA(Qld); *Daily Standard*, 14 June 1919.
11. Lieutenant J. Wearne, raids, 27 March 1919, BP4/1, 66/4/3660, AA(Qld); D. Burns to P. Laidler, 3 April 1919, MP367, 512/1/898, AA.
12. M. Considine, Question sheet, 4 July 1919, BP4/1, 66/4/2165; Legge to Irving, 26 and 27 March 1919; Irving to Defence Dept, 28 March 1919, BP4/1, 66/4/3660, AA(Qld); Theodore to Watt, 26 March 1919, CP447/3, SC5[1] AA.
13. Intelligence report, 23 March 1919, CP447/3, SC5[1].
14. *Daily Standard*, 8 May 1919; *Daily Mail*, 3 April 1919; Censor's notes, 16 and 30 October 1918, QF 2214 and 2080, AA(Vic.).

15. *Telegraph*, 31 March 1919; A.M. Short, report, 1 April 1919, BP230/4, AA(Qld).
16. *Daily Standard*, 31 March 1919; *Brisbane Courier*, 1 April 1919; *Telegraph*, 31 March 1919; *Bulletin*, 10 April 1919.
17. *Brisbane Courier*, 1 April 1919; J. Scott Griffiths to Jerry Cahill, 8 June 1919; G. Taylor to Harry Holland, 9 June 1919 (copies in possession of author); *Daily Standard*, 26 April 1919; *Daily Mail*, 14 April and 1 July 1919.
18. Lieutenant J. Wearne, raid on Norman Jeffery's residence, 27 March 1919, BP4/1, 66/4/3660, AA(Qld); *Brisbane Courier*, 1 and 3 April 1919; *Daily Standard*, 3 April 1919; Intelligence file on Red Flag prisoners, April 1919, BP4/1, 66/4/2165, AA(Qld).
19. Intelligence file on Red Flag prisoners, April 1919, BP4/1, 66/4/2165, AA(Qld); *Daily Mail*, 3 April 1919; J.G. Cahill, Court statement, BP4/1, 66/4/2165, AA(Qld).
20. Comptroller General of Prisons, report, 25 April 1919, Col/A1154, 5916 of 1919, QSA; *Daily Mail*, 23 April 1919.
21. *Telegraph*, 9 April 1919; Intelligence file on Red Flag prisoners, April 1919, BP4/1, 66/4/2165; *Daily Standard*, 3 April 1919; *Brisbane Courier*, 5 April 1919; *Daily Mail*, 15 April 1919.
22. File on J. Doyle (Samsonvale), 1919, BP4/1, 66/4/2165, AA(Qld).
23. This table is taken from a listing in BP4/1, 66/4/2165 AA(Qld). The listing concluded with the sentiment: *"GOD SAVE THE KING!!! (and Billie Hughes)"*.
24. T. Botham, "The Red Flag Riots: Conservative Reactions", 16; *Truth*, 20 April 1919; *Daily Mail*, 8, 11 and 15 April 1919; *Brisbane Courier*, 8, 9 and 15 April, 1919.
25. Watt to Military Command, 27 March 1919; Irving to Legge, 28 March 1919; Legge to Irving, 28 March 1919, BP4/1, 66/5/142, AA (Qld); *Telegraph*, 28 March 1919; Russell, Defence to Watt, 29 March 1919, CP447/3, SC5(1), AA; *Daily Standard*, 13 July 1919.
26. Intelligence memos on "Madorsky", "Melville" and "Weinberg", 4-5 April 1919; Urqhart to Irving, 4 April 1919, BP4/1, 66/4/3660, AA(Qld); G. Meredith, Censor, report, 6 June 1917, BP4/1, 66/5/115, AA(Qld).
27. W. Weinberg to Minister of Defence, 23 May 1919; Memo on Weinberg, 11 June 1919; W. Weinberg's personal effects, 8 April 1919; Intelligence, Sydney, memo, 22 April 1919, BP4/1, 66/4/3660, AA(Qld).
28. Legge to Irving, 1 April 1919, BP4/1, 66/4/3660, AA(Qld); (my emphasis) *Daily Standard*, 2 May 1919; *Brisbane Courier*, 3 April 1919; Intelligence notes of RSSILA meeting, 2 April 1919, BP4/1, 6/4/2165, AA(Qld). In the Queensland Parliament, Sutton's statement was reported differently and more bluntly. He allegedly stated, "You know how to make bombs and how to use them . . . Boys, there are plenty of jam tins about still", *QPD*, 82, 16 September 1919, 772.
29. Russell, Defence to Watt, 4 April 1919, CP447/3, SC5[1], AA; Arrest file on deportees, April 1919, BP4/1, 66/4/3660, AA(Qld); Irving, deportation list, April 1919, BP4/1, 66/4/3660, AA(Qld); Irving, reports, 3 and 5 April 1919, BP4/1, 66/4/3660, AA(Qld); Irving to Watt, 5 April 1919, CRS/A3934, SC5[1], AA.
30. Lee to Dept of Defence, 31 March and 1 April 1919; Defence to Premier, NSW, 27 March 1919, 479/25/190, AA.; Irving to Defence Dept, 1 April 1919, BP4/1, 66/4/3660, AA(Qld) (my emphases).
31. Ainsworth to SIB, 26 March 1919, CRS AA1969/224, AA (my emphases); R. Jensz, "A 'pathetic sideshow': Australians and the Russian intervention, 1918-19", *Journal of the Australian War Memorial* 7 (October 1985): 14; D. Saunders, "Aliens in Britain and the Empire During the First World War", *Immigrants and Minorities* 4 (March 1985): 16.

32. Irving to Defence, 17 April, 5 and 28 June 1919, BP4/1, 66/4/3660, AA(Qld).
33. Defence memo, 8 April 1919, CP447/3, SC5[1]; Russians in Australia file, 1919-21, CP78/22, 1921/67, AA; Censor's report, 7 May 1919, AF3998, AA(Vic.); Inspector Ferguson, report, 28 April 1919; Legge, memo, 23 April 1919, BP4/1, 66/4/3660, AA(Qld); Deputation to NSW Chief Secretary, 20 May 1919, CRS, 42 PI, AA; Intelligence report, 4 November 1919, BP4/1, 66/5/115, AA(Qld); P. Simonoff to Souse of Brisbane Workers, 26 July 1919, BP4/1, 66/4/2165, AA(Qld), (my emphasis).
34. P. Kreslin to Mousoviet, undated, BP4/1, 66/4/3660, AA(Qld), (my emphases).
35. *Daily Mail*, 8 and 10 April 1919.
36. Lee to Mailer, 4 April 1919, and subsequent memos; Lists of personal effects, April 1919, BP4/1, 66/4/3660, AA(Qld).
37. "Bolsheviks in Darlinghurst", protest, 16 April 1919; BP4/1, 66/4/3660, AA(Qld); "Russian Deportees!", leaflet; *Daily Standard*, 14 June 1919.
38. *Daily Standard*, 26 April and 12 May 1919.
39. G. Taylor to P. Carney, Townsville, 26 May 1919; G. Taylor to Harry Holland, New Zealand, 9 June 1919, BP4/1, 66/4/2165 AA(Qld); *Nabat*, 6 August 1919; *Knowledge and Unity*, 36.
40. Russell to Watt, 31 March 1919, CP447/3, SC5[1], AA; *Daily Standard*, 25 March 1919; Irving to Defence, 27, 28 and 29 March 1919, BP4/1, 66/4/3660, AA(Qld); Irving to Pearce, 27 March 1919, CP447/3, SC5[1], AA. The Governor-General praised Theodore's actions as being "quite satisfactory . . . in spite of his past association with the extreme Labor Movement", Affairs report, 1 April 1919, CO418/176, 184, PRO.
41. Irving to Defence, 12 April 1919, MP367, 512/1/898; P. Simonoff to Souse of Russian Workers, 26 July 1919, BP4/1, 66/4/2165, AA(Qld); Brown and Broad to Irving, 25 March 1919, BP4/1, 66/4/3660, AA(Qld); *Brisbane Courier*, 27 March and 14 April 1919; Wills, report, 8 June and 8 August 1919, BF4/1, 66/4/3660, AA(Qld); P. Boormakin to Watt, 28 May and 21 July 1919, PRE/A627, 7140 of 1919, QSA.
42. *Brisbane Courier*, 12 April 1919; *Daily Standard*, 26 April 1919; Theodore to Huxham, 26 April 1919 Col/A1154, 6090 of 1919; *Daily Standard*, 14 June 1919; Censor, memo, 7 May 1919, QF3998, AA(Vic).
43. P. Shohnovsky et al. to N. Ulianoff (Lenin), 18 June 1919, BP4/1, 66/4/3660, AA(Qld).
44. Intelligence report, 8 April 1919, BP4/1, 66/4/3660, AA(Qld); *Brisbane Courier*, 9, 12 and 24 April 1919. A year later, J.A. Walsh was a member of the trio who formed a pastoralists' deputation to London to press successfully for a loans blockade against the Queensland "socialist" government. See T. Cochrane, "The Danger is Real".
45. *Brisbane Courier*, 7 April 1919; *Daily Mail*, 7 April 1919; Constables Rowe and Kiddell, reports, 7 April 1919, COL/A1148, 4256 of 1919, QSA.
46. *Daily Mail*, 11 April 1919; *Daily Standard*, 2 May 1919; *The Leader*, 1919; Urquhart to Under Home Secretary, 7 April 1919, COL/A1148, 4256 of 1919, QSA.
47. Urquhart to Home Secretary, 24 April 1919, COL/A1152, 4961 of 1919; Irving to Defence Dept, 29 April 1919; Irving to Defence Dept, 29 April 1919, BP4/1, 66/4/2165, AA(Qld); Short, report, 30 April 1919, BP230/4, AA(Qld); Wills, report, 26 May 1919, BP4/1, 66/5/115, AA(Qld); *Daily Standard*, 2 May 1919.
48. *Daily Standard*, 2 May 1919; Censor's report, 1 May 1919, BP4/1, 66/4/2165, AA(Qld); *Daily Mail*, 6 May 1919 (my emphases).
49. *Daily Standard*, 6 May 1919; *Daily Mail*, 6 May 1919; *Brisbane Courier*, 6 May 1919.

Conclusion: Militants are Hard to Kill

1. *Brisbane Courier*, 3 May 1919; *Daily Standard*, 21 May 1919.
2. *Brisbane Courier*, 1 and 6 May 1919: H. McQueen, "The 'Spanish' Influenza Pandemic in Australia, 1912-1919", in *Social Policy in Australia*, ed. Jill Roe (Stanmore: Cassell, 1976), 135; A. Boesch, Brisbane, to E. Boesch, Switzerland, 21 May 1919, MP95/1, Q4254, AA(Vic.); *Australian Highway*, July 1919; *Queensland Government Gazette*, 31 May 1919.
3. *The Leader*, May 1919; R. Evans, "'Some Furious Outbursts of Riot': Returned Soldiers and Queensland's 'Red Flag' Disturbances, 1918-19", *War & Society* 3,2 (1985): 89-90. *Brisbane Courier*, 21 April 1919; J.J. Stable, "Review of Industrial and Political Situation in Queensland", 9 February 1919, CP447/3, SC5[1], AA.
4. *Brisbane Courier*, 21 April, 3 May and 5 July 1919; A. Langley Simmons to Military Intelligence (undated), BP4/1, 66/5/115, AA; "Queensland Trade Union Statistics", *The Movement*, March 1920, 5-6.
5. King and Empire Alliance to John Adamson, March 1920, MP367/1, 502/2/69, R. Darroch, *D.H. Lawrence in Australia* (Melbourne: Macmillan, 1981), 48-9.
6. C.E.W. Bean, *The Australian Imperial Force in France During the Allied Offensive, 1918* (Sydney: Angus & Robertson, 1942), 190; *Brisbane Courier*, 2, 4 and 12 July 1919.
7. Barrington Moore, Jr, *Injustice. The Social Bases of Obedience and Revolt* (London: Macmillan, 1978), 418.
8. *Brisbane Courier*, 22 April 1919; F. Culverhouse, "Three Black Lights", Oxley Library Ms.
9. P. Fussell, *Abroad. British Literary Travelling Between the Wars* (New York: Oxford University Press, 1980), 3-23; *Aussie*, March 1919; Evans, "Furious Outbursts".
10. *Aussie*, April 1920; Barrington Moore, Jr, *Injustice*, 419-23.
11. *Daily Mail*, 11 April 1919; *The Leader*, December 1918; *Brisbane Courier*, 1 July 1919;
12. E. Leed, *No Man's Land. Combat and Identity in World War I* (London: Cambridge University Press, 1979), 186-92; K. Inglis, "Returned Soldiers in Australia, 1918-1939", *Collected Seminar Papers on the Dominions between the Wars*, Institute of Commonwealth Studies, 1971, 59; P. Gibbs, *Now It Can Be Told* (New York: Harper and Brothers, 1920), 547-48; *Daily Mercury*, 16 April 1919; *Daily Standard*, 2 May 1919.
13. Barrington Moore, Jr, *Injustice*, 399 and 423; Evans, "Furious Outbursts of Riot".
14. R. Evans, "Loyalty and Disloyalty:" 489-99; *Labor Call*, 3 April 1919.
15. E. Leed, "Class and Disillusionment in World War I", *Journal of Modern History* 50 (1878): 698; Barrington Moore, Jr, *Injustice*, 339.
16. T. Jackson Lears, "The Concept of Cultural Hegemony: Problems and Possibilities", *American Historical Review* 90(1985): 579.
17. G. Ainsworth to H.E. Jones, 26 March 1919, CRS AA 1969/224, AA.
18. V. Burgmann, *"In Our Time". Socialism and the Rise of Labor, 1885-1905* (Sydney: Allen and Unwin, 1985), 3; Barrington Moore, Jr, *Injustice*, 472.
19. *Brisbane Courier*, 26 March, 3 April and 3 May, 1919; R. Evans, K. Saunders and K. Cronin, *Exclusion, Exploitation and Extermination. Race Relations in Colonial Queensland* (Sydney: ANZ Book Co., 1975), *passim*.
20. *Daily Standard*, 27 May 1919; Acting Sergeant A. Bock, report, 21 May 1919; Sergeant McNaullty, report, 3 June 1919; J. Huxham, memo, 27 May 1919, col/A1154, 6169 of 1919, QSA.
21. M.H. Ellis, evidence in libel action, T.J. Ryan v *Hobart Mercury*, 1921, in

Jennie Scott Griffiths' cutting books (privately owned); Barrington Moore, Jr, *Injustice*, 483-85.

22. *The Times*, 25 August 1919; *Brisbane Courier*, 28 April 1919; R. Evans, *Loyalty and Disloyalty*, 175-76.

23. *Daily Standard*, 24 July 1919; *Melbourne Socialist*, 1 August 1919; CIB, Information file for E.G. Theodore, 2 October 1919, Pre/A639, 10583 of 1919, QSA; K. Richmond, "Reactions to Radicalism: Non–Labour Movements, 1920-9", *Journal of Australian Studies* 5 (1979): 50-63.

24. T. Cochrane, "The Danger is Real".

25. D.J. Murphy, *T.J. Ryan: A Political Biography* (St Lucia: University of Queensland Press, 1975), 413; *Daily Standard*, 30 June 1919; *Telegraph*, 30 June 1919.

26. Barrington Moore, Jr, *Injustice*, 86, 276, 336 and 470; N.G. Butlin et al., *Government and Capitalism. Public and Private Choice in Twentieth Century Australia* (Sydney: Allen and Unwin, 1982), 75-6.

27. Barrington Moore, Jr, *Injustice*, 351.

28. Ibid., 81-82.

29. Intelligence report, 19 July 1919, CP447/2, SC 294/22, AA; J. Scott Griffiths to Red Flag Prisoners, 8 June 1919, CRS (Russia/Qld), 42/PI, AA.

30. Agent "77" reports, 26 July, 17-21 September, 19-29 November 1919, BP4/1, 66/5/115 and 66/4/3557, AA; Longreach "Red Flag" case, July 1919, Goombungee "Red Flag" case, July 1919, Dululu "Red Flag" case, November 1919. Eton "Red Flag" case, July 1919, BP4/1, 66/4/2165 AA; Babinda "Red Flag" case, October 1919, BP4/1, 66/5/115, AA; *Melbourne Socialist*, 8 August 1919.

31. *Daily Standard*, 18 September 1919; Intelligence reports, re Resanoff, August 1919, BP4/1, 66/4/2165, AA; Lieutenant-General Legge, memo, 17 April 1919, BP4/1, 66/4/3660, AA(Qld); *Daily Mail*, 10 April 1919; *Brisbane Courier*, 10 April 1919; Commissioner Urquhart to Military Command, 25 October 1919, BP4/1, 66/4/3660, AA(Qld); *Sydney Morning Herald*, 25 September 1919.

32. "Summary of Communism", 5, 26 July 1922; 6, 11 August 1922; 9, 18 September 1922; 19, 16 February 1923 and 21, 26 April 1923, AA1979/199, 1, AA; E. Fried, "Russians in Queensland, 1886-1925", 95; Information on Civa Rosenberg was gratefully received from Eric Fried, who visited her in 1985 and returned with photographs and impressions of her warm welcome and graciousness.

33. Secretary, Defence Department to Peter Simonoff, 19 March 1920, MP367/1, 502/2/82, AA; Prime Minister to Acting Premier, Queensland, 12 May 1920, Col/A1199, 4749 of 1920, QSA; Secretary, Prime Minister's Department, to Official Secretary to Governor-General, 23 February 1921, CP78/22, 1921/67, AA; Memos on stranded Russians, February-August 1920, Pre A671, 7870 of 1920, QSA.

34. I. Turner, *Industrial Labour and Politics. The Dynamics of the Labour Movement in Eastern Australia* (Canberra: Australian National University Press, 1965), 206-10; E. Fried, "Russians in Australia", 91; "Summary of Communism", 6, 5 December 1921, CP447/2, SC292, AA; "Light Horseman", North Queensland to Sir H. Chauvel, November 22, CP447/2, SC294, AA; "Communist Movements in Australia", Secret, (undated), CP447/2, SC292[1], AA.

35. G. Lewis, "Queensland Nationalism and Australian Capitalism", in *Essays in the Political Economy of Australian Capitalism* II, ed. E.L. Wheelwright and Ken Buckley (Sydney: ANZ Book Co., 1978), 111.

36. J. Tilanus, Report on Jerome Cahill, (undated), BP4/1, 66/4/2165, AA(Qld).

Bibliography

Official Material, Unpublished

Public Records Office

Governor-General's Despatches. Co418/157-59, 169-70, 176-78 (1917-19).
Governor's Despatches, Queensland. Co418/419, 161, 171, 179, 193, 209, 221 (1916-22).

Australian Archives, Canberra and Brighton

Attorney General's Department. CP406 series (1918).
Defence Department. BP4 series (1918-20); BP230 series (1917-29); BP 197 series (1914-18); MP 95 series (1915-19).
Office of the Governor General. CP78 series (1901-21).
Prime Minister's Department. CP103 series (1916-19); CP 189 series (1916-17); CP 29 series (1917); CP 447 series (1918-19); CRS/A457 series (1907-23); CRS/A458 series (1916-29); CRS/A658 series (1918-19).

Australian Archives, Brisbane

Censor's Reports 1914-19. BP4/2.
Correspondence files 1914-22. BP4/1.
Investigation Branch, Queensland 1919-46. CA753.
Miscellaneous Papers of Queensland Branch Office, Military Intelligence 1915-19. BP230/12.
Miscellaneous Papers, Queensland 1917-20. BP 230/4.
Papers seized from Australian Communist Party, Queensland 1919-26. BP230/6.
Special Intelligence Bureau, Brisbane 1917-19. CA752.

Queensland State Archives

Governor's Office. Official letters received 1914-18 Gov/A67-78; Secret and Confidential Outward Despatches and Telegrams 1912-18 Gov/68-90.

Home Office. In-letters 1912-20. COL/A937-1225. Correspondence and papers on various matters regarding the Great War COL/155.

Justice Department. Correspondence and Associated Papers...related to the Great War 1915-18. JUS/74.

Police Department Files 1913-23. POL/J 1-39.

Official Material, Published

Commonwealth of Australia. *Gazette* 1915-20.

Commonwealth of Australia. *Parliamentary Debates* (1916-20).

Commonwealth of Australia. *Parliamentary Papers* 1916-20.

Commonwealth of Australia. *Senate Debates* (1916-20).

Labour and Industry. Branch Reports, nos.8-11.

Official Yearbook of the Commonwealth of Australia 1917-20. Melbourne: G.H. Knibbs.

Queensland. *Government Gazette* 1916-20.

Queensland. *Journals of Parliament* 1914-20.

Queensland. *Parliamentary Debates* 1916-21.

Queensland. *Parliamentary Papers* 1916-19.

Other Sources

Abse, Dannie. *Ash on a Young Man's Sleeve*. Harmondsworth: Penguin, 1982.

Allen J. "Aspects of Vere Gordon Childe". *Labour History* 12 (1967): 52-59.

Armstrong, J. "Closer Unity in the Queensland Trade Union Movement 1900-1922". M.A. thesis, Department of History, University of Queensland 1975.

Ashworth, A.E. "The Sociology of Trench Warfare". *British Journal of Sociology* 19 (1968): 407-20.

Atkinson, C. "Was There Fact in D.H. Lawrence's *Kangaroo?*" *Meanjin* 24 (1965): 358-59.

Atkinson, Meredith. "The Russian Soviets". *Stead's Review*, 20 September 1919, p.9.

Age, 1918-19.

Amos, Keith. *The New Guard Movement, 1931-1935*. Melbourne: Melbourne University Press, 1976.

Argus, 1917-19.

Armstrong, Robert. *The Kalkadoons, A Study of an Aboriginal Tribe on the Queensland Frontier*. Brisbane: W. Brooks & Co., nd.

Aussie: The Australian Soldiers Magazine, 1917-20.

Australian Highway, 1919-23.

Bean, C.E.W. *The Australian Imperial Force in France During the Allied*

Offensive, 1918. Official History of Australia in the War of 1914-18, Volume 6. Sydney: Angus & Robertson, 1942.

Beattie, B. "Memoirs of the IWW". *Labour History* 26 (1974): 33-39.

Bedford, I. "The Industrial Workers of the World in Australia". *Labour History* 26(1974): 40-46.

Bennet, H. Scott, and R.S. Ross. *The Story of the Red Flag*. Melbourne: Socialist Party of Victoria, 1918.

Bingham, Colin. *The Beckoning Horizon*. Ringwood: Penguin, 1983.

Blackeney, Michael. *Australia and the Jewish Refugees 1933-1948*. London: Croom Helm, 1985.

Boote, H.E. *A Fool's Talk*. Sydney: Worker Press, 1915.

Boston, R. *The Admirable Urquhart: Selected Writings*. London: Gordon Fraser, 1975.

Botham, Trevor. "The Red Flag Riots: Conservative Reactions". Australian National University, B.A. (Hons) thesis. 1975.

Bradley, J. *Allied Intervention in Russian 1917-1920*. London: Wiedenfeld and Nicholson, 1968.

Brisbane Courier, 1916-21.

Brown, Gordon. *My Descent from Soapbox to Senate*. Brisbane: Co-operative Press 1953.

Brugger, Suzanne. *Australians and Egypt 1914-1919*. Melbourne: Melbourne University Press, 1980.

Bulletin, 1916-20.

Burgmann, Verity. "The Iron Heel. The Suppression of the IWW during World War I". In *What Rough Beast. The State and Social Order in Australian History*, ed. Sydney Labour History Group, pp. 171-91. Sydney: Allen and Unwin, 1982.

_____. *"In Our Time". Socialism and the Rise of Labor, 1885-1905*. Sydney: Allen and Unwin, 1985.

Bussey, G., and M. Tims. *Pioneers for Peace, Women's International League for Peace and Freedom 1915-1965*. London: WILPF, 1980.

Butlin, Noel, A. Barnard, and J.J. Pincus. *Government and Capitalism. Public and Private Choice in Twentieth Century Australia*. Sydney: George Allen and Unwin, 1982.

Cain, Frank. *The Origins of Political Surveillance in Australia*. Sydney: Angus & Robertson, 1983.

Calazer, L. "When the Plague Came to Queensland". In *Brisbane Housing, Health, the River and the Arts*, ed. Rod Fisher, pp. 79-89. Brisbane History Group Papers 3 (1985).

Campbell, H.A. *Socialism at Work in Queensland*. London: National Labour Press, 1919.

Canetti, E. *Crowds and Power*. Harmondsworth: Penguin, 1973.

Carsten, F.L. *War Against War. British and German Radical Movements in the First World War*. London: Batsford Academic and Educational, 1982.

Challinor, Raymond. *The Origins of British Bolshevism*. London: Croom Helm, 1977.

Chatsfield, Charles. "World War I and the Liberal Pacifist in the United States". *American Historical Review* 75 (1970): 1920-37.

Childe, V.G. *How Labour Governs. A Study of Workers' Representation in Australia*. Melbourne: Melbourne University Press, 1923.

Clarke, F.G. *Will-o'-the-Wisp. Peter the Painter and the Anti-Tsarist Terrorists in Britain and Australia*. Melbourne: Melbourne University Press, 1984.

Cochrane, R. "The Danger is Real: Capitalist Response to an Australian Socialist Programme. A Study of Queensland 1920-24". M. Phil. thesis, Griffith University, 1984.

Communist, 1920.

Conroy C. *Political Action*. Sydney: Worker Print, 1918.

————. *Fools or Traitors*. Sydney: Worker Print, 1920.

Copland, D.P. "Australia in the World War: Economic". In *Cambridge History of the British Empire*, Volume 7. Cambridge: Cambridge University Press, 1933.

Coward, Dan. "The Impact of War on New South Wales: Some Aspects of Social and Political History 1914-17". Ph.D. thesis, Department of History, Australian National University, 1974.

Crawford, R.M. "The Australian Pilgrimage of Arnold Wood". *Journals of the Royal Australian Historical Association* 48 (1963): 405-26.

Crouch, R. *The Australian Labor Party and the War*. Melbourne: Labor Call, 1927.

Croydon Mining News, 1917-19.

Culverhouse, F.V. "Three Black Lights 1914-18", Oxley Library, Ms.

Cunneen, C. *King's Men. Australia's Governor-Generals from Houpton to Isaacs*. Sydney: Allen and Unwin, 1983.

Curthoys, A., and A. Markus. *Who Are Our Enemies? Racism and the Working Class in Australia*. Sydney: Hale and Iremonger, 1978.

Daily Mail, 1916-20.

Daily Standard, 1916-20.

Darling Downs Gazette, 1916-20.

Darroch, R. "The Man Behind Australia's Secret Armies". *Bulletin*, 2 May 1978 pp. 60-62.

Davison, Graeme. "Unemployment, race and public opinion: reflections on the Asian immigration controversy of 1888". In *Surrender Australia? Essays in the Study and Uses of History*, ed. A. Markus and M.C. Ricklefs. Sydney: George Allen and Unwin, 1985.

————. *D.H. Lawrence in Australia*. Melbourne: Macmillan, 1981.

Denholm, B. "Some Aspects of the Transitional Period from War to Peace 1918-1921". *Australian Quarterly* (1944): 39-50.

Denny, W. *A Digger at Home and Abroad*. Melbourne: Popular Publications, nd.

Direct Action, 1914-17.

Douman, M. "Townsville 1914-1919. A Study of Group Attitudes and Behaviour". B.A. thesis, Department of History, Townsville University College, 1969.

Dubovsky, Melvin. *We Shall Be All. A History of the Industrial Workers of the World*. New York: Quadrangle, 1969.

Dukes, Paul. *October and the World: Perspectives on the Russian Revolution*. London: Macmillan, 1979.

Durham, Martin. "British Revolutionaries and the Suppression of the Left in Lenin's Russia, 1918-1924". *Journal of Contemporary History* 20 (1985): 203-19.

Echo, Australia, 1912.

Ellis, Malcolm. *Handbook for Nationalists*. Brisbane: NPD, 1918.

_____. *The Red Road*. Sydney: Sydney & Melbourne Publishing Co., 1932.

Ely, Richard. "The First Anzac Day: Invented or Discovered?" *Journal of Australian Studies* 17 (1985): 41-58.

Englander, David. "Troops and Trade Unions, 1919". *History Today* 37 (1987): 8-13.

Evans, Raymond. "Loyalty and Disloyalty. Social and Ideological Conflict in Queensland During the Great War". Ph.D. thesis, Department of History, University of Queensland, 1981.

_____. "'Some Furious Outbursts of Riot': Returned Soldiers and Queensland's 'Red Flag' Disturbances". *War and Society* 3 (1985): 75-98.

_____. "The Battles of Brisbane: The Conscription Struggle 1916-17". In *Brisbane at War*, ed. Helen Taylor, pp.5-15. Brisbane History Group Papers 4 (1986).

_____. "A Bad Time for Balalaikas: Australia's First Red Scare 1918-20". *The History Teacher* 39 (1986): 10-17.

_____. *Loyalty and Disloyalty. Social Conflict on the Queensland Homefront, 1914-18*. Sydney: Allen and Unwin, 1987.

Evans, Raymond, Kay Saunders and Kathryn Cronin. *Exclusion, Exploitation and Extermination. Race Relations in Colonial Queensland*. Sydney: ANZ Book Co., 1975. Reprinted St Lucia: University of Queensland Press, 1988.

Evatt, H.V. "Australia and the Home Front 1914-1918". *Australian Quarterly* (1937): 68-75.

Ferro, Marc. *The Great War 1914-18*. London: Routledge and Kegan Paul, 1969.

Fewster, Kevin. "Politics, Pageantry and Purpose. The 1920 Tour of Australia by the Prince of Wales". *Labour History* 38 (1980): 59-66.

_____. "The Operation of State Apparatuses in Times of Crisis: Censorship and Conscription, 1916", *War and Society* 3 (1985): 37-54.

Fishman, W.J. *East End Jewish Radicals 1875-1914*. London: Duckworth, 1975.

Fitzgerald, Ross. *From 1915 to the Early 1980s. A History of Queensland*. St. Lucia: University of Queensland Press, 1984.

Fitzhardinge, Lloyd. *The Little Digger 1914-1952. William Morris Hughes. A Political Biography*. Vol. 2. London: Angus & Robertson, 1979.

Florinsky, M.T. *Encyclopedia of Russia and Soviet Union*. New York: McGraw Hill, 1961.

For Australians, 1919.

Fried, Eric. "Russians in Queensland, 1886-1925". B.A. (Hons) thesis, University of Queensland, 1980.

Fry, Eric. "Tom Barker 1887-1970". *Labour History* 18 (1970): 75.

Fussell, Paul. *The Great War and Modern Memory*. London: Oxford University Press, 1975.

_____. *Abroad. British Literary Travelling Between the Wars*. New York: Oxford University Press, 1980.

Gammage, Bill. *The Broken Years. Australian Soldiers in the Great War*. Canberra: Australian National University Press, 1974.
_____. "Australians and the Great War." *Journal of Australian Studies* 6 (1980): 26-35.
Gerritson, R. "The 1934 Kalgoorlie Riots: A Western Australian Crowd". *University Studies in History* 5 (1967-70): 42-75.
Gibbney, H.J. "Ainsworth, George Frederick (1878-1950)". In *Australian Dictionary of Biography*, vol. 9, ed. Bede Nairn and Geoffrey Serle, pp. 21-22. Melbourne: Melbourne University Press, 1986.
Gibbs, P. *Now It Can Be Told*. New York: Harper and Brothers, 1920.
Glynne, T. *The Communist International to the IWW*. Sydney: NPD, 1920.
Good, K. "The World View of the Returned Serviceman's League". M.A. thesis, Department of History, University of Queensland, 1965.
Gordon, Amanda. "The Conservative Press and the Russian Revolution". In *Australian Conservatism. Essays in Twentieth Century Political History*, ed. Cameron Hazlehurst, pp.29-49. Canberra: Australian National University Press, 1979.
Gregory, Helen, and John Thearle. "Casualties of Brisbane's Growth: Infant and Child Mortality in the 1860s". In *Brisbane Housing, Health, the River and the Arts*, ed. Rod Fisher, pp. 57-70. Brisbane History Group Papers 3 (1985).
Grey, J. "A 'pathetic sideshow': Australians and the Russian Intervention, 1918-19". *Journal of the Australian War Memorial* 7 (1985): 12-17.
Griffiths, Jennie Scott. Cutting Books (privately owned).
Hall, R. *The Secret State. Australia's Spy Industry*. Melbourne: Cassel, 1978.
_____. "The Secret Army". *National Times*, 23-28 January 1978, pp. 12-13.
Hardach, G. *The First World War 1914-1918*. London: Allen Lane, 1977.
Harris, Joe. *The Bitter Fight. A Pictorial History of the Australian Labour Movement*. St. Lucia: University of Queensland Press, 1970.
Haupt, G. *Socialism and the Great War. The Collapse of the Second International*. Oxford: Clarendon Press, 1972.
Hayes, Paul. *Fascism*. London: Allen and Unwin, 1973.
Henderson, G. "The Deportation of Charles Jerger". *Labour History* 31 (1976): 61-78.
Holton, E. *British Syndicalism 1900-1914. Myths and Realities*. London: Pluto Press, 1976.
Holton, Robert. "The crowd in history: some problems of theory and method". *Social History* 3 (1978): 219-33.
Hornibrook, J.H. *Bibliography of Queensland Verse, with Bibliographical Notes*. Brisbane: A.H. Tucker, 1953.
Howie, J.B. *Australia and the Coming Peace*. Melbourne: NPD, 1915.
Hunt, D.W. "A History of the Labour Movement in North Queensland". Ph.D. thesis, University of Queensland, 1979.

Hunter, R. *Violence and the Labour Movement.* London: Routledge and Kegan Paul, 1916.

Hutt, A. *The Post-War History of the British Working Class.* London: Victor Gollancz, 1937.

Hyslop, Robert. "Mutiny on 'HMAS Australia'. A Forgotten Episode of 1919 in Political Naval Relations." *Public Administration* 29 (1970): 284-96.

Inglis, Ken. "Returned Soldiers in Australia, 1918-39". *Collected Seminar Papers on the Dominions Between the Wars.* Institute of Commonwealth Studies, 1971.

International Socialist, 1916-17.

Iremonger, J., J. Merritt, and G. Osborne (eds). *Strikes. Studies in Twentieth Century Australian Social History.* Sydney: Angus & Robertson, 1973.

Irving, Terry. "Sources of Australian Intolerance: Some Reflections". In *A Pluralist Australia,* ed. George Shaw, pp. 34-43. Australian Studies Centre, University of Queensland, 1984.

Isaac, J.E., and G.W. Ford. *Australian Labour Relations Readings.* Melbourne: Sun, 1971.

James, John. "The Guardsmen are Born". *Nation* 64 (1961): 8-10.

Jauncey, L.C. *The Story of Conscription in Australia.* Melbourne: Macmillan, 1968.

Jensen, H.I. "The Darwin Rebellion". *Labour History* 11 (1966): 3-13.

Kellow, H.A. *Queensland Poets.* London: George Harrap, 1930.

Kennedy, B. *Silver, Sin and Sixpenny Ale. A Social History of Broken Hill.* Melbourne: Melbourne University Press, 1978.

Kennedy, David. *Over Here, The First World War and American Society.* New York: Oxford University Press, 1980.

King, Terry. "The Tarring and Feathering of J.K. McDougall: 'Dirty Tricks' in the 1919 Federal Election". *Labour History* 45 (1983): 54-67.

Knibbs, G.H. *The Private Wealth of Australia and Its Growth.* Melbourne: McCarron, 1918.

Knowledge and Unity, 1918-21.

Kristianson, G. *The Politics of Patriotism. The Pressure Group Activities of the Returned Servicemen's League.* Canberra: Australian National University Press, 1966.

Lake, Marilyn. *A Divided Society. Tasmania during World War One.* Melbourne: Melbourne University Press, 1975.

———. "An Aspect of Tasmania Patriotism in the Great War: The Persecution of Aliens". *Tasmanian Research Association Papers and Proceedings* 19 (1972): 87-99.

Lane, Ernest. *Dawn to Dusk, Reminiscences of a Rebel.* Brisbane: W. Brooks, 1939.

Lawson, Ronald. *Brisbane in the 1890s: A Study of an Australian Urban Society.* St Lucia: University of Queensland Press, 1973.

Leader, 1919.

Lears, T. Jackson. "The Concept of Cultural Hegemony. Problems and Possibilities". *American Historical Review* 90 (1985): 576-973.

Leed, Eric. *No Man's Land. Combat and Identity in World War I.* London: Cambridge University Press, 1979.

———. "Class and Disillusionment in World War I". *Journal of Modern History* 50 (1978): 680-99.

Leibknecht, K. *Militarism and Anti-Militarism.* Cambridge: River Press, 1973.

Lewis, Glen. "Queensland Nationalism and Australian Capitalism". In *Essays in the Political Economy of Australian Capitalism*, vol. 2, ed. E.L. Wheelwright and K. Buckley, pp. 110-47. Sydney: ANZ Book Co., 1978.

Lindsay, Jack. *Life Rarely Tells. An Autobiography in three volumes.* Ringwood: Penguin, 1982.

Lloyd, M. *Sidelights on Two Referenda.* Sydney: Worker Print, 1952.

Lone Hand, 1916-21.

Love, Peter. *Labour and the Money Power. Australian Labour Populism 1890-1950.* Melbourne: Melbourne University Press, 1984.

Low, S. "Ten Little Aliens". Mitchell Library Ms.

McGuire, M. "The IWW in Australia". *Red and Black* 8 (1978-79): 32-36.

McHugh, J. and B.J. Ripley. "Russian Political Internees in First World War Britain: The Cases of George Chickerin and Peter Petroff". *Historical Journal* 28 (1985): 727-38.

McKernan, Michael. *The Australian People and the Great War.* Melbourne: Nelson, 1980.

McLachlan, N. "Nationalism and the Divisive Digger: Three Comments". *Meanjin* 27 (1968): 302-8.

McLaughlin, J. *A Happy Revolution.* Brisbane: Worker Press, 1918.

McQueen, Humphrey. "Shoot the Bolshevik! Hang the Profiteer! Reconstructing Australian Capitalism 1918-21". In *Essays in the Political Economy of Australian Capitalism*, vol. 2, ed. by E.L. Wheelwright and K. Buckley, pp. 185-206. Sydney: ANZ Book Co., 1978.

———. "The 'Spanish' Influenza Pandemic in Australia, 1912-19". In *Social Policy in Australia. Some Perspectives 1901-75*, ed. Jill Roe, pp. 131-47. Stanmore: Cassell, 1976.

———. *Gallipoli to Petrov, Arguing with Australian History.* Sydney: Allen and Unwin, 1984.

Meaney, N. "Australia's Secret Service in World War I: Security, Loyalty and the Abuse of Power". *Quadrant* 23 (1979): 19-23.

Militant, 1919-20.

Moore, Andrew. "Guns across the Yarra. Secret armies and the 1923 Melbourne police strike". In *What Rough Beast? The State and Social Order in Australian History*, ed. Sydney Labour History Group, pp. 220-33. Sydney: Allen and Unwin, 1982.

Moore, Barrington Jr. *Injustice, The Social Bases of Obedience and Revolt.* London: Macmillan, 1978.

Morris, Richard. "Mr Justice Higgins Scuppered: The 1919 Seamen's Strike". *Labour History* 37 (1979): 52-62.

Morrison, A. "Militant Labour in Queensland 1912-17". *Journal of the Royal Historical Society of Australia* 38 (1952): 209-34.

Moscovici, Serge. *The Age of the Crowd. A Historical Treatise of Mass Psychology.* Cambridge: Cambridge University Press, 1985.

Mosse, George L. "National Cemeteries and National Revival: The Cult of the Fallen Soldiers in Germany". *Journal of Contemporary History* 14 (1979): 1-20.

Muirden, B. *The Puzzled Patriots. The Story of the Australia First Movement.* Melbourne: Melbourne University Press, 1968.

Munro, Craig. *Wild Man of Letters. The Story of P.R. Stephensen.* Melbourne: Melbourne University Press, 1984.

Murphy, D.J. *T.J. Ryan. A Political Biography.* St Lucia: University of Queensland Press, 1975.

————. "Religion, Race and Conscription in World War I". *Australian Journal of Politics and History* 20 (1974): 155-63.

Murray, R.K. *Red Scare. A Study of National Hysteria.* New York: McGraw Hill, 1955.

Myers, R.I. "Ernest Sandford Jackson". *Trephine* 4 (1955): 89-90.

Nabat, 1919.

National Leader, 1915-19.

New York Times, 1919.

Nolan, Carolyn. "Beirne, Thomas Charles (1860-1949)". In *Australian Dictionary of Biography*, vol. 9, ed. by Bede Nairn and Geoffrey Serle, pp. 248-50. Melbourne: Melbourne University Press, 1986.

Normington-Rawling, J. "Foundation of the Communist Party in Australia". *Quadrant* 37 (1965): 71-77.

O'Connor, H. *Revolution in Seattle. A Memoir.* Seattle: Left Bank Books, 1981.

O'Farrell, Patrick. "The Russian Revolution and the Labour Movements of Australia and New Zealand, 1917-1922". *International Review of Social History* 8 (1963): 177-97.

————. "The Irish Republican Brotherhood in Australia: the 1918 Internments". In *Irish Culture and Nationalism 1750-1950*, ed. O. MacDonagh, W.F. Mandle and P. Travers, pp. 182-93. London: Macmillan, 1983.

O'Rockie, J. *The Coming Slavery and the Future of the Workers.* Brisbane: Workers Press, 1918.

Parker, Neville. "Dr. E. Sandford Jackson". In *People, Places and Pestilence. Vignettes of Queensland's Medical Past*, ed. M. John Thearle, pp. 13-24. Brisbane: University Department of Child Health, 1986.

Patrick, Alison. "Brookes, Herbert Robinson (1867-1963)". In *Australian Dictionary of Biography*, vol. 9, ed. Bede Nairn and Geoffrey Serle, pp. 425-27. Melbourne: Melbourne University Press, 1986.

Patrick, Ross. "Jackson, Ernest Sandford (1860-1938)". In *Australian Dictionary of Biography*, vol. 9, ed. Bede Nairn and Geoffrey Serle, p. 457. Melbourne: Melbourne University Press, 1986.

Perks, M. "A New Source on the Seventh ALP Federal Conference, 1918". *Labour History* 32 (1977): 75-79.

————. "Labour and the Governor-General's Recruiting Conference, 1918". *Labour History* 34 (1978): 28-44.

Perry, W. "The Police Strike in Melbourne in 1923". *The Victorian Historical Magazine* pp. 43-44 (1972-73): 896-935.

Phillips, J.A. "The Townsville Meatworkers' Strike: A Perspective on Social Conflict in Queensland 1918-1919". B.A. thesis, Department of History, University of Queensland, 1977.

Philp, James. *Songs of the Australian Fascisti*. Brisbane: Edward Dunlop, nd.

Poole, Tom and Eric Fried. "Artem: A Bolshevik in Brisbane". *Australian Journal of Politics and History* 31 (1985): 243-54.

Potter, S.B. *Socialism in Queensland*. London: ILP, nd.

Potts, D. *The Twenties*. Melbourne: F.W. Cheshire, 1971.

Preston, W. Jr. *Aliens and Dissenters. Federal Suppression of Radicals, 1903-1933*. New York: Harper and Row, 1963.

Proletariat, 1919.

Protest, 1916.

Pryor, L.J. "Back from the Wars: The Ex-Serviceman in History". *Australian Quarterly* (1946): 43-50.

Quail, J. *The Slow Burning Fuse. The Lost History of the British Anarchists*. London: Paladin, 1978.

Quarterly Review, 1849-50.

Queensland and Queenslanders. Brisbane: Australian History Publishing Co., 1936.

Queenslander, 1916-20.

Queenslanders As We See 'Em. Brisbane: Newspaper Cartoonists Association, 1917.

Queensland Police Union Journal, 1919.

Rabinowitch, A. *The Bolsheviks Come to Power*. New York: W. Norton, 1978.

Rawson, D.W. "Political Violence in Australia". Parts 1 and 2. *Dissent* 22 and 23 (1968): 18-27 and 35-39.

Reed, John. *Ten Days That Shook The World*. New York: Random House, 1935.

Reid, Gordon. *A Nest of Hornets: The Massacre of the Fraser Family at Hornet Bank*. Melbourne: Oxford University Press, 1982.

Returned Sailors' and Soldiers' Labor League. *Soldiers and the Labor Movement*. Brisbane: Worker Press, 1919.

Richmond, K. "Response to the Threat of Communism: The Sane Democracy League and the People's Union of New South Wales". *Journal of Australian Studies* 1 (1977): 70-83.

Riddell, E., ed. *Lives of the Stuart Age, 1603-1714*. London: Osprey Publishing Co., 1976.

Rivett, Rohan. *Australian Citizen. Herbert Brookes 1867-1963*. Melbourne: Melbourne University Press, 1965.

Robbins, Keith. *The Abolition of War. The Peace Movement in Britain, 1914-1919*. Cardiff: University of Wales Press, 1976.

Robson, L. *The First AIF. A Study of its Recruitment 1914-1918*. Melbourne: Melbourne University Press, 1970.

Roe, M. "Comment on the Digger Tradition". *Meanjin* 24 (1965): 357-58.

Rosa, S.A. *The Invasion of Australia*. Sydney: Judd Publishing, 1920.

Rosenbaum, H.J. and P.C. Sederberg. *Vigilante Politics*. Pennsylvania: University of Pennsylvania Press, 1976.

Roskill, S.W. "The Dismissal of Admiral Jellicoe". *Journal of Contemporary History* 4 (1969): 69-93.

Ross, E. "Australia and 1917". *Australian Left Review* 4, (1967): 40-44.

Rothstein, A. *The Soldiers' Strikes of 1919*. London: Macmillan, 1980.

Rushton, P.J. "Communal Anxiety: An Aspect of the Conscription Campaigns". *Tasmanian Historical Research Association Papers* 19 (1972): 49-60.

Rydon, Joan. *A Biographical Register of the Commonwealth Parliament.* Canberra: Australian National University, 1975.

Saunders, D. "Aliens in Britain and the Empire During the First World War". *Immigrants and Minorities* 4 (1985): 5-27.

Schedvin, B. "E.G. Theodore and the London Pastoral Lobby". *Politics* 6 (1971): 26-41.

Shute, C. "Blood Votes' and the 'Bestial Boche': A case study in propaganda". *Hecate* 2 (1976): 6-22.

"Secret Service". *Queer Queensland: The Breeding Ground of the Bolshevik*. Brisbane: privately published, 1918.

Serle, G. "The Digger Tradition and Australian Nationalism". *Meanjin* 24 (1985): 149-58.

Shaw, A.G.L. "Violent Protest in Australian History". *Historical Studies* 60 (1973): 545-60.

Shaw, G.P. "Conscription and Queensland 1916-1917". B.A. thesis, Department of History, University of Queensland, 1966.

_____. "Patriotism versus Socialism: Queensland's Private War 1916". *Australian Journal of Politics and History* 19 (1973): 167-77.

Socialist, 1914-19.

Soldier, 1919-20.

Soldiers and the Labor Movement. Brisbane: Worker Print, 1919.

Soltow, L. "The Censuses of Wealth of Men in Australia in 1915". *Australian Economic History Review* 12 (1972): 125-41.

Soule, George. *Prosperity Decade, From War to Depression: 1917-29*. New York: M.E. Sharpe, 1947.

Souter, Gavin. *"Lion and Kangaroo: The Initiation of Australia"*. Sydney: Collins, 1976.

Squeri, Lawrence. "The Italian Local Elections of 1920 and the Outbreak of Fascism". *Historian* 65 (1983): 324-36.

Stocks, D. "The Little Adventure. Australian Involvement in the British Intervention in Northern Russia". B.A. (Hons) thesis, University of Queensland, 1985.

Strength of Empire, 1919-20.

Sturma, Michael. "Myall Creek and the Psychology of Mass Murder". *Journal of Australian Studies* 16 (1985): 62-70.

Summers, Anne. "The Unwritten History of Adela Pankhurst Walsh". In *Women, Class and History. Feminist Perspectives in Australia 1788-1978*, ed. E. Windschuttle, pp. 388-402. Melbourne: Fontana, 1980.

Sun, 1918-19.

Sydney Morning Herald, 1917-20.

Telegraph, 1917-19.

Thompson, F.W. *The IWW: Its First Seventy Years 1905-1975*. Chicago: IWW Press, 1976.

Thorpe, William. "A Social History of Colonial Queensland. Towards a Marxist Analysis". Ph.D. thesis, University of Queensland, 1985.

Times, 1918-20.

Toland, John. *No Man's Land. The Story of 1918*. London: Eyre Methuen, 1980.

Toowoomba Chronicle, 1917-19.

Townsville Daily Bulletin, 1916-19.

Trask, D. *World War I at Home: Readings on American Life 1914-20*. New York: John Wiley and Sons, 1970.

Triad, 1919-21.

Trotter, W. *Instincts of the Herd in Peace and War*. London: T. Fisher Unwin, 1916.

Truth, 1917-20.

Tuchman, Barbara. *The Proud Tower. A Portrait of the World Before the War 1890-1914*. London: Hamish Hamilton, 1966.

Unemployed Clarion, 1921.

Unemployment Problem — Proposed Solution by the Government of Queensland. Brisbane: Government Print, 1919.

Urquhart, F.R. *Camp Canzonettes, being Rhymes of the Bush and other things*. Brisbane: Gordon and Gotch, 1891.

Vernadsky, G. *A History of Russia*. New Haven: Yale, 1961.

Voice of Australian Democracy, 1916.

Waites, B.A. "The effect of the First World War on class and status in England, 1910-20". *Journal of Contemporary History* 11 (1976): 27-43.

Walker, R.B. "Violence in Industrial Conflicts in New South Wales in the late Nineteen Century". *Historical Studies* 86 (1986): 54-70.

Walker, S.E. "Schooldays with Percy Stephensen 1914-19". Fryer Library MS.

Ward, Stephen. "Intelligence Surveillance of British Ex-Servicemen, 1918-1920". *Historical Journal* 16 (1973): 179-188.

Waters, Malcolm. *Strikes in Australia. A Sociological Analysis of Industrial Conflict*. Sydney: Allen and Unwin, 1982.

Watson, Frederick. *A Brief Analysis of Public Opinion in Australia During the Past Six Years*. Sydney: Tyrell's, 1918.

Wildman, O. *Queenslanders Who Fought in the Great War*. Brisbane: Besley and Pike, nd.

Wilks, Ivor. *South Wales and the Rising of 1839*. London: Croom Helm, 1984.

Winter, J. *Socialism and the Challenge of War. Ideas and Politics in Britain 1912-18*. London: Routledge and Kegan Paul, 1974.

Withers, Glenn. "The 1916-1917 Conscription Referenda: A Clinometrical Appraisal". *Historical Studies* 78 (1982): 36-47.

Woolf, Leonard. *After the Deluge. A Study of Communal Psychology*. Harmondsworth: Penguin, 1937.

Worker, 1914-20.

Workers' Life, 1917.

Index